DATE			
OCT 1 4 1991 DE 28 '08			
AUG 1 5 '93 DEC 18 '00			
AUG 3 '94 NO 23 09			
NOV 17 '94			
MAR 17 '95			
SEP 21 '95			
OCT 21 '95			
OC 12 '97			
MY 01 '98			
MY 16 '98			
DE 10 '98			

SEVEN
DECISIVE BATTLES
OF THE
MIDDLE AGES

SEVEN
DECISIVE BATTLES
OF THE
MIDDLE AGES

Joseph Dahmus

NELSON-HALL nh CHICAGO

Library of Congress Cataloging in Publication Data

Dahmus, Joseph.
  Seven decisive battles of the Middle Ages.

  Bibliography: p.
  Includes index.
  1. Battles. 2. Military history, Medieval.
I. Title.
D128.D33 1983   909.07   83-13490
ISBN 0-8304-1030-9

Manufactured in the United States of America

10 9 8 7 6 5 4 3 2 1

The paper in this book is pH neutral (acid-free).

CONTENTS

PREFACE

WHEN IS A BATTLE DECISIVE? FLETCHER PRATT SAYS THAT TO BE decisive a battle "must really mark one of those turning points after which things would have been a great deal different if the decision had gone in the other direction."[1] Since he omits the battle of Hastings from the battles he considers decisive, one that most other authors have included, we might conclude that what is a decisive battle and what is not frequently is a subjective matter.

A Serb would judge the battle of Kossovo in 1389 decisive, since the Turks ended Serbian ambitions of establishing an empire in the Balkans. Other European nationals would judge Kossovo differently. Or consider the query Paul the Hermit put to Antony in the fourth century when, after many years in desert solitude, he emerged to ask, "How fares the human race...and whose empire is it that now sways the world?"[2] To Paul nothing strictly human could be viewed as decisive, a position which even the late Otto Maenchen-Helfen seemed willing to endorse. Talking of those scholars who are at pains to justify their particular historical writing, he observed, "May I point out that I fail to see why the history of, say, Baja California is more respectable than, say, that of the Huns in the Balkans in the

460s. *Sub specie aeternitatis,* both dwindle into nothingness."[3]

All seven of the battles described here must be considered of major importance, since truly significant consequences followed upon their outcome. There were other battles in the Middle Ages which may have had equally decisive results. A case might be made for the battle of Tours (732), the battle of Legnano (1176), the battle of Agincourt (1415), or others. But the chosen battles merit classification as among the most decisive battles, even though admittedly an effort was made to spread their selection so as to cover the time span of the Middle Ages (Chalons, 451, to Angora, 1402) and to introduce the reader to the Muslim world of the Near East (Yarmuk, 636, and Hattin, 1187).

1

MEDIEVAL WARFARE

FOR AN INTRODUCTION TO A HISTORY OF WARFARE IN THE MID-
dle Ages, one must turn back to the decline of Rome. Most of
the nations of medieval Europe first came to view along the
northern borders of that empire. Their mores, their cultures,
and their institutions felt to some degree the influence of
Rome, and this included the way they carried on war. The
ancestors of many of the peoples of these areas had helped
defend the frontiers of the Roman Empire during the centuries of its decline. From the second century A.D., Rome
had first recruited from the noncitizens who had been living
within the empire, then from newly arrived folk from
beyond the frontier. Marcus Aurelius introduced the practice of settling thousands of Germans within the empire,
where they were expected to shore up the frontier. Later the
emperor Julian brought in entire tribes and gave them the
status of *foederati* (allies) with the responsibility of holding
their part of the frontier against other alien peoples beyond.
So non-Roman had the Roman army become by the fourth
century that the Latin term *barbarus*, meaning barbarian,
had acquired the connotation of soldier.

It is generally maintained that Rome's greatest contribu-
tion to history was preserving much of the culture of the
ancient world, notably the Greek, and passing this on to the

1

West. This suggests that if Rome (and Greece) influenced
the thought, language, law, religion, art, and technology—
that is, the civilization of the future nations of western
Europe—she should also have left her mark on the art of war
which these budding nations practiced. That she surely did,
but only to a limited degree. It is a curious fact that whereas
Rome had much to offer these semicivilized peoples, in the
area of warfare they were almost Rome's equal. The best
soldier in the world of Julius Caesar when he conquered
Gaul (58-51 B.C.), was the citizen foot soldier who made up
the famed Roman legions. By the fourth century A.D., that
erstwhile warrior was only a memory. The most effective
warrior of this later age was the armed horseman, a type of
soldier that Rome had never developed and indeed had
depended upon non-Roman peoples to supply when the need
arose. It was this horseman who was destined to rule the
field of battle for the greater part of the Middle Ages.

The superiority of the armed horseman was painfully
brought home to Rome in August 378 at Adrianople when
the cavalry of the "barbarian" Visigoths annihilated the
Roman army and left its emperor dead on the field. The
Visigoths had moved from the steppe lands north of the
Black Sea to the Danube in order to escape the on-pressing
Huns, who had ridden in from Asia and already had subjugated their cousins, the Ostrogoths. When the Visigoths
reached the Danube, Emperor Valens reluctantly granted
them permission to cross and settle on lands in Thrace.
There, because of mistreatment at the hands of Roman officials, they rose in revolt, then destroyed the army of Imperial Rome at Adrianople with weapons and horsemen
which were "barbarian," not Roman. What is also significant about the battle of Adrianople is that though Rome continued to raise armies, they became appreciably less Roman
and more barbarian as time passed.

The battle of Adrianople signaled the rapid disintegration of the Roman Empire in the west. (The eastern half of the empire, known as the Eastern Roman Empire, the Byzantine Empire, or Byzantium, continued on for another thousand years.) In the year 410 these same Visigoths who had destroyed the Roman army at Adrianople, now led by their most famous king, Alaric, "sacked" the city of Rome. Shortly after Alaric's death they moved west and established the first of the "barbarian" kingdoms in southwestern France (Gaul) and Spain. Because Rome had denuded her defenses along the northern frontier in order to meet the challenge of Alaric and the Visigoths, this frontier collapsed, and a flood of "barbarian" Vandals, Sueves, Burgundians, Alans, Franks, Angles, and Saxons crossed over and marked off states of their own on lands formerly ruled by Rome. The majority of these peoples consented to save Rome's face by recognizing her sovereign power and accepting the status of *foederati*. It cost them nothing to do this and would assure them cheap grain from Rome's African provinces. It also provided a measure of stability in a world that was falling apart. Indeed, in 451, many of these peoples—Visigoths, Franks, and Burgundians among others—allied themselves in a common cause against an enemy whose approach impelled them for the moment to set aside their own animosities.

This enemy was the Huns, who, about the year 375, forced their way into the lands above the Black Sea and established a sprawling empire with its center in Hungary. Within a few years they forced the neighboring German tribes to accept their rule. From their capital on the Theiss River they collected tribute from both Rome and Constantinople. The demands they made on Constantinople, which were much the larger, continued to grow until the year 450, when the Byzantine emperor, Marcian, defied the Hunnic king, Attila, and announced an end to tribute. This defiance provoked Attila into leading his huge army of Huns and Germans westward into Gaul. In 451 at Chalons he confronted the "Roman" army and its allies, Visigoths, Franks, Burgundians, and Alans, in one of the decisive battles of history. A threat that might have led to a rapid extinction of Roman culture lifted when Attila and his horde suffered defeat and returned to Hungary. Attila appeared again the following year, this time in northern Italy, but the Hunnic peril ended shortly and the Germanic nations were left pretty much to themselves to create states of their own.

The most successful of the newly created states proved to be that of the Franks. Unlike most of the German peoples who had crossed into the empire, such as the Visigoths and Vandals, the Franks had not pulled up their roots and migrated to distant lands. They simply spread farther to the west from their homeland east of the Rhine. Under their most famous king, Clovis, they extended Frankish rule over the greater part of what is known today as France. A crucial step in the rise of Clovis was his acceptance of baptism as a Catholic Christian. This act won him the adherence of the hierarchy of the church of Gaul, the only organized institution which still survived in that part of Europe.

Gregory, the sainted bishop of Tours, credited the God of the Christians with the victories Clovis gained in forcing most of the "kinglets" of Gaul to recognize his rule. Still, even with heaven's assistance to supplement his own sagacity, Clovis needed warriors and weapons to accomplish what he did. The period is an obscure one, but two reasonably acceptable generalizations concerning the art of war may be offered: first, the kind of warfare Clovis and his warriors fought, including the weapons they used, were not greatly different from those of their neighbors; and second, these remained largely unchanged until the second half of the eighth century.

What constituted the core of Clovis' army was his own band of retainers. These were men whose loyalty he secured by sharing with them the fruits of conquests and by ruthlessly destroying anyone who dared question his authority. Such armed bands were not uncommon during these troubled times when Roman authority had disappeared and most German kings were such in name only. These monarchs lacked the wealth, the administrative machinery, and the force of popular acceptance to enable them to rule effectively except over limited areas.

For the origin of these war bands one might find a clue in the ancient *comitatus*, a practice that the Roman historian Tacitus ascribed to the Germans of his day. The young men of a tribe submitted themselves to the leadership of a warrior they admired "to defend and protect him, to put down one's own acts of heroism to his credit."[1] A more immediate prototype is seen in the armed bands that prominent Romans began to recruit, when imperial power waned, to provide protection for themselves and their estates. The leaders of such bands—they might be known as counts (Latin *comes*, companion) or dukes (Latin *dux*, leader)—composed the backbone of royal authority during this, the Merovingian age (481–752).

Together with the *comitatus* Tacitus also mentions the practice that the Germans had of requiring military service from all able-bodied men. To fight was their principal if not sole responsibility as far as the tribe was concerned. From this tradition one may trace references to the levy, which scholars encounter in the documents of the Merovingian period. The reference might be to a general levy, although only rarely so, since most men so recruited would lack both the experience and the sense of discipline to be useful. A more select levy, however, could be quite valuable in defending the walls of a city, in doing garrison duty, in helping in the siege of a town, or in holding prisoners captive. No doubt many men engaged in this kind of military service inherited their posts from their fathers and forefathers, who had been similarly employed in the late empire.

The more fortunate members of these armed bands of the Merovingian period wore helmets and coats of mail, although neither of these approached the near invulnerability of those used in the feudal age to come. The warriors also carried shields and for weapons chose from a variety of javelins, lances, swords, axes, bows and arrows, and knives, which differed in kind and size depending on whether the fighting was on foot or on horseback. This point raises the controversial question concerning the art of war at this time, namely, did the war bands of Clovis, his sons, and grandsons ride horses merely for purpose of transport or did they actually fight on horseback?

The evidence is meager and not convincing. Some Frankish units that served in the Roman army of the early fifth century apparently did fight as horsemen. But the evidence suggests that as late as 732 at Tours, the army of Charles Martel, leader of the Franks, rode to do battle with the Moors on horseback, dismounted when they reached the battlefield, defeated the enemy, then mounted again and pursued on horseback. That these Merovingian kings maintained some horsemen appears highly probable, since they had in their service such peoples as Alans, Sarmatians, and Goths, all of whom had a long tradition of fighting on horseback. The tardiness of the Franks to adopt this method of warfare has been traced to the traditions of their home in the Rhineland where thick forests militated against the use of cavalry.

Although Tours was the only great battle fought during the Merovingian period, there was a great deal of petty fighting, and this frequently centered about towns and cities. It was in such places that the enemy could hope to find loot, and it was in fortified cities that an opponent's strength would be concentrated. Documents make mention of siege engines, of battering rams mounted on wagons and covered with sheds of wood to protect those inside from the missiles, of rope ladders, and of the besieged throwing down caldrons of burning oil and pitch on the besiegers. There is also reference to naval craft being used in this period. This might be traced back to imperial times when Rome policed the rivers of Gaul or simply credited to the ingenuity of the people.

In 752 Pepin the Short, son of Charles Martel, had himself proclaimed king and founded the second of the Frankish dynasties, the Carolingian. This dynasty took its name from Charlemagne, son of Pepin, who proved the most famous representative of that line. Above all his other notable accomplishments military success accounted most for his title, "The Great." He destroyed the Lombards and Avars, subjugated the stubborn Saxons, and erected an empire which reached from Denmark to Croatia and from below Rome to across the Pyrenees into Spain.

With regard to the art of war, Charlemagne's reign witnessed a quickening of the trend which was to make the armed horseman the unquestioned master of the battlefield. Charlemagne had no choice but to place greater reliance on horsemen, since the armies of three of his principal enemies—the Moors in Spain, the Lombards in Italy, and the Avars in eastern Europe—consisted principally of cavalry. If Charlemagne wished to destroy these enemies that ringed his kingdom, he had no choice but to recruit horsemen of his own who could contend with them on their terms.

A less personal explanation for the trend toward armed horsemen was a development that some scholars trace to the early eighth century. This is the introduction of the stirrup. Speculation continues as to the origin of the stirrup and its precise appearance in western Europe, but there is no question concerning the importance of its impact upon the art of war. Up to this point the armed horseman could prove himself a formidable warrior with his javelins, bow and arrows, and sword. But since he lacked a firm base from which to operate, his accuracy suffered as did the force with which he could use his weapons. The stirrup furnished him such a base. Once he found himself firmly attached to the back of his steed, he could throw his lance with far greater speed and accuracy, he could deliver a far more powerful thrust with his sword, and he could rise in his stirrups and with the greater leverage thus afforded, deliver a shattering blow with his mace or battle-ax.

All this did not happen overnight, and even during Charlemagne's reign a considerable portion of his army continued to consist of foot soldiers. It is interesting to note that capitularies (laws) from his reign required all men who held benefices—estates sufficiently productive to furnish them the means—to serve as horsemen and to equip themselves with shield, lance, sword, dagger, bow, quiver, and arrows. In all probability it was not long before the requirement of bow and arrow disappeared once the knight found his other weapons far more effective and easier to handle.

The emergence of the armed horseman to a position of unquestioned superiority on the field of battle in the ninth century not only transformed the art of war but altered to a considerable degree both the social and political structure of society. What chiefly accounted for this heavy impact upon society was the high cost of the horse. It has been calculated that the horse in this period was roughly the equivalent in value to two dozen oxen, at a time when a peasant who owned a single ox was considered fortunate. The crucial problem facing the king and other lords was where to find the means to enable them to transform their armies or bands of retainers from relatively inexpensive foot soldiers to costly horsemen.

Since this was a period of agrarian economy, when the king could realize but little revenue from tolls and other levies on trade, he had to fall back on land to provide the means to equip his knights. He did this first by giving out to selected warriors parcels of his own estates; revenues from the estates would finance the procurement of horse, armor, and weapons. When his own estates threatened to become exhausted, the king turned to the church, as had Charles Martel, and insisted that bishops and abbots turn benefices over to his warriors to provide them with what they required. Within a few years all men holding a specified amount of land, as noted in the capitulary above, were required to come equipped with horse, armor, and weapons when the king or lord should summon them.

With such emphasis placed upon land as providing the means for equipping armed horsemen, the inevitable consequence was the rise of a land-owning aristocracy who were to dominate almost all phases of life during the balance of the medieval period. While the social and political prominence of this class carried on long after it had lost its original *raison d'etre*—the ability to supply armed horsemen and to lead them in battle—this was clearly their role during the period from the ninth to the twelfth century, the so-called feudal period. During these centuries the power of a king or other lord was counted in terms of the knights he maintained together with those his vassals were pledged to supply him.

That the military superiority of the knight during this feudal age had such an impact on medieval society was due principally to the high cost of his armor, his weapons, and his mount. His chief offensive weapons consisted of lance, mace, and sword. He wore a conical steel cap, usually with a nasal bar to protect the face and later a metal panel behind to shield the back of his neck, a shirt of chain mail that reached to his knees (hauberk), and a large shield that grew smaller as his armor became stronger. By the close of the twelfth century a pot helm, largely cylindrical in shape and with slits for the eyes, had become popular. By this time, too, the knight's mail shirt had grown sufficiently long to divide itself at the bottom into leg coverings that reached down to his shoes. Straps of iron also protected his feet. So completely protected by iron were these knights of the twelfth century that the Turks referred to them as the "iron people." But all these improvements cost more and more money, the result being a steady drop in the number of heavily armed knights and the appearance of a more lightly armed class of horsemen called sergeants.

As vital to the knight's effectiveness on the field of battle as his armor and weapons was his horse. On the back of his favorite steed he could confront any enemy; unhorsed he was liable to be stabbed by some lowly foot soldier or captured and held for ransom. As he put on more and heavier armor to protect himself, he did what he could for his mount. He draped its body with chain metal that reached as close to the ground as mobility would permit. Unfortunately, this was never far enough to guard the horse's under-quarters from the thrust of a dagger or knife or the sharp point of a pike that the enemy had stuck into the ground. The knight's horse often proved his Achilles' heel.

There was another factor in feudal warfare which contributed to the creation of a proud aristocracy of landed magnates. This was the castle. Castles made their appearance during the Carolingian period, the greater number of them during the unsettled years of the late ninth and tenth centuries, when the Carolingian empire disintegrated and kings lost most of their power. In England many sprung up during the reign of the weak Stephen (1135–54). Their number and prominence marked in general the presence of a monarch who reigned rather than ruled.

The first castles were blockhouses protected by a palisade and moat and often constructed on a hill to furnish added strength and visibility. In the twelfth century, largely as a result of experience gained on the Crusades when Christian knights learned of the more formidable fortifications in Syria, stone castles gradually replaced those of wood. The usual type of castle was the motte-bailey, which consisted basically of a mound and courtyard. On the mound stood a citadel, known as a donjon or keep, which sometimes reached a height of a hundred feet or more, a courtyard protected by a high, thick wall and deep moat, and a drawbridge which controlled movement in and out of the castle. Until the advent of gunpowder and artillery in the fifteenth century, the walls of such castles might defy the efforts of any attacker who lacked the means to maintain a blockade for an extended period and starve out the besieged. In an age when transport was difficult and the service required of knight and foot soldier limited, such a blockade was not easy to maintain.

With so much attention ordinarily given the aristocracy and the knight in books and pictures describing the feudal period, one is apt to forget that the foot soldier never disappeared from the scene. True, at no time in the history of warfare had he fallen so low. The knight almost pushed him off the battlefield, while in the social order his low position fell even lower as the land-owning class rose to a commanding position. Yet the foot soldier retained some importance. He was useful in garrisoning a castle and in helping defend walled cities, especially in Italy and the Low Countries. He assisted in the transport of the equipment and the materials needed by the knightly class. He was expected to have another horse ready should the knight lose his first mount. He could penetrate the ranks of opposing knights and stab or cripple their mounts, and he could kill or capture any unhorsed knight he might come upon. Still, all these functions remained auxiliary.

The history of the armies of foot soldiers that were ready to take the offensive in the fifteenth century does not lead back to these foot soldiers scattered among the ranks of knights but to foot soldiers who had always fought as warriors. These could be found in Wales, Scotland, and Switzerland, where the mountainous terrain discouraged the use of cavalry, or in the Low Countries and in northern Italy, where walled cities and towns had always demanded their presence for garrison and siege duties. Only after much effort did the English kings extend their rule over Wales, something they never succeeded in doing to the Scots. The Alpine passes in Switzerland enabled the mountaineers there to inflict a series of bloody defeats on the feudal armies of the Hapsburgs and gain their independence. The foot soldiers of Flanders repeatedly thwarted the ambitions of the French kings to absorb them, as at Courtrai in 1302. In Italy it was the foot soldiers who assured the victory of the northern Italian cities over Frederick Barbarossa, the Holy Roman emperor, at Legnano in 1176.

The weapons used by these foot soldiers varied to some degree with the era, country, and terrain. Some were unique, such as the Danish two-handed battle-ax, which the Anglo-Saxons adopted from the Danish invader. A weapon popular with the Swiss was the halberd, a sort of pike as much as twenty feet in length, which carried an assortment of cruel attachments on its head: a hook with which to drag the knight from his horse, a spear, and an axe which a sturdy foot soldier could swing with such force as to crush the armor of the best equipped horseman. The Welsh were famed for their long bows which they used with unusual force and accuracy. Their garrulous chronicler, Gerald of Wales, claimed he saw points of an arrow shot by such a bow sticking through four inches of an oak door. He also told of a knight nailed to his horse by an arrow that had pierced the flap of his mail shirt, his mail breeches, his thigh, the wooden saddle, and had lodged finally in the flank of his horse.

An even more destructive weapon, though less accurate and more difficult to fire, was the crossbow. This has usually been associated with the Genoese mercenaries, who were among the first nationals of Europe to let themselves out for hire. Its missile struck with such dreadful force as to cruelly maim anyone it did not kill. It was so brutal a weapon that the church declared it outlawed. Then there was the pike. With its butt buried in the ground or pressed against the ground with the foot, it could disembowel a charging horse. Apart from these special weapons there were the more common knives, daggers, swords, axes, falchions, fist-shields, javelins, and lances that made up the arsenal of the foot soldier's weapons. For protection he wore what he could secure, a helmet when available, a shield, a short shirt of mail and iron gloves.

While the foot soldiers could challenge the arrogance of the feudal aristocracy and his knights in such places as the Low Countries and Switzerland, this proud class was ultimately brought into reasonable submission by the rise of a strong ruler. Circumstances which had contributed to the weakening of the state in the earlier Middle Ages began to work in its favor after the close of the feudal period. By the end of the eleventh century, after the last of the "barbarian" invaders, the Vikings and Magyars, had been pacified or assimilated, Europe began to enjoy a state of relative stability and peace. Industry and trade expanded, towns and cities increased in number and size, and an increasing measure of fluid capital began to energize the economy of western Europe. Within a short time kings were collecting revenues large enough to enable them to finance much of the cost of warfare and take its direction out of the hands of the landed aristocracy upon whom they had earlier depended. Henry II of England, for example, permitted his vassals to pay a fee, called scutage, in lieu of military service. With this money Henry could hire mercenaries and appoint captains of his own choosing. The Crusades and the church favored

the rise of monarchs since it was to kings that popes generally appealed to lead armies against the Infidel. And it was the
strengthening of the monarchy which the church felt held
greatest promise for the establishment of a peaceful
Christendom.

One of the first rulers to succeed in managing his feudal
aristocracy with a firm hand was William, duke of Normandy, better known as William the Conqueror for his victory at Hastings in 1066, which made him king of England.
A little later Louis VI, king of France, laid the foundation of
French royal power which his grandson, Philip II Augustus
(1180-1223), used to extend his authority over much of
France. Philip's most striking achievement was depriving
John, king of England, who as his vassal was ruling the
western provinces of France, of Normandy and other fiefs
north of the Loire River. In 1214, when Philip defeated
John's ally Otto IV of Germany at Bouvines, he guaranteed
his hold on those provinces. Roughly a hundred years later,
in 1356, at the battle of Crecy, Philip VI hoped to complete
the work begun by Philip II and push England completely
out of France, but instead he suffered a startling defeat. It required another century of conflict, the Hundred Years' War,
(1337-1453), before this was accomplished.

As noted above, one of the factors in the rise of royal power
was the Christian church. In the eleventh century, the
papacy, which almost had been swept under in the mire of
Italian political strife, struggled to its feet with the help of
the German king. It then assumed the leadership of Europe
in urging a series of offensive campaigns against Islam called
the Crusades for the purpose of restoring Christian control
over Palestine and the Holy Land. No king took part in the
First Crusade (1096-99). That was the height of the feudal
age when kings were usually no more powerful than the
more ambitious of their vassals. But the kings of France and
Germany led the Second Crusade (1147-49), and thereafter

it was usually monarchs to whom the pope appealed and who led their countries' armies.

No problem so absorbed papal concern and effort from the eleventh century to the close of the Middle Ages as the organization of Crusades against the Turks. For the background to these expeditions one must reach back to the rise of Islam, the state which Mohammed established as a theocracy in 630 when he occupied Mecca, the holy city of the Arabs. After Mohammed's death, his successors, called caliphs, carried the expansion of Islam beyond the confines of Arabia. At the Yarmuk River in 636 they gained a tremendous victory over the Byzantine army, which gave them control of Syria and opened the way to the rapid conquest of Egypt and North Africa. Exactly a hundred years after the death of Mohammed, Charles Martel finally succeeded in blunting Islamic expansion when he defeated the Moors at Tours in 732.

By this time, even though the Islamic state stretched from the Indus River across Mesopotamia, Syria, Egypt, North Africa and through Spain into southwestern France, western Europe remained only mildly disturbed. What afforded the Christian West a feeling of security and insulated it from any major attack from Islam was the Byzantine or Eastern Roman empire, whose control of Anatolia and Constantinople appeared to block permanently Islam's moving up into the Balkans. In 1095 the Byzantine emperor sent an appeal to Pope Urban II for assistance against the Seljuk Turks who had conquered the greater part of Anatolia. It was partly to shore up Byzantine power, and more directly to drive the Muslim from Jerusalem and Bethlehem, that the West undertook the Crusades under papal leadership.

The First Crusade proved the most successful. It not only resulted in the capture of Jerusalem but led shortly to the establishment of a series of Christian states that stretched along the coast of Syria to the north. Still, a glance at the

map should have warned any westerner that it was unrealistic to think of holding these territories once Islam became
united. The man who succeeded in unifying much of Islam
and then demonstrated the weakness of the Christian position was Saladin. His overwhelming victory over the army
of the Crusades in 1187 at Hattin, followed by the capture of
Jerusalem, was the capstone of his brilliant career.

Saladin's success in capturing Jerusalem and thus nearly
ending Christian rule in Syria provoked the three leading
kings of Europe—Richard of England, Philip Augustus of
France, and Frederick Barbarossa of Germany—to undertake
the well known Third Crusade (1189–92). Other Crusades
followed without great success, and Louis IX of France died
in 1270 on what is generally identified as the Last Crusade.
With the rise of the Ottoman Turks in the fourteenth century, Islam went on the offensive, and all thought of a Christian conquest of Syria evaporated. Now it became the
anxious concern of the papacy and Christian Europe to halt
the Turkish drive into the Balkans. Under the prodding of
the pope, western Europe organized a huge army in 1396
which moved triumphantly down the Danube until it
reached Nicopolis. Here Bayazid, the sultan of Turkey, and
his army annihilated it. Bayazid, called the Thunderbolt,
had his eye on Constantinople. Its capture would give him
complete control of southeastern Europe and the greatest
metropolis in the Western World. He could have taken the
city at this time had it not been for Timur the Lame, the
Mongol khan. At the battle of Angora in 1402, Bayazid lost
his army to Timur and shortly after died a prisoner in
Timur's capital at Samarkand.

The battle of Angora holds a double distinction for the
Middle Ages. It probably counted more warriors, surely
more horsemen, than any battle prior to modern times, and
it was one of the last major battles in which gunpowder and
artillery did not play a prominent role. Their impact came
with the modern age, which was about to dawn.

2

THE BATTLE OF CHALONS

AMONG THE INTRIGUING HISTORICAL PICTURES WHICH THE ART-
ist Raphael painted is his fresco entitled "Pope Leo the Great
and Attila." The fresco shows the pope, flanked by cardinals
and other churchmen, confronting the Hunnic king and his
warrior hordes. Smoke and devastation have already announced Attila's approach, and a similar fate seems to await
the city of Rome, some of whose famous structures, including the Colosseum, furnish the picture's background.
Leo's right hand is raised, and he appears to be ordering the
Hunnic king to return whence he had come. The most ar-
resting figures in the scene are the Apostles Peter and Paul.
They hover in the sky above Leo, swords in hand, threatening Attila with death should he defy the pope's command.
The story upon which this scene is based tells how Attila
turned about, impressed either by the stern presence of the
saintly pontiff or by the swords of the Apostles, and took his
barbarian army back to Hungary.

As is often true of dramatic episodes from the past which
skeptics are apt to dismiss as legend, this story does have
some basis in fact. Pope Leo did meet Attila, probably late in
the summer of 452, some sixty miles north of Rome near the
southern shore of Lake Garda, where the Hunnic king had
his camp. Leo's companions on this mission were not

17

cardinals—they and their red hats do not make their appearance until much later—but two prominent Roman senators, Trygetius and Avienus. The nature of their discussions with Attila is not known. Pope Leo makes no mention of the incident, nor does the Christian chronicler Prosper who wrote an account of what happened a few years after the event. The Apostles with their drawn swords appear in a later embellishment of Prosper's story. The fact remains, however, that following his meeting with Leo, Attila did return to Hungary. But this is getting ahead of the story.

Attila was the most illustrious of the "barbarian" leaders who ravaged the Roman Empire during the period of its decline. There were other barbarian kings who did the same, the word *barbarian* being used loosely in the sense of non-Roman and semicivilized. Alaric, king of the Visigoths, was the first of several German chieftains who "sacked" the city of Rome. He did this in 410 A.D. Forty-five years later another German king, the Vandal Gaiseric, ruler over most of North Africa west of Egypt, looted the Eternal City a second time. After Attila came Odovacar, probably a Scirian German, not so formidable a leader as the others, although he enjoys enduring fame as the man who deposed Romulus Augustulus, the last of the "Roman emperors" in the West. Following Odovacar came Theodoric, who made Italy the base of an imposing Ostrogothic kingdom which he carved out of the dying empire. These and other barbarian kings figured more prominently in the history of the decline of the Roman Empire than did Attila the Hun. Attila continues, nonetheless, to be best known as the most destructive and dreaded of the enemies that the weakening empire encountered in its decline.

What gave Attila this fearsome reputation was the wont of medieval writers to refer to him as the "Scourge of God."[1] To these Christian writers all evil that befell man was visited by

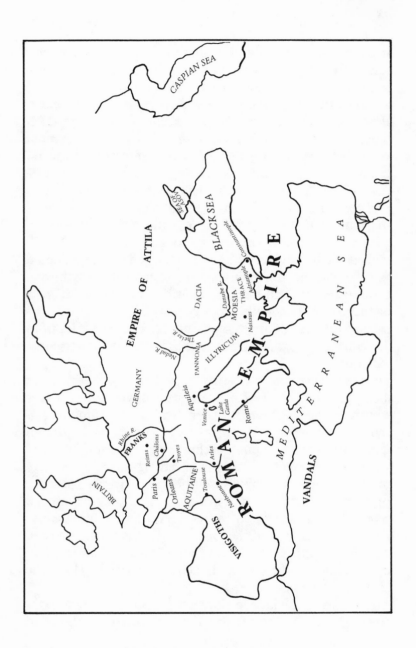

an angry God intent on punishing human beings for their sins. Few disasters had a purely natural origin, certainly nothing so destructive as the appalling devastations worked by Attila and his Huns. True, Attila never occupied the city of Rome. Yet there were special features about him and his people which left the Romans more terrified at the thought of his coming than they were of Alaric, for instance, who did actually "sack" the city. First of all, Attila was not a Christian as was Alaric, even though Alaric was an Arian and therefore a heretical Christian. But heretics were considered an improvement over pagans like Attila. Then, the descriptions which contemporaries gave of the Huns caused civilized people to shudder. Who but Attila and his hordes could have led so many different peoples to forge their own mutual animosities and join forces against him at Chalons in 451? At this battle, as the historian Edward Gibbon put it in his *Decline and Fall of the Roman Empire*, all the peoples from the Volga to the Atlantic were either leagued with or against the dour king of the Huns.

Few Romans had ever seen Huns. They had heard about them and their diabolical ways from travelers and slaves who may have suffered at their hands. According to Jordanes, they were the offspring of witches and unclean spirits. No wonder, then, that they were "a stunted, foul and puny tribe, scarcely human, and having no language save one which bore but slight resemblance to human speech." So terrifying was their appearance that more powerful peoples fled in horror to escape them, for "their swarthy aspect was fearful, and they had, if I may call it so, a sort of shapeless lump, not a head, with pinholes rather than eyes.... Though they live in the form of men, they have the cruelty of wild beasts."[2]

These words about the Huns are from the pen of a sixth-century Goth, a poor historian at best, and one who lived when the Hunnic peril was only a dark memory. What is considered the most reliable description of the Huns is that left by a Greek soldier, Ammianus Marcellinus by name, whose history of the Roman Empire survives for the years 353 to 378. Ammianus died about the year 400. The impressions he had of the Huns were probably not based upon personal contact, however, and it may be significant that while he names eleven Gothic leaders, he mentions not a single Hun. He located the home of this savage race as east of the Sea of Azov. What accounted in part for their ill-favored physical appearance was one of their traditional practices: "The cheeks of the children are deeply furrowed with an iron from their very birth." Because of the wrinkled scars this practice left, "they grow old without beards and without any beauty, like eunuchs. They all have compact, strong limbs and thick necks, and are so monstrously ugly and misshapen that one might take them for two-legged beasts."

Ammianus reassures his reader that fearful though the appearance of these Huns might be, "they have the form of men, however ugly." Still they did not use fire to prepare their food as civilized people did, nor did they live in houses, which they shunned the way ordinary people avoid tombs. They were nomadic. "No one in their country ever plows a field or touches a plow-handle. They are all without fixed abode, without hearth, or law, or settled mode of life, and keep roaming from place to place, like fugitives, accompanied by the wagons in which they live." They made their clothes from linen or the skins of field mice, and these they never changed, but "when they have once put their necks into a faded tunic, it is not taken off or changed until by long wear and tear it has been reduced to rags and fallen from them bit by bit." The men spent the greater part of their lives on the backs of their horses. There they did what buying and selling their simple needs required. There they ate and drank; there they slept when on the march; and there they conducted what little government they tolerated.

Possibly the most reliable portion of Ammianus' description of the Huns concerns the weapons they used and their manner of fighting. Since they spent so much of their time on horseback, they were superb horsemen. Because "they are lightly equipped for swift motion, and unexpected in action, they purposely divide suddenly into scattered bands and attack, rushing about in disorder here and there, dealing terrific slaughter." Ammianus was ready to call them "the most terrible of all warriors, because they fight from a distance with missiles having sharp bone, instead of their usual points, joined to the shafts with wonderful skill; then they gallop over the intervening spaces and fight hand to hand with swords, regardless of their own lives."

Amoral traits compounded the ferocity of the Huns. "In truces they are faithless and unreliable, strongly inclined to sway to the motion of every breeze of new hope that presents itself, and sacrificing every feeling to the mad impulse of the moment. Like unreasoning beasts, they are utterly ignorant of the difference between right and wrong; they are deceitful and ambiguous in speech, never bound by any reverence for religion or for superstition." What aggravated these base instincts and brought them into play was their "infinite thirst for gold." In summary, Ammianus wrote: "This race of untamed men, without encumbrances, aflame with an inhuman desire for plundering others' property, made their violent way amid the rapine and slaughter of the neighbouring peoples."[3]

It is unfortunate that from the time these early writers penned their harsh descriptions of the character and mores of the Huns of the fourth and fifth centuries, no written source of any consequence has come to light which might relieve the darkness of the picture they left. Archaeological discoveries have helped to a degree; if nothing more, they have furnished bits of evidence indicative of the kind of life the Huns lived while still east of the Caspian.

The most powerful factor that determined the character of the Huns and their way of life was surely the climate of the land in which they lived. Because little rain fell in Inner Asia, that is, over the immense reaches of steppe which stretched east of the Urals into Mongolia, historians in the past have classified these people as nomads. They were a folk who had no permanent homes. Their search for food for themselves and for their stock kept them forever on the move. But the discovery of relatively extensive grave sites in Hunnia have led scholars to modify this earlier view of the Hunnish nomadism to one of seminomadism. The Huns appear to have occupied reasonably permanent sites and, furthermore, to have moved about in one general area. They drove their herds north in the spring to the pastures they had occupied the year previously, then in the fall returned to their customary winter quarters. This suggests a significant advance over a purely nomadic existence since it permitted the evolution of the kind of mores only a more stable society could produce.

From the beginning of time, the mainstay of nomads and seminomads has been animal husbandry, and the Huns were no exception. They maintained large herds of horses and sheep along with some cattle. Horses provided them means of transportation and mounts in time of war together with a good part of their meat and milk. They boiled chunks of horse meat in huge caldrons and particularly on the march depended on the milk of their mares for drink. Their sheep furnished food, clothing, and shelter—milk, cheese, and meat for food, sheepskins, woven fabric, or felt for their tents and clothing, and leather for their shoes. On occasion game and fish relieved the monotony of their diet, as did millet, which they managed to raise despite the lack of

rainfall and shortness of the growing season. But that was
the extent of their agriculture. What Ammianus Marcellinus
wrote about their never touching a hand to a plow may be
true, since not a single plowshare has been unearthed in
Hunnia.

While the economy of the Huns was one of self-suffi-
ciency, they did carry on some trade with the peoples along
their borders. Their principal exports were horses and slaves.
They raised the horses and captured the slaves on their raids
and in time of war. They had no use for slaves themselves,
although the few wealthy among them might keep slaves as
domestic servants. With the gold they received in exchange
for their goods or seized on their raids, they might buy wine
and silk, both of which were in great demand. Or they might
be content to let their hoard of gold accumulate, as did the
Avars in Hungary.

On their slow trek to northern pastures and their return to
winter homes the Huns moved those who required transportation—small children, the aged, and infirm—in four-
wheeled wagons. When greater speed was necessary, as on a
raid, they used two-wheeled wains, and when they wished
the most speed they rode their horses. It was the speed of
their horses which impressed the western observer, along
with the unusual endurance and toughness of these animals.
No doubt conditions in Hunnia inured them to circumstances which western steeds would not tolerate, as the
fourth-century Roman writer Vegetius lamented. Vegetius
did find the Roman horse superior in intelligence and looks,
but he had high praise for the patience, dependability, and
durability of the Hunnic horses. True, they were ungainly
beasts, with large hooked heads, protruding eyes, manes
hanging below the knees, large rib cages, wide-spreading
hooves—but with "beauty even in their ugliness."[4]

As suggested above, what Ammianus Marcellinus had to
say about the military prowess of the Huns was probably the

most accurate part of his description. They excelled as horsemen and bowmen. These skills they had learned and practiced from boyhood. Beside bow and arrow, the Hunnic warrior carried a sword and lance, and perhaps a lasso, a weapon fairly common among the steppe peoples and a favorite with the Alans. For protective covering the Huns depended upon padding of leather and wool unless he was able to seize or buy something of iron from his more civilized neighbors. Those so fortunate might wear a cuirass and helmet of metal. He also carried a small shield of wickerwork which might be covered with leather.

Much of the advantage which the Huns enjoyed over the armies they encountered derived from the speed and endurance of their horses. Long distances meant little to them, and they regularly arrived sooner than their troubled enemies expected. As they approached their foe they made a fearful noise, then let fly a heavy volley of arrows, after which they would close in for hand-to-hand fighting. Western writers say nothing of the stratagem of the feigned flight which they are believed to have shared with other warriors of the steppe world. They used neither spur nor stirrup, although they managed a kind of wooden saddle which helped secure them on their mounts.

Jordanes and Ammianus Marcellinus comment on the evil ways of the Huns but say nothing about religious beliefs and practices. And the work of archaeologists has done little to clarify the problem of their religion. They had seers and men who divined omens, as well as amulets and idols of precious metals, stone, and chalk, and there is evidence which suggests they sacrificed animals to their gods. But the closest scholars have come to identifying a god who was the object of Hunnic worship was a sacred sword which for them represented the god of war. If they worshipped gods in human or animal form, there are no names to identify these, and no scholar ventures to say whether they had priests.

By the middle of the fifth century when Attila was preparing to take his army westward into Gaul, Ammianus Marcellinus and his contemporaries would have found the thought of these Huns and the threat of their coming less appalling. Since food was more plentiful north of the Black Sea than it had been in the semiarid reaches east of the Caspian whence they had come, these Huns had shed some of the ways of their earlier nomadic existence. Convincing evidence of their greater stability are the large grave fields which have been discovered. Although wagons or tents of felt probably continued to serve the majority as homes, the more ambitious and wealthy lived in wooden dwellings. Animal husbandry persisted as their principal source of food, and they raised some millet and drank two beverages not unlike the mead and beer of the Germans. They also consumed considerable quantities of wine which Roman peddlers smuggled from south of the Danube. Hunnish leaders discouraged trade with the Romans and restricted it to an annual fair on the Danube, which after 447 was held at Naissus (Nis). The commodities which the Roman most wanted from the Huns were slaves and horses.

Social stratification that surely existed among the Huns east of the Caspian is clearly revealed from the description western writers give of Attila and his people in Hungary. Beneath the king and enjoying a position of great influence was an aristocracy based upon birth and service. Its leaders formed a sort of council of state which advised the king. He recruited his bodyguard from its members. The chief privilege which the aristocracy enjoyed was that of having first choice to any captured booty or slaves. In Attila's day, one of the members of the aristocracy, Onegesius by name, held a position similar to that of a prime minister or vizier. He occupied the place of honor on formal occasions and lived in a house of wood second only to Attila's in size.

Given the low cultural development of the Huns, no great dividing line separated the aristocracy from the mass of free men and women below them. Most Huns fell under this latter classification. The great majority of Huns were free, among other reasons because their nomadic culture militated against the evolution of large-scale slavery. Their social tastes were also simple, and they preferred gold to any slave for whom it might be bartered. The only slave noted by the fifth-century teacher and historian Priscus was the Roman architect whom Onegesius had commissioned to build a bathhouse where he might enjoy what he considered the epitome of Roman luxury. The disappointed Roman had hoped his ingenuity would at least have gained him his freedom.

The Huns paid no taxes. The simple needs of their nomadic civilization made these unnecessary, as the lack of any administrative machinery made their collection impossible. Each male Hun carried the weapons he had made for himself, and beyond war there existed no national need for which funds were required. Yet while their nomadic ways left the Huns more personal freedom than a more stable society would have permitted, these same nomadic mores may account for the failure of the Huns to develop an assembly of free men. This institution did evolve among the Germans and placed the ultimate authority of the tribe in the hands of the majority.

Ammianus Marcellinus and his contemporaries were especially ignorant about the origins of the Huns. They knew little more than that these people had come from the unknown land beyond the Caspian and that they had established themselves in the region east of the Danube, largely unknown country to writers of the early Middle Ages. Ancient writers had usually been content with identifying any people beyond the Danube simply as Scythians. By the fifth century Byzantine writers were distinguishing the Huns from other northern barbarians, but that was all. They knew nothing concerning the ancient homeland of these Huns in Asia. The Hunnic language provided no clues, nor, for that matter, has it given modern philologists much to work with. There still remains the question whether these Huns may be identified with the Hsiung-nu who attacked China during the second and first centuries B.C. and against whom the Chinese erected the Great Wall. They are best classified simply as Asiatic Mongoloids and therefore the cousins of the Avars and Magyars who later followed them from the steppe country beyond the Caspian Sea into southern Russia.

It was in the plains north of the Black Sea about the year 375 that the Huns made their appearance. There they encountered the Alans, another Asiatic people,[5] whom they subjugated after several years of raiding each other's camps. Some of the Alans managed to make their way west, where they joined various German tribes in overrunning Gaul. Most of the Alans accepted Hunnic authority and joined them in subduing the Ostrogothic people, who lived just to the west of the Alans. Some of the Ostrogoths succeeded in escaping westward to join their cousins, the Visigoths (West Goths), who were already on the move toward the Danube in order to get away from the Hunnic menace.

It was only then that the Roman world became aware of the existence of these Huns, and high time, too. For the Huns, more than any other barbarian people, were chiefly responsible for accelerating what had been a gradual infiltration of the empire by semicivilized Germans from across the Rhine and Danube. This activity became a powerful movement and heralded the early end of the classical world in the west. In 375 the Visigoths received permission from the apprehensive Roman emperor, Valens, to cross the Danube into imperial territory and put that mighty river between them and the Huns. Two years later these Goths, together with the Ostrogoths and Alans who had joined them, rose in rebellion and destroyed Valens and his Roman army at Adrianople. The empire never quite recovered from this disaster.

The fears which many Romans must have had in 376 that the Huns would shortly follow the Visigoths across the Danube did not materialize. A general history of the Roman Empire during the period 376 to 450 would have given the Huns little note. During those seventy-five years other northern barbarians were making history. First there were the Visigoths. For a time these Goths were satisfied to remain on unoccupied lands in Thrace and Moesia which Valens's successor, Theodosius, had assigned them, but not for long. When Theodosius died in 395 they again rose in rebellion, this time under Alaric, their most illustrious leader. For more than a decade Alaric led his people and Alan allies through Greece and Illyricum, pillaging and looting as they looked for a new homeland. As long as Stilicho, the Vandal commander in chief of the Roman army in the west, was alive, there was no getting into Italy, where Alaric hoped to lead his people. In 408 the weak western emperor, Honorius, who stood in fear of Stilicho, had him executed. In August of 410, Alaric and his Visigoths occupied Rome, looted the city for three days and then moved to the south. When Alaric died, his brother-in-law, Athaulf, led the Visigoths back to northern Italy, crossed the western Alps into Gaul, and eventually established the first of the Germanic kingdoms in Aquitaine. In 415 they crossed the Pyrenees into Spain.

Other Germans were on the move into the empire. They found little to hinder them since Stilicho had eliminated the Roman legions from the Rhine frontier and Britain in his efforts to keep Alaric out of Italy. Accordingly, during the year 405–406 there was a general crossing of the Rhine by a number of German tribes. One of these, the Vandals, pillaged their way across Gaul and into Spain, then some years later established a powerful kingdom in North Africa. Unique about this Vandal kingdom was its refusal to accept the face-saving arrangement other German tribes had made of recognizing the suzerain authority of Rome.[6] More of a threat to Rome than this defiance, however, was the navy which the Vandals fitted out and with which they secured control of the western Mediterranean. This fleet enabled them to block grain shipments from Africa which Rome needed to feed its populace and to barter satisfactory arrangements with the German *foederati* (allies) to the north.

Still other Germans were making history during the period 376 to 450. Shortly after Stilicho had summoned the legions from Britain, Angles and Saxons began crossing over to the island in ever increasing numbers once they found the native Britons unable to prevent their coming. Though the invaders did not complete their conquest of Britain until the close of the sixth century, that distant province, to all intents and purposes, was lost to the empire soon after 410. The Salian Franks, whom the emperor Julian had permitted to occupy the area between the Meuse and Scheldt, now extended their rule to the Somme. Alemanni, Ripuarian Franks, and Burgundians also crossed the Rhine, the latter pushing their way far down into the valley of the Rhone.

And where were the Huns during this time and what were they doing? A few may have joined the Visigoths in the fighting at Adrianople in 378, although this is doubtful. It is more likely that they had held themselves aloof from imperial affairs, content for the time being with looting their neighbors and enslaving whomever came within their reach. If any Huns did cross the Danube to share in ravaging Thrace after the tragedy at Adrianople, they returned shortly to their homeland north of the Danube. There is a record of Hunnic raids across that river in 384, by which time they were encountering not Romans, but Visigoths, to whom Emperor Theodosius had entrusted the defense of that region. In return for the extensive tracts of Moesia and Dacia that Theodosius had surrendered to them, these Visigoths were to serve as "an unconquerable bulwark against the inroads of the Huns."[7]

What proved to be the principal role of the Huns vis-a-vis the Roman Empire during the half-century following the battle of Adrianople was that of furnishing troops for its defense. Hunnic horsemen were in great demand, both by the legitimate emperors as well as by occasional pretenders who sought that position. In 388 Emperor Theodosius defeated the pretender Maximus with the assistance of Huns and other barbarian auxiliaries. Stilicho kept Huns in his employ during his campaigns against Alaric, as he did when he fought the imperial pretender Eugenius. Even Rufinus, the "strong man" in Constantinople during the reign of the incompetent Arcadius, had a bodyguard composed of Huns. Rufinus even permitted thousands of Huns to cross over into Thrace with their wives and children, where they settled on lands provided them by the imperial government.

It was during the closing years of the fourth century that a Hunnish kingdom slowly emerged out of the scattered and largely independent hordes that had first appeared north of the Black Sea. Here in this fertile region it was easier for the abler and more ambitious chieftains to assert a measure of authority. No doubt the example of the neighboring German tribes who had long accepted the leadership of a chieftain or king influenced the Huns in their gradual acceptance of the same arrangement.

The first Hunnic ruler that Roman writers identify as a king was Uldin. From the ambivalent character of his behavior toward the empire scholars conclude that his authority was largely titular. He extended aid to the Romans, as he had to Stilicho, then led raids across the Danube, seemingly as the opportunity recommended or his chieftains suggested. He apparently lacked the authority to prevent other Hunnic leaders from dealing directly with the empire or from attacking it. In 408 Uldin took advantage of the critical situation which faced Stilicho and the empire because of Alaric's threat and led his Huns across the Danube into Thrace. But he hurried back to Hungary for safety when he learned that several Hunnic chieftains had accepted imperial money and had refused to support him.

There remains little firm information about the Huns during the decades of the 420s and the 430s. Long before this time those Alans who had been subdued had disassociated themselves and had crossed the Rhine into Gaul. Even Hunnish raids fell off during this period. All this suggests the absence of strong leadership. That the centralization of Hunnic authority had not come completely undone is clear from the fact that Aetius, commander in chief of the Roman armies in the west in 425, was able to recruit several thousand Hunnic horsemen to serve under him.

A new Hunnish king came forward during this obscure period, Ruga (Rua, Rugi'la, Roas, Ruila) by name, but whether he was Uldin's successor or a chieftain who managed to reestablish the kingship is not clear. While little is known of this ruler, scholars find him employing the policy which became a constant in Hunnic diplomacy, that of dealing with the Roman Empire as two separate states, a western and an eastern empire. Such a policy, of course, made sense. It not only reduced the firmness with which the Romans could deal with the Huns, it also enabled the latter, when the opportunity offered itself, to force concessions more easily from one half or the other. So Ruga furnished horsemen to Aetius, who handled military and imperial policies of the western empire. To the eastern emperor, not only did he refuse auxiliaries but he forbade his chieftains to supply any. At the same time he demanded an annual tribute of 350 pounds of gold from the eastern emperor, Theodosius II. When a group of Huns did take service with the eastern emperor in defiance of Ruga's orders, he set out to attack Constantinople. He died in 434 before he could get his army underway.

The news of Ruga's death set off general rejoicing in Constantinople. The capital hoped that since Ruga had no son capable of succeeding him Hunnic power would weaken, and there would be a return to the largely passive policy which the Huns had been pursuing prior to his emergence. Constantinople's expectation proved a forlorn hope, for without any known difficulty the sons of Ruga's brother Mundzuc (Mundiuch), the one Bleda and the other Attila, presently appeared as joint kings. Constantinople accepted the new rulers without hesitation and without extended negotiations even agreed to a new treaty. This treaty pledged Constantinople to surrender all fugitives from Hunland and to pay a ransom of 8 *solidi* for any Roman prisoner who had escaped and was not returned. Constantinople also undertook not to treat with any barbarian people with whom the Huns were at war. Huns and Romans were to share equal privileges at what fairs might be held on the Danube. Finally, the annual tribute of 350 pounds of gold was increased to 700. That the two new rulers meant to administer affairs with an iron hand became evident upon the return of the two sons of a chieftain who had taken service with Constantinople. Both youths were promptly crucified.

For more than a decade the two brothers, Attila and Bleda, shared the responsibilities of leadership. Bleda was the elder and appears to have enjoyed a position of precedence, although the stronger personality of Attila assured him superiority even before 445 (or 446) when he had his brother murdered. Meantime, once the new treaty had been forced upon Constantinople, the two brothers devoted themselves to confirming Hunnic authority over the different hordes as well as over the German peoples who had once recognized Hunnic rule. The most important of these peoples to accept Hunnic rule were the Gepids and the Ostrogoths. There were also Rugians, Heruli, Scirians, Turcilingi, Sueves (Quadi), and others. The only major German tribe north of the Danube which succeeded in maintaining its independence was the Lombards. Though Attila himself may not have known the precise limits of his empire, historians believe he exercised effective authority over the peoples of Austria, Hungary, Roumania, southern Russia, and a part of Pannonia south of the Danube. His headquarters were located in Hungary somewhere between the Danube and the Theiss rivers. Because buildings were constructed of wood, archaeologists have failed to find any trace of his capital.

Attila, the man who ruled this enormous empire and later aspired to conquer all of Europe, takes his place alongside Genghis Khan and Timur the Lame as one of the three most fearsome conquerors the steppe peoples of Asia ever produced. Only brief sketches of the man remain. Priscus, a contemporary, has a little to say, while somewhat more comes from the pen of Jordanes, who wrote a century after Attila's death. In his history of the Goths he gives this picture of the Hunnic king: "He was a man born into the world to shake the nations, the scourge of all lands, who in some way terrified all mankind by the dreadful rumors noised abroad concerning him. He was haughty in his walk, rolling his eyes hither and thither, so that the power of his proud spirit appeared in the movement of his body. He was indeed a lover of war, yet restrained in action, mighty in counsel, gracious to suppliants, and lenient to those who were once received into his protection. He was short of stature, with a broad chest and a large head; his eyes were small; his beard thin and sprinkled with gray; and he had a flat nose and a swarthy complexion, showing the evidences of his origin."[8]

This sketch does not differ substantially from that of the historian Priscus, who had seen Attila in 448 when he accompanied an embassy from Constantinople to the Hunnic king's court. Priscus offers a clue to Attila's ability to exercise such a strong hold over both his own people and so many other nations as well. He writes how Attila held himself aloof, allowed only members of his family circle and his most intimate advisers to approach him, and insisted upon the most punctilious observance of court ceremonials. His eating habits and the garments he wore set him off from those about him. While his aristocratic companions ate and drank from silver and gold vessels, he ate from a wooden plate. "His dress too was plain, having care for nothing other than to be clean, nor was the sword by his side, nor the clasps of his barbarian boots, nor the bridle of his horse, like those of other Scythians, adorned with gold or gems or anything of high price."[9]

Attila showed himself different from his chieftains in the way he responded to the entertainment that followed the banquet which Priscus and the other members of the embassy shared with him and his court. When a sort of clown "came forward, and by his appearance, his dress, his voice, and the words he confusedly uttered (for he mixed the tongue of the Huns and the Goths with that of the Latins), he softened everyone except Attila and caused unquenchable laughter to arise. But Attila remained unmoved and his expression unaltered, nor in speech nor action did he reveal that he had any laughter in him."[10]

Nowhere did Attila afford more convincing proof of his shrewdness than in his treatment of subject peoples. He assured himself of their respect and cooperation by dealing honorably with their leaders and by calling upon them for counsel. Among his most trusted advisers was Ardaric, king of the Gepids, and Walamir, one of the Ostrogothic kings.

His German subjects were obliged to contribute only armed men when war threatened. However, other subjects whom it was safe to treat less honorably, such as the Slavs, did not enjoy that privileged status. It was their duty to pay a share of the products of their farms, herds, and flocks.

Another mark of Attila's sagacity, unless it was simply the force of tradition, was his refusal to alter the mores of his people lest they permit themselves to be assimilated into the more numerous Germanic and Slavic peoples about them. In contrast to Theodoric, king of Ostrogoths, who entertained a high regard for Roman culture, Attila made no pretense to do other than despise the civilization of Rome. What he admired about the empires south of the Danube and Rhine, and what he demanded of them, was their gold. In terms of intellectual and spiritual values, Attila remained as much a barbarian as his fellow Huns, and he apparently had no wish to change this.

In his relations with the eastern and western empires Attila continued the policy of his predecessors. He dealt with them as separate states. Only by preventing them from working together could he hope to force concessions and gold from them. To further cripple the eastern empire he increased his demands for gold and hounded its emperors with continuous embassies which could be expected to accept satisfaction for grievances they had trumped up only upon receipt of rich gifts. From the year 449 the western emperor paid him gold, not as formal tribute, but under the guise of a salary which Attila was entitled to by virtue of his honorary office as master of the soldiers.[11] The arrangement was not lost on contemporaries, and Priscus identified it simply as a pretext for concealing the payment of tribute. Attila's most effective weapon in dealing with the western empire, however, and a policy that almost guaranteed its good behavior, was his control of the supply of auxiliaries upon which that half of the Roman Empire had come to depend for its survival.

The man who made it a policy to depend principally upon Hunnic auxiliaries to maintain the frontiers of the western empire was Aetius, actual master of the soldiers. In 425 he had used an army of Huns to help secure the succession of Valentinian III following the death of Emperor Honorius. Then in 433, again with the help of his Hunnic friends, Aetius forced Valentinian and his mother, Placidia, the regent, to recognize him as the chief master of the soldiers. From that year until his death in 454 Aetius was the real ruler of the western empire and the director of imperial policy.

This man Aetius, known somewhat gratuitously as "the last of the Romans," was born in Lower Moesia. His father was a native of that country, his mother an Italian, which was the basis for his classification as a Roman. Since his father had served Rome as a general, young Aetius began his career early. He was actually a hostage, first with Alaric and later with the Huns. During the years he spent with the Huns, he learned their language and established a warm friendship with King Ruga. Later, his son Carpilio also spent some years as a hostage at the Hunnic court.

Both contemporary writers and later historians deal kindly with Aetius. Some of this good fortune may be traced to one of the few documents which survives that troubled period, a panegyric by Renatus Profuturus Frideridus. This poet refers to Aetius as a man "free from avarice and greed" and concerned only with the good fortunes of the empire. Emperor Valentinian III was not so sure, and in 454 he had Aetius executed. There is no question that Aetius was an able general. He had earlier blocked the Visigoths in their attempt to take Arles and to occupy Narbonese Gaul. In 436 one of his captains gained a spectacular victory over the

Burgundians, the historical event around which the German epic, the *Nibelungenlied*, was woven.

Rome's first major trouble with Attila came in 441 when Huns slaughtered the Roman merchants who had come to do business on the Danube. What prompted Attila to choose this particular moment to disrupt relations with Rome was probably the news that Theodosius II, emperor in Constantinople, had sent an expeditionary force to help Valentinian III against the Vandals in Sicily. Under the circumstances, his Huns could attack these merchants without much danger of retaliation.

There is less likelihood that Attila had reached some sort of understanding with Gaiseric, king of the Vandals, as a contemporary writer declares. In any event, when Roman emissaries protested to Attila about these attacks, he placed the onus for the trouble on the Romans. They had neglected to pay him his annual subsidy, they had continued to shelter fugitives, and they had despoiled Hunnish royal graves. The first two charges had an oft-repeated ring. Whether true or not, they were conveniently at hand. The charge about the graves was a new one and might have been true. At least the bishop of Margus, whom the Huns had specifically charged with despoiling Hunnic cemeteries, secretly arranged a deal with his accusers which promised him immunity if he handed over the city of Margus. This he did, and so without a struggle a major city of Moesia was abandoned to the Huns.

Other Hunnic companies were ravaging Thrace and Illyricum and capturing Danubian fortress cities. A lull came in 442, possibly by way of a formal truce, but the following year found the Huns back at it again. They captured and destroyed Ratiaria (Arcar) on the Danube, Singidunum (Belgrade), Naissus (Nis), and Sardica (Sofia), then marched toward Constantinople and took Philippopolis. When they inflicted a disastrous defeat upon the imperial army under

Aspar, Constantinople had no choice but to ask for terms. The new treaty tripled the annual subsidy, raising it from 700 pounds of gold to 2,100, repeated the usual demand for the return of fugitives, and increased the ransom for escaped Roman prisoners from 8 *solidi* to 12.

The four years of peace which this humiliating treaty bought ended in 447 when Attila again sent his pillaging hordes down across the Danube. If he had an official pretext for doing so, this is not known. His real purpose was probably to continue the drain on the resources of the empire and demoralize it to the point of complete impotency. His warriors carried their devastating raids through the Balkan provinces as far south as Thermopylae and in their progress captured and destroyed some seventy cities and fortresses. In 448 helpless Constantinople asked for terms. The new treaty insisted upon a payment of 6,000 pounds of gold to cover the arrears in the tribute, required the return of all Hunnic fugitives, and obligated the emperor not to recruit any Huns in the future. He was also ordered to evacuate a strip of territory five days journey in depth and running along the south bank of the Danube from Singidunum to Novae (Sistova). Once this area had been evacuated and left desolate, Huns could carry their raids across this no-man's land into Thrace and Illyricum without hindrance of any kind. The presence of this wide strip, which was barred to Romans, would also make it more difficult for the empire to recruit auxiliaries from among the peoples to the north.

This year, 448, saw Attila at the height of his power. In 443, when the earlier treaty had been negotiated, the situation had been somewhat different. Although Theodosius then had agreed to the increased annual tribute of 2,100 pounds of gold, he apparently had no real intention of paying this and he did not. His failure to do so accounts for the 6,000 pounds of gold in arrears covered by the treaty of 448.

The empire could safely take such a position in 443, or so it thought. After 448 Attila and the Huns would no longer tolerate any such violation of treaty terms.

For a few years the situation held. Attila appears to have been content to collect the heavy annual tribute from the eastern empire to go along with the "pay" he received from the western empire as "master of the soldiers." There was some excitement in 449 over the plot which Chrysaphius, the most influential minister of Theodosius II, had hatched to bring about the death of Attila. Chrysaphius thought he had corrupted Edecon, Attila's leading counselor. Edecon accepted a bribe to assassinate Attila, but when he returned to Hungary he instead revealed the plot. At first Attila demanded the death of Chrysaphius, but then relented and promised no retaliation.

The summer of 450 witnessed an event which proved of far-reaching importance. This was the death of Emperor Theodosius II in July. On August 26, four weeks after his death, the senate elected Marcian, a retired tribune, to succeed him. Since Marcian's military accomplishments had been undistinguished, other considerations must have recommended him to the senate. Among these was the fact that he had once served as aide-de-camp to Aspar, the most powerful of the masters of the soldiers in the eastern empire. Marcian must also have given the senate assurance that he would terminate tribute payments to Attila. It was the senate and the class which that body represented that had been suffering most heavily from the tribute paid to Attila since it had been the policy of Chrysaphius to saddle them with its payment.

If Marcian had promised the senate to cut off the tribute, he was true to his word. After he had ordered the execution of Chrysaphius, he sent his ambassador, Apollonius, to Attila to announce there would be no more tribute. When Attila learned the nature of Apollonius' mission, he refused to meet him, although he demanded the gifts such emissaries traditionally brought. Some of Marcian's courage must have rubbed off on Apollonius, for he announced that since Attila had refused to see him he was not entitled to these gifts. Attila might have taken the gifts and had Apollonius' head as well, but he thought the better of it. He wanted no war with Constantinople, neither did he wish to lose face with his subject German kings by mistreating the person of an ambassador. That would have violated one of the most ancient rules of society.

In the spring of 451 Attila started his huge army toward the Rhine in a move which he hoped would establish his lordship over the western empire. The ending of tribute by Constantinople must have provoked his action, while among other considerations which helped determine Attila's decision to march against the western empire rather than the eastern was surely the impregnability of Constantinople. He and his Huns could ravage the Balkan provinces at will, but earlier raids had left these areas picked so clean any forays into that region would net the Huns little. To capture Constantinople, on the other hand, would be out of the question. The line of fortifications which Emperor Anthemius had erected in 431 had been reinforced in 439 and again in 447. During assaults the Huns might make on these fortifications, there was no way of preventing the Byzantine fleet from bringing in all the supplies the city might require. Furthermore, to have attempted the capture of the city and failed would have endangered the very existence of the Hunnic empire. At the first sign of weakness, the German kings would repudiate Attila's authority, and the loyalty of the leaders of the more distant Hunnic hordes would be eroded.

The western empire by contrast offered no such obstacles, and Gaul and Italy had long since recovered from the earlier ravaging suffered at the hands of the Visigoths and Vandals. The cities of those provinces promised far richer loot than any expedition into the Balkans could be expected to produce. There was, of course, the opposition which Aetius might throw in Attila's way, although the Roman general's source of Hunnic auxiliaries had dried up and this would leave his army considerably weakened. If Attila could prevent the Visigoths from joining Aetius, he would have no great difficulty overrunning the West.

The question remains why Attila chose this particular time to make his move against the western Roman Empire. The repudiation of the tribute by the eastern emperor might provide explanation enough. Contemporaries offer several other explanations, but the serious historian may have difficulty accepting any of them as plausible. One story has it that a herdsman had dug up "the sword of Ares," a sacred object honored among the Scythian kings, which discovery left Attila convinced that he would become master of the entire world.

Another story which sounds equally imaginative concerns Honoria, the strong-willed sister of Valentinian III. She had been caught in an amorous affair with her steward, whereupon her indignant brother had executed the man. Then to prevent similar incidents in the future, he had Honoria betrothed to a wealthy senator who could be expected to keep her quiet. Honoria, in her bitterness and in an effort to prevent this marriage, secretly sent the eunuch Hyacinthus to Attila to solicit his help and entrusted her messenger with her ring in order to convince the Hunnic chieftain of the genuineness of her appeal. Attila interpreted the ring as an offer of marriage and forthwith demanded Honoria's hand and half the empire as her inheritance. This demand he presumably sent to Theodosius II, the senior emperor in Constantinople, who liked the idea and urged Valentinian to ship Honoria off to Hungary. Valentinian III thought otherwise. He had Hyacinthus beheaded and would have done the same to Honoria but for the pleading of their aged mother,

Placidia. To put an end to any further such difficulties with his sister, however, he had her married immediately to the wealthy senator.[12]

Another story links Attila's invasion of the western empire with Gaiseric, king of the Vandals, who feared the Visigoths were about to attack his kingdom. This is the account as Jordanes gives it. "Now when Gaiseric, king of the Vandals...learned that his [Attila's] mind was bent on the devastation of the world, he incited Attila by many gifts to make war on the Visigoths, for he was afraid that Theodoric, king of the Visigoths, would avenge the injury done to his daughter. She had been joined in wedlock with Humeric, the son of Gaiseric, and at first was happy in the union. But afterwards he was cruel even to his own children, and because of the mere suspicion that she was attempting to poison him, he cut off her nose and mutilated her ears. He sent her back to her father in Gaul thus despoiled of her natural charms. So the wretched girl presented a pitiable aspect ever after, and the cruelty which would stir even strangers still more surely incited her father to vengeance. Attila, therefore, in his efforts to bring about the wars long ago instigated by the bribe of Gaiseric, sent ambassadors into Italy to the Emperor Valentinian to sow strife between the Goths and the Romans.... [For] Beneath his great ferocity he was a subtle man, and fought with craft before he made war."[13]

Historians generally dismiss Jordanes' account as fiction except the concluding statement which speaks of Attila's shrewdness. This they accept, and there is evidence that Attila did try to prevent the Visigoths and Romans from joining forces against him by seeking to convince each that his intended war was with the other. In any event, his hope that he could keep these potential foes of his apart was a reasonable one. They had long been enemies, actually at war from 436 to 439 over Narbonese Gaul and Arles, which the Visigoths claimed belonged to them. In 446 their king Theodoric had given haven to Sebastian, who had attempted to block Aetius's bid for the office of master of the soldiers. Still later, in 446, Theodoric had received Attila's blessing, and Hunnic troops as well, in his efforts to conquer Spain.

Attila's failure to divide Rome and the Visigoths saved the empire in the West. For a time Theodoric did appear to waver, wondering whether it would not be to his advantage to have Roman and Hun fight each other, perhaps to the point of mutual exhaustion. Given that happy circumstance, he could have occupied Narbonese Gaul without opposition. As it happened, the magnitude of Attila's threat proved too overwhelming. Theodoric offered to join Aetius and, significantly, without demanding the surrender of Arles as the price of his cooperation. His decision is all the more surprising since the army which Aetius was bringing against Attila was probably one of the weakest he had ever had under his command. Most serious was the absence of the Hunnic auxiliaries upon which he had always depended. The army which he led across the Alps in the spring of 451 consisted of regular Roman troops which would be joined by the *laeti*[14] and *foederati* he could expect to come to his assistance when he reached Gaul.

Aetius could also count on some help from those Ripuarian Franks who had recognized the succession of the younger son of the dead king. The elder son had appealed to Attila for his recognition, and it may have been the prospect of insuring the Frankish alliance for himself that impelled Attila to move when he did. Whatever the case, Aetius had earlier adopted the younger son and had promised him Rome's assistance.

Sangiban, king of the Alans, ruled a small state that included the city of Orleans where he made his headquarters. Sometime previous, when it became clear to Aetius that he could not expect to receive Hunnic mercenaries any longer, he had given these lands to the Alans with the understanding that they would fight to preserve Roman authority in that area. But Jordanes, our principal authority for informational background to the battle of Chalons, states that Sangiban was only a treacherous ally at best and that Aetius feared he had been treating with Attila. But some historians have charged that Jordanes, a Goth, in his endeavor to credit the Visigoths with the coming victory over Attila at Chalons, may have deliberately blackened the record of Sangiban and the Alans. Whatever the case, Aetius could also hope to have the assistance of other scattered allies: Salian Franks, Burgundians from Savoy, Celts from Armorica (Brittany), and some Saxons who lived north of the Loire. Far and away the most important of all of his friends was the powerful Visigothic army, which the aged king Theodoric was bringing with him.

The army which Attila took with him to the Rhine was appreciably superior in terms of numbers to that with which Aetius and Theodoric could hope to confront him. That it did not approach the half-million figure reported by contemporaries goes without saying. To these writers his host was terrifying both in numbers and in savagery, and the suggestion of a half-million was their way of expressing this terror. Like Aetius' army, Attila's too was composed of a variety of peoples. Beyond his own Huns there were a number of German peoples: Heruli from the Black Sea, Scirians from Galicia, Rugians from the region of the upper Theiss, Thuringians, Ostrogoths under their several kings, Gepids from the mountains of Dacia under their king Ardaric, as well as Burgundians from east of the Rhine, and those Ripuarian Franks who adhered to the elder brother in the dispute over the throne. While the Germans fought under their own leaders, Attila held the position of commander in chief and decided the final strategy.

That Attila might boast a superiority in numbers over his "Roman" foe counted for little, since the disparity was probably not sufficiently large to be decisive. It might indeed have proved a liability. Smaller but better organized armies had often gained the victory in ancient times, *viz.* the Greeks at Marathon, Alexander the Great against the Persians, Hannibal against the Romans, and Julius Caesar against his enemies. The following century would find Belisarius, Justinian's ablest general, winning consistently over larger armies. In an age when armies lived off the land, the larger the army, the sooner it would outrun its supply of food and fodder. Only by keeping on the march and constantly making new conquests could Attila be sure of retaining the loyalty of the Germans he had forced to join him.

Attila's questionable advantage in numbers was probably more than neutralized by the superior weapons and protective gear some of his opponents could boast. Both armies included contingents of foot soldiers and both had cavalry units, but of the heavy-armed cavalry as opposed to the light-armed, the Romans possessed a clear superiority. During the period of the Republic, Rome had depended solely upon foot soldiers. Only reluctantly, and not until the third century A.D. did she begin to recruit horsemen in order to counter the mounted archers of the Parthians and Sassanid Persians. The fourth and fifth centuries brought increased dependence upon horsemen, although Rome generally found it cheaper to rely upon barbarian auxiliaries to supply these. These horsemen fought under their own chieftains, although they would accept orders from a man like Aetius when he was in command.

The best horsemen of the period were probably the cataphracts that were used extensively by the emperors in Constantinople. The cataphract wore a steel helmet and mail shirt and carried a dagger, battle-ax, sword, lance, bow, and an oblong shield. Procopius, writing some seventy-five years after Chalons, judged these horsemen to be the best in the world. It is doubtful that Aetius had any cataphracts, but he did boast some heavily armed horsemen. The greater number of his horsemen were more lightly equipped and carried little beyond bow and lance. They ordinarily fought in support of the more heavily armed cavalry and in the defense of fortresses.

The Huns' association with horses from their youth and their ancient traditions made them unmatched as horsemen. They could move more quickly than any other cavalry and could ride for longer periods of time. Like the cataphract they carried bows and arrows, which they probably used with greater dexterity than any soldiers in the world. They also carried long lances, swords, and daggers, as did the cataphracts. What they lacked was heavy defensive armor. Only the wealthier Huns were able to equip themselves with protective gear, although Hunnic horsemen generally wore metal helmets that extended to the nose. Lest a larger shield impede their mobility, they carried small shields of wickerwork that were covered with leather. It was the practice of mounted bowmen to shower their foe with arrows, then close in for hand-to-hand fighting with lance and sword. The lasso also appears in the arsenal of Hunnic weapons, although there is no mention of the Huns using this weapon in the battle of Chalons.

Except for the Goths, the Germans were slow in adopting the horse for war purposes. The Goths had learned the importance of cavalry from the eastern Roman armies and from the Persians long before the Hunnic horsemen began swarming over the lands north of the Black Sea. It was the mounted Visigoths in addition to some Ostrogothic and Alan horsemen who decimated the Roman foot soldiers at Adrianople in 378. At Chalons, as will be seen, it was the heavily armed cavalry of the Visigoths that turned the fortunes of battle against Attila and his Huns. Alan horsemen, probably the equal of the Huns in skill, may also have contributed to Attila's defeat.

The Franks, on the other hand, and the majority of other German tribes stayed principally with their foot soldiers.[15] As late as 732, at the famous battle of Tours, Charles Martel and his Franks rode to the battle site on their horses and there dismounted and fought to victory over the Moors with their heavy swords. But Attila and his Huns had a contempt for infantry. Jordanes relates how Attila sought to fire the spirits of his followers by ridiculing the foot soldiers that his enemy had brought against them. Some of his own German allies may have been on foot for Jordanes states that the night before the battle of Chalons the Gepids fought a bitter battle with the Franks in Aetius' army and 15,000 men were left dead on the field.

Early in the spring of 451 Attila moved his army from Pannonia into Lorraine, and on April 6, the day before Easter, captured and destroyed Metz. Rheims suffered a similar fate, but Paris escaped because of the holy counsels of St. Genevieve, so tradition has it. Attila's immediate objective may have been Orleans. This is where Sangiban, king of the Alans, had his capital, and if one is to believe the prejudiced Jordanes, that monarch may have promised to cooperate with Attila. What little evidence exists tends to disprove Jordanes' charge, however, and it apears Orleans may have suffered a bloody siege and fallen to Attila had not the arrival of Aetius and the Visigoths forced the Hunnish chieftain to retire.

Whatever the actual story about Orleans, Attila drew back to the northwest into the province of Belgica, perhaps with the Visigoths and Aetius in pursuit. About five miles from the town of Troyes, at a place identified as *locus Mauriacus* (Mauriac place) and commonly referred to as the Catalaunian Fields, he pitched his camp and prepared to make his stand. The exact site where the great battle took place remains a matter of some controversy. The written sources are not clear, nor have any archaeological findings come to view to aid scholars in establishing the precise spot. Because the battle site was believed for centuries to have been Chalons, it has retained that identification even though it was fought nearer to Troyes. One fact of significance about the site was that it constituted a large open field, no doubt chosen by Attila to furnish his cavalry the greatest possible room for freedom of action.

The battle began late in the afternoon scarcely more than three hours before sunset, and there is a story which offers an explanation for the late hour. It is said that soothsayers whom Attila consulted before the battle had warned him that he would suffer defeat even though the opposing general would be slain. By this time Attila had come to bear Aetius a bitter hatred, so the story goes, and he was willing to accept defeat if it meant the death of his adversary. He delayed hostilities until the afternoon in order to prevent the enemy from having time to gain a decisive victory. The reader who believes in omens will be relieved to learn that an opposing general did die at Chalons. It was not Aetius, however, but Theodoric, king of the Visigoths.

The obscurity which shrouds so many aspects of the battle of Chalons does not extend to the actual disposition of the warriors in the opposing armies, that is, if one accepts Jordanes' account as accurate.[16] According to Jordanes, Aetius assigned the place of honor, the right wing, to Theodoric, king of the Visigoths. This gesture of good will would have pleased Theodoric, whose loyalty Aetius wished to keep at all costs. As a precautionary step he had Thorismund, Theodoric's eldest son, join him and the "Romans" who made up the left wing. The knowledge that Thorismund was in Aetius' company would reduce the danger of Theodoric's switching sides or withdrawing from the battlefield if things went poorly. Again as a safety measure Aetius placed Sangiban and his Alans in the center, where their questionable dependability would do least injury. Not only did it not materialize, according to a recent scholar who dismisses Jordanes' allegations concerning Sangiban's loyalty as unfounded, but the Alans proved themselves a bulwark of strength against the fiercest charges Attila could muster against them.[17]

Because the weakest part of Aetius' army was the center, according to Jordanes, some scholars have suggested the possibility that the Roman general had read Polybius' account of the spectacular victory Hannibal gained over the Roman army at Cannae in 216 B.C. The Carthaginian commander deliberately weakened the center of his line in the hope that the Romans would drive forward so quickly they would be unaware of the two powerful wings of the Punic army encircling them. If this was also the plan and hope of Aetius at Chalons, Attila fell into the same kind of trap as had the Romans at Cannae. He placed the strongest of his troops in the center where they would be facing the "treacherous" Sangiban and his Alans. To his left and opposing the Visigothic army he stationed the Ostrogoths and Gepids, who were the best of his German allies. He left a mixed group to face Aetius.

Just before the major battle began Aetius gained a tactical advantage of some significance. This had to do with the occupation of the crest of a hill which broke the general flatness of the area.[18] After some fighting Aetius managed to gain control. While this victory was "only a skirmish before the big battle began," the higher ground may have furnished Aetius a better view of the enemy's movements and beyond this provided his army a psychological lift. Jordanes, at least, judged Aetius' success of such importance that he had Attila haranguing his men following this setback in an effort to rally their dampened spirits.

Of the actual fighting itself only the briefest accounts remain, and they are not clear. Aetius and Thorismund seem to have pushed forward against the weak right of the Hunnic army, while Attila in turn aimed his most powerful thrust at the center of the Roman line where the Alans were stationed. As he did so, he exposed his left flank to a formidable charge by Theodoric and the heavy-armed horsemen of the Visigothic army.[19] Before it was too late Attila realized the danger of finding himself encircled by the two wings of the Roman army, so once the sun began to set he fell back to his camp. The same day, or more probably the following morning, Aetius and the Visigoths laid siege to Attila's camp, since they did not wish to risk a direct assault. It was in the course of this siege that the body of Theodoric was discovered.

Contemporary writers agree on two points about the battle: first, that the casualties on both sides were heavy and, second, that the battle ended in no clearcut victory for either Aetius or Attila. Idatius states that 300,000 warriors lost their lives, which is only a more absurd figure than the 165,000 which Jordanes suggests. Modern scholars are inclined to agree on three points: that both sides suffered severe losses; that while Aetius did not win a decisive victory, Attila was clearly on the defensive following the battle; and that what proved the most crucial development was the death of Theodoric, the king of the Visigoths.

An analysis of the aftermath to the battle as based principally upon Jordanes' account is as follows: had Theodoric lived, he and Aetius would have continued the attack on Attila, presumably to a successful conclusion. Thorismund, whom the Visigothic army promptly acclaimed king after they had discovered the body of Theodoric, also wished to press the advantage gained at Chalons, but Aetius demurred. He feared that a decisive victory over Attila would serve only to replace a dangerous Hunnic threat to the empire with a Visigothic one. By themselves the Romans could not hope to withstand the victorious Visigothic army. So Aetius warned Thorismund that while the army may have hailed him king, he could not be at all certain the court circle back in Tolosa (Toulouse) would accept him. Aetius urged him to hurry back home to his capital before the news of Theodoric's death arrived there lest one of his brothers usurp the throne. Thorismund thought the advice good and led his army away to the south. That Aetius' counsel was not an empty warning was revealed two years later when a brother, Theodoric II, murdered Thorismund and took over the throne.

Opposed to this interpretation of Thorismund's withdrawal from Chalons is the view that he left not with the blessing of Aetius, but very much against his wishes. Theodoric, Thorismund's father, had been willing to cooperate with Aetius and to accept his leadership in the deadly struggle with Attila, whom he may have considered as much an enemy to the Visigoths as to Rome. Not so Thorismund, who must have judged Aetius and Roman power as much a threat to the Visigothic state as that posed by Attila and the Huns after the victory gained over them at Chalons on the first day. Thorismund must have reasoned that the future of the Visigoths would best be served by permitting the Germans along the Rhine and the Huns to continue to dispute Roman authority in Gaul.

Why did Aetius wish to continue the war against Attila until a total victory had been won? The easiest answer is the most obvious one. After all the strenuous efforts he had made to weld an alliance of so many different peoples against a man who had been threatening the very existence of the empire, he could not permit an opportunity to destroy that man to slip through his fingers. A second objective may also have been in Aetius' mind, that of again being able to recruit Hunnic horsemen for Rome. Attila had absolutely forbidden this. Aetius had found these Huns the most dependable and most effective auxiliaries in his efforts to defend the empire. Without their continued assistance, he may have reasoned, that empire could not long be preserved.

For two or three days Attila puzzled over the failure of the enemy to follow up their victory, then led his horde and allies back across the Rhine. In Hungary he licked his wounds until the following summer, when he marched another large army across Pannonia, through the Julian Alps, and into Italy. Hatred of Aetius and a desire for revenge may have inspired this campaign. Or it may simply have been the demand of his followers for loot. They had probably taken little back to Hungary from their campaign the previous year which had ended in the defeat at Chalons.

The capture of Aquileia late in the summer of 452 constituted Attila's principal achievement on this Italian campaign. So thoroughly did his troops devastate the city that a century later Jordanes could find few traces of it remaining. Just as completely razed as Aquileia but destined to have a brighter future was Patavium (Padua). Other cities which opened their gates suffered less grievously. These included Vicenza, Verona, Brescia, Bergamo, Milan, and Pavia. To the south of Milan and in the vicinity of the Mincio, Attila found himself confronted not by Aetius, who had disbanded his army, but by an embassy from Rome headed by Pope Leo I (the Great). The pleas and arguments of this embassy, coupled with a variety of other factors—historians suggest restiveness among the German allies in Attila's army, a shortage of food and fodder, an outbreak of dysentery, news of the approach of the eastern Roman emperor, Marcian, with an army—impelled Attila to withdraw from Italy and return to Hungary.

Attila had but a few more months to live and not much more time was vouchsafed his empire. In the spring of 453 he added the "very beautiful" Ildico to his coterie of wives, but on his wedding night died from a nosebleed. Had he not been in a drunken slumber, so writes Jordanes, the blood from his nose would not have suffocated him. The following year the German peoples who had accepted Attila's authority rose up in rebellion, annihilated the Hunnic army at Nedao in Pannonia, and killed Ellac, Attila's eldest son. The death of Dinzic, another of Attila's sons, in a battle against a combined Roman and Ostrogothic army in 469 announced the formal end of the empire which Attila had created.

The Huns made their appearance in Europe about the year 375 A.D. A century later they had disappeared from history. Since their empire had endured a relatively short time and since they had never appropriated for themselves any large part of the Roman Empire, one might well ask why so much significance attaches to the battle of Chalons, which marked for them the beginning of the end. Why might the battle fought there in the spring of 451 be classified as decisive?

Chalons proved to the western Roman Empire and to the Germans that the Huns could be defeated. Had Attila lived another twenty-five years and had there been no defeat at Chalons to destroy his image of invincibility, he might well have conquered the whole of the western empire. Tradition and history occasionally make mistakes as, for instance, in the case of the Vandals, who are undeserving of the reputation of being the wanton destroyers their name suggests. But tradition and history make no mistake about the Huns. Chalons hurried to its end the existence of the most ruthless "barbarian" invader Europe had ever suffered. The words *Huns* and *Attila* quite properly conjure up the image of razed cities, slaughtered communities, and enslaved populations.

The Huns showed themselves indifferent to the influences of a higher culture. Had Attila won at Chalons, the cultural level of the West would have suffered further and immediate decline. Scholars question the accuracy of Venice's claim that its original settlers were refugees who fled Attila's approach. No one will doubt the fear that the prospect of Attila's might evoked in the minds of most contemporaries. Some fifteen years after Attila's death the whole of Constantinople turned out to carry the head of his slain son, Dinzic, in triumphant procession. "The real significance of Attila [and of Chalons] lies in the fact, that the pressure of his Huns forced the Romans and the Teutons to recognize that the common interest, yes civilization, was at stake, and thus drove them to make the great alliance, on which the future progress of the world depended."[20]

3

THE BATTLE OF THE YARMUK

IT HAS BEEN SAID THAT HAD ABRAHA, RULER OF YEMEN, SUC-
ceeded in his attempt to overrun the Hijaz in 570 A.D, Christianity would have won out in Arabia, "the Cross would
have been raised on the Kaaba, and Muhammad might have
died a priest or monk."[1] The year 570 was the Year of the
Elephant, so called because Abraha brought an elephant
with him, perhaps with the hope that the sight of that
strange monster would frighten the Bedouins into submission. Abraha's expedition failed, but the year of his invasion
has remained a memorable one in the world of Islam.

It was in the Year of the Elephant that Mohammed was
born. When the Prophet died in 632 he left his new theo-
cratic state so firmly established that within a century some
of his disciples were penetrating India, while others were
fighting Franks in Gaul more than three thousand miles to
the west. The event that opened the way to the establishment of this enormous empire, which stretched from the Indus to beyond the Pyrenees and was surely the largest empire to be conquered in so short a time, was the decisive victory the Muslims won over the Byzantine army at the Yarmuk river in the summer of 636.

Among the circumstances which rendered the conquest of this huge empire especially remarkable were the general ignorance the Mediterranean world had of Arabia and its people and the near contempt felt for them on the part of the few who did know about them. From prehistoric times Arabia had remained outside the sweep of history. Empires of the ancient Near East had come and gone—Babylonia, Egypt, Assyria, Chaldea, Persia, and that of Alexander the Great—with little concern in western Europe about the people who lived in that hot, dry peninsula. Had Arabia possessed a rich supply of commodities to bring to the markets of Egypt, Syria, and Babylonia, a thriving trade might have resulted and close associations maintained with the peoples who dwelt there. But Arabia could boast of little, only a few spices and frankincense, and while these were prized, they were not actively sought out. Had it not been for the caravans that moved irregularly up from the Punt with tropical products from Africa for Egypt and Syria, Arabia might have been completely bypassed.

Not that the Arabian peninsula had existed in complete isolation from the rest of the ancient Near East. One of the curious circumstances about Arabia is the fact that so many famous peoples of history traced their origins to that desert country. There were first the Akkadians whom scholars tell us moved from Arabia into Babylonia about 2300 B.C. After them came the Assyrians, Chaldeans, Amorites, Aramaeans, Phoenicians, and Hebrews, all Semitic peoples, all leaving the Arabian peninsula when their numbers grew too many for that barren land to sustain and making their way into the rich valleys of the Tigris and Euphrates. By the time these peoples were making history, they and the rest of the world had all but forgotten their origins in the arid Arabian peninsula. Not so the Arabs who accepted Mohammed as Prophet. When he died his followers carried his message throughout the greater part of the Mediterranean world and

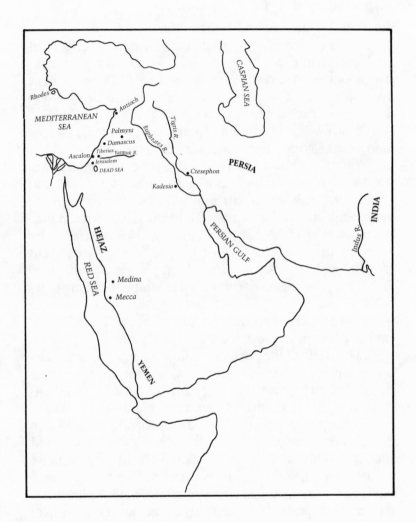

RED SEA

MEDITERRANEAN
SEA

Rhodes

Antioch

Palmyra

Damascus

Ascalon

Tiberias

Yarmuk R.

Jerusalem

DEAD SEA

Euphrates R.

Tigris R.

CASPIAN SEA

PERSIA

Ctesephon

Kadesia

PERSIAN GULF

INDIA

Indus R.

HEJAZ

Medina

Mecca

YEMEN

convinced many of the peoples they found there to respect
Allah as the one and only, all-powerful deity and to revere
dusty, largely unknown Mecca as the Holy City.

Arabia's enormous size would have made it an important
land in ancient times had it not been for the lack of rainfall.
It is about one-third the size of the United States, a huge
peninsula almost surrounded by water but itself mostly a
desert. Its location adjacent to Egypt, Syria, and Babylonia
would have been ideal from the point of view of trade had the
land much to offer. But few lands are so hot, so dry, and so
unproductive. Only around the periphery of the peninsula is
vegetation found. Along the western coast to the south in
Yemen and Asir, sufficient rain does fall to permit some
systematic cultivation of the soil. In the Hijaz to the north,
the homeland of Mohammed, life was made possible by
oases and the coming of spring rains that caused the desert to
green up and provide the Bedouins grazing for their camels.
Still it was the very poverty of Arabia which led many of its
tribes in ancient times to emigrate to Babylonia, the same
poverty that played an indirect part in the military expansion of Islam in the seventh century.

The hard life of the Arabian peninsula bred a tough, independent people. Existence there was a constant struggle for
survival, a situation which explains the practice of infant-
icide that prevailed until Mohammed and the expansion of
Islam brought it to an end. The Arabs generally divided into
two classes, the settled folk who lived in the villages and
such larger communities as Mecca and Medina and the more
numerous nomadic Bedouins who moved about the desert
sands and oases in an unending search for food. Bedouin life
was most characteristic of central and northern Arabia,
which included Mohammed's country of Hijaz. The
Bedouins constituted the most restless element in the population of Arabia, and it was with them that the raid, the *razzia*, became almost a national institution. So poor and un-

productive was the land that raiding the camps of those who had more became a necessary means of survival. As a Bedouin poet once observed: "Our business is to make raids on the enemy, on our neighbor and on our brother, in case we find none to raid but a brother!"[2] It was this element, the Bedouins, which proved most receptive to the appeal of Mohammed's successors to carry his message and the sword to the peoples outside Arabia.

Almost as typical of Arabia as its intense heat and aridity are the date palm and the camel. Without them life in that peninsula would have been impossible. The date which was introduced from Babylonia became a staple and together with the milk of the camel constituted the chief item in the Bedouin's fare. "Honour your aunt, the palm," the Prophet is said to have enjoined, "which was made of the same clay as Adam."[3] The camel furnished the Bedouin milk and flesh for food, hair for his tent, dung for fuel, and the principal means of transportation. The history of human society in Arabia begins, indeed, with the domestication of the camel. The camel is the special gift of Allah (*Koran* 16:5-8).

The climate of Arabia together with the scattered character of its sparse population long discouraged the establishment of political states. In Yemen in the southwest, the Sabaean kingdom had emerged by the eighth century B.C., but for Arabia generally the most typical political and social unit was the clan. Each family had its tent, a number of tents made up a clan, and a number of clans might recognize a common ancestor and form a tribe. The sheik, senior member of the clan or tribe, enjoyed a position of leadership, although it was an office he exercised with the good will of the other leaders of the group. In a larger community such as Mecca, authority rested in the hands of an oligarchy of wealthy merchants who were the leaders of the ten or more clans that composed the one Kuraish tribe which dominated the city. Mohammed was born into the Hashim clan, a socially poor one. The most famous of Mecca's clans was the Umayyad clan, which was destined to found the most powerful dynasty (661-750) in the history of Islam.

Arabia entered history about the tenth century B.C. when the queen of Sheba (Saba) in Yemen visited Solomon with her caravan of camels (3 *Kings* 10). Saba afterwards absorbed other southern Arabian kingdoms; one of these was Ma'in, which had been active in colonizing the land known today as Abyssinia. Arabia's first conflict with a major power came in the seventh century when Saba's affluence attracted the attention of Assyria to the north. In the fourth century B.C., the Nabataeans, an Arab tribe to the north, established a kingdom in the Negev desert with a capital at Petra. The earlier attempt Rome had made to occupy the Hijaz during the reign of the emperor Augustus had failed, but Petra itself fell to the emperor Trajan in 106 A.D. Another north Arabian state, Palmyra, enjoyed a brief period of prominence in the third century, first as a Roman ally, then as an independent state, until reviving Roman power snuffed out its existence in 272.

The state of Abyssinia extended its influence into Yemen, successfully for the most part until the late second century B.C., when a native Himyarite dynasty rose to contest its supremacy. From the close of the fourth century A.D. two powerful empires undertook to interfere in the affairs of Yemen. One was the Sassanid Persian empire, which had its capital at Ctesiphon on the Tigris river; the other was the eastern Roman (Byzantine) Empire with its capital at Constantinople. Not only did both empires seek to gain influence in Yemen, but both maintained small Arab states or kingdoms in northern Arabia. The Persians were allied with the kingdom of the Lakhmids on the eastern fringe of the Syrian desert, while Constantinople befriended the Ghassanids to the west.

This was Arabia about the year 570 when Mohammed was born. Who could have predicted that this man, born of poor parents and early left an orphan, would take the history of Arabia out of the hands of its mighty neighbors and lay the foundation of its future greatness. Several circumstances advanced Mohammed's ambition to make himself the spiritual and political leader of Arabia. One was his birth in Mecca, the principal city of Arabia. Another was the presence in Mecca of the Kaaba, the shrine which made Mecca the Holy City for all Arabs. Inside this rectangular, roofless structure were gathered several hundred idols that Arabs from all over the peninsula came to worship during the time of the spring truce. Tradition has it that Abraham, the father of the Arabs, constructed the Kaaba and placed in one of its walls the Black Stone sent down from heaven. Once Mohammed made himself master of Mecca, he purged the Kaaba of its idols but retained the Black Stone. It remains there to this day, the most precious relic from the past to the tens of thousands of faithful Muslims who annually make the pilgrimage to the Holy City.

Little is known about Mohammed until his early twenties when he served as a caravan leader to a wealthy widow named Khadija, whom he married. About the age of forty he began to preach a gospel of strict monotheism, of man's duty to worship the one god Allah, of his obligation to assist his poor neighbors, of a belief in heaven and hell. The majority of Mohammed's ideas can be traced to the Bible of the Jews and the New Testament of the Christians, and it is significant that when he urged his followers to undertake a war of extermination against unbelievers, he excepted from slaughter the people of the Book (Bible). No doubt similarities between his views and the beliefs of the Jews and Christians hastened the conversion of many of these peoples to Islam.

The word *Islam* means submission to God's will, a virtue which perhaps remains the most striking feature of the religion practiced by Mohammed's adherents. Mohammed also preached the necessity of almsgiving (*zakat*, similar to the tithe), of observing a strict fast during the month Ramadan, of making a pilgrimage to Mecca, and of praying daily (in later years five times a day) with one's face turned toward Mecca. He accepted polygamy, but he banned the *razzia* and the use of alcoholic beverages. He assured his followers an eternity in paradise should they die fighting the infidel.

If Mohammed's gospel proved readily acceptable to millions within a few years of his death, it did not to the leaders of Mecca when he was still alive. They objected to the unyielding monotheism he preached, since the economic life of Mecca benefited greatly from the flow of pilgrims who came to worship the idols in the Kaaba. They feared the introduction of a dictatorship which the recognition of Mohammed as Prophet would likely entail. They resented his relegation of their honored ancestors to hell because of their polytheism; and they feared the disciples of Mohammed would assist him in carrying out a social and economic revolution that would bring an end to their leadership.

In the summer of 622 Mohammed fled Mecca and found a haven in Medina, a community two hundred miles to the north. His life had been in some danger, now that Khadija was dead, as was his uncle, Abu Talib, the leader of the Hashim clan, who had protected Mohammed from his persecutors. Within a few years of his arrival in Medina he had made himself master there and then began to organize raids against the caravans moving to and from Mecca. After Mecca failed in a massive attempt to capture Medina in 627 and destroy the Prophet, the number of his adherents in the Holy City increased rapidly, leading to his own occupation of the city in 630. He prudently retained the Kaaba and so preserved Mecca's character as the Holy City. He himself continued to make Medina his home, and there he died in 632.

Mohammed made no provision for his succession. Even had he left a son, his death would have posed a real problem. What ordinary man could succeed a prophet? The urgency of the situation was not lost upon the leaders of Mecca, and early on the morning after his death they designated the aged Abu Bakr, father of the Prophet's favorite wife, Aishah, as caliph (successor, deputy). Their action guaranteed the loyalty of Mecca but it did nothing to stay the repudiation of Meccan leadership by a number of tribes who had only reluctantly recognized Mohammed's rule. Some tribes resented payment of the *zakat*, a tax which helped finance the newly established theocracy. Others could argue that since their agreement with Mohammed had been of a personal nature, as between tribal chieftains, it had lapsed with his death. And almost immediately "false" prophets appeared throughout Arabia who preached a gospel more suited to the traditional polytheism of the Arabs and one they could practice untrammeled by an authority other than their own.

Abu Bakr and his counselors met the challenge to Mecca's leadership head on. All men of fighting age were called up, divided into eleven groups, and each group assigned a particular region of Arabia to pacify. The conflict which ensued between Mecca and these rebellious tribes has received the name Riddah Wars, that is, wars of succession or apostasy. Since the extent of the fighting went beyond that required to bring recalcitrant tribes back into the fold, the term is not entirely satisfactory. Possibly two-thirds of Arabia—lands and tribes which had never recognized Mohammed as Prophet—were shortly forced to acknowledge Mecca's leadership for the first time.

So ambitious a goal as the conquest of all Arabia would have been impossible even if Mecca's foes had been united, but the lack of communications and the proud indepen-

dence of Arabia's tribes made such cooperation impossible.
The pacification of the most dangerous area, that of the central region which was occupied by the Banu-Haifa, was an
assignment entrusted to Khalid b. al Walid, probably the
ablest of the early Islamic captains. His victory over this
tribe at Akraba in 633 when the "false" prophet Musailima
was slain, led quickly to the submission of all Arabia and the
end of the Riddah Wars. The policy of conciliation which
Abu Bakr adopted in dealing with the defeated tribes as-
suaged the bitterness of their defeat and brought the peninsula the first peace that land had known.

Still, the coming of peace left Arabia an armed camp, and
so a new crisis confronted Abu Bakr and Mecca. How long
could they expect the restless tribes of the peninsula to
respect the ban against intertribal warfare which denied the
Bedouins the only occupation they had known and the raids
by which they had supplemented the meager products of
their flocks? A new outlet must be found for their warlike
spirit and for their rapaciousness, one that would furnish the
military excitement, the food, and the booty to which the
razzia had accustomed them. The solution was another kind
of razzia, this one on a much larger scale than any before. It
was to be undertaken not against the tribes of Arabia, which
had all accepted Mecca's leadership, but against the peoples
outside the peninsula.

That kind of razzia Mohammed had himself anticipated
when in 630 he sent an expedition of some 3,000 men to
pillage the community of Mu'tah located just southeast of
the Dead Sea. Byzantine forces had annihilated this raiding
party, but the precedent had been established. Given the
presence of thousands of armed and restive Bedouins with
nothing to do, Abu Bakr and Mecca had no choice. In the fall
of 633 they organized three raiding expeditions with instructions to plunder the settlements along the southern borders
of Syria. These areas were familiar to the Arabs, since Busra

and Gaza, important terminal points for caravans from the south, were located there. Although the size of these raiding parties—some 3,000 men each—suggested objectives more important than any yet undertaken by the Arabs, their leaders surely did not contemplate anything beyond punishing raids, a sort of grand *razzia*. Level-headed men the like of Abu Bakr and his counselors would have considered preposterous the goal of depriving the imposing Byzantine and Persian empires to the north and east of their cities and territories. It was only after early successes had raised the possibility of greater and more ambitious objectives that these goals received serious consideration and systematic campaigns were organized to bring them to fruition.

The astonishing success the Arabs enjoyed on these raids, followed by the even more astounding victories they gained over the larger and better-equipped armies of Byzantium and Persia, have scholars searching for explanations. How could untried forces from a culturally backward region, inferior in numbers, equipment, and experience, achieve the remarkable victories of these Arabs, particularly during the early years between 633 and 642? Mention has been made of the armed character of the peninsula following the conclusion of the Riddah Wars and also of the ban against the *razzia* and against intertribal warfare. Beyond this there were the repeated exhortations of Mohammed that his disciples carry on a holy war (*jihad*) against the unbelievers. While scholars have questioned the degree of religious motivation these Arab warriors may have felt,[4] there is no question that the gospel of the Prophet served as a cohesive agent in supplying a measure of unity to a land and a people which had never known them.

The desire for loot was surely the most compelling motive in the minds of the Bedouins who joined the forces going north. But soon the pleasant climate of Syria and Palestine and the high standard of living found there suggested to these weather-beaten warriors from hot, dusty Arabia the desirability of moving themselves and their families permanently to these new lands. An eminent authority on Arabic history has called this movement out of Arabia "the last great Semitic migration."[5] While it was the pressure of growing populations which had inspired the earlier exoduses, here it was the quest for booty and a more comfortable life.

To the endurance of the Arab and to his ferocity must be credited in large measure the early victories he won over the armies of Byzantium and Persia. He was one of the fiercest warriors of his day. From boyhood he learned horsemanship and fighting as well as the constant need of joining his efforts with those of his fellow clansmen in beating off a raid or of going on one of their own. Still, the exigencies of tribal warfare made few demands other than that he be able to ride swiftly and fight with spirit. Against the professional soldiers Byzantium and Persia employed to maintain the frontiers of their empires, he would have been helpless but for the organizing genius of a Khalid and the mistakes of his enemies.

The Arab carried few weapons, a sword and javelin, and he lacked protective gear. The only organization he knew, that of advancing swiftly against the enemy in successive waves of horsemen, scarcely carried beyond the initial attack. So short of weapons were the Arabs that the only major expedition that moved up into Syria during the lifetime of the Prophet was an expedition of 3,000 Bedouins against Mu'tah, a city located just east of the southern extremity of the Dead Sea, for the purpose of seizing swords manufactured in that region. No sooner had the Arabs encountered and defeated the armies of Byzantium than they adopted both the arms and the strategy of their defeated foe.

The Arab did most of his fighting under physical conditions with which he was most familiar. It is no accident that the huge empire Islam gained within a century of the Prophet's death encompassed arid and semiarid lands for the most part, regions often as hot and dry as Arabia itself. Two battles of decisive importance in the rise of Islam, one at the Yarmuk and a second one at Kadesiya, were won in sandstorms. Where water was available, Arab horses were the fastest in the world. Where water was lacking and long stretches of desert posed a seemingly insurmountable barrier to forward movement, the Arab had his camel and continued his march. It was this kind of daring, novel maneuver that enabled Khalid to cross the Syrian desert and confront the astonished Byzantine forces on the other side, who were confident the desert effectually blocked Khalid.[6]

Granted the Arabs' prowess and zeal as warriors, what may explain their success as much as their merits were the deficiencies of their foes. Had the Byzantine and Persian empires not exhausted themselves by long years of heavy fighting, most notably during the reign of Emperor Heraclius (610–641), the rise of the Islamic empire would have been inconceivable. By the year 630 when Mohammed took over Mecca, Byzantine resources had become so depleted that Constantinople was obliged to abandon a number of fortresses along the desert frontiers to the south and to cut off the subsidies it had paid its Arab allies in the area.

Both the Byzantine and Persian empires had present within their borders large Semitic populations that had never fully accepted the rule of their conquerors. They objected to the high taxes these "foreign" governments imposed, taxes which kept mounting as the wars continued. They objected to the religious policies. The rulers of Persia favored the Medaean religion, a policy which displeased the Semitic population of Iraq. The Semitic populations of Syria and Egypt, although Christian for the most part, objected to what the "orthodox" Christian emperor in Constantinople was ordering them to believe. Imperial law demanded that the Monophysite Christians there recognize both a human and divine nature in Christ, not the single divine nature they had come to accept.

For these reasons the peoples of Syria and Palestine generally refused to support the imperial armies against the Arab invaders. Against the initial Arab raiders they quite naturally defended themselves, since they were fighting for their lives and property. When they found the Byzantine forces unable to defend them and learned that the intruder promised them both religious toleration and lower taxes, they opened their arms and their city gates. The story is told, and it is probably true, that when the Arabs who had captured Emesa (Hims) decided to evacuate the city at the approach of the Byzantine army rather than defend it, the Christian populace protested: "We like your rule and justice far better than the state of oppression and tyranny in which we were."[7] And when the Arabs did leave, the Christians closed the gates to the Byzantine forces and would not let them enter. The Jews, too, welcomed the Arabs because of the discrimination they had long suffered under Byzantine rule, and so did the Samaritans. So valuable did the Arabs consider the assistance given them by Samaritans in their struggle with the Byzantine army that the Samaritans were exempted from the poll tax which the Arabs customarily levied upon subject peoples.[8]

Yet the prospects for the survival of Byzantine rule in Syria were not entirely gloomy. The soldiers with which Byzantium opposed the fierce raids of the Arab tribesmen were the best equipped in the world. Under normal circumstances and given proper leadership, they might have kept these desert raiders out of Syria indefinitely, however great the discontent of the Monophysite majority who lived there. The principal strength of the Byzantine army lay in its divisions of heavy cavalry. The individual warrior, known as a cataphract (Greek, "clad in full armor") carried a lance, broadsword, bow, quiver, and dagger. He wore a steel cap, a long mail shirt which reached from his neck to his thighs, gauntlets, and steel shoes. The horse he rode was considerably heavier than the light and fast Arab steed, and the horses of the officers and the warriors in the front rank were equipped with steel frontlets and poitrails.

While the most efficient coordination of horsemen and infantry remained to be worked out during the period of the Crusades, Byzantium was already using heavy-armed foot soldiers although ordinarily only for the defense of frontier fortresses and for carrying out expeditions of a small order into mountainous regions where the use of horsemen was impractical. Such a foot soldier wore a steel helmet, mail-shirt, and at times gauntlets and greaves. For weapons he carried a lance, sword, and an axe, which had a cutting blade at one side and a spike at the other. He protected himself with a large round shield. Because of his lack of mobility and the problem of water, the Byzantine heavy-armed foot soldier rarely took part in desert engagements. To supplement the limited number of cataphracts and to have warriors more capable of counteracting the skirting attacks of the swiftly moving Arabs, Constantinople regularly contracted with tribes along its southern frontiers and with other peoples, such as the Armenians, for light-armed cavalry that used equipment and tactics similar to those of Arab horsemen. Had it not been for the defection of such mercenaries at the Yarmuk, that decisive battle would probably have had a different ending.

In the fall of 633, with the Riddah Wars ended, Abu Bakr invited all Arab tribes, including those of southern Yemen, to send volunteers for a holy war against the Unbeliever in Syria. Since the objective of this offensive was to be spoil, not territory, the war resembled the raids with which the Arabs were familiar, except that it would be larger and better organized than any yet undertaken. Three units of 3,000 men each were recruited, principally from the more restless and warlike of the tribes. As these units moved toward Syria their numbers increased, and by the time they crossed into Christian country they may have reached more than 7,000 each. Moslem chroniclers say that Abu Bakr gave orders to the leaders of the different expeditions not to injure old people, women, or children, not to devastate any cultivated areas or cut down fruit-bearing trees, and not to slay any animals. These orders were in keeping with Abu Bakr's benevolent nature, although his instructions concerning the sparing of animals and cultivated fields raise the possibility that he may have considered holding on to what lands his raiders might overrun.

The first detachment that left Arabia for Syria early in 634 was composed of tribesmen of the Hijaz and western Arabia, the warriors upon whom Mecca had chiefly relied in the Riddah Wars. That they were privileged to move first stood in the nature of a reward for these services. Being unexpected, their attack promised to be materially most rewarding. Amr b. al 'As, who later gained fame for his conquest of Egypt, commanded this unit. A second detachment moved under command of Yazid b. abi-Sufyan, the brother of Muawiyah, who was destined to become an illustrious general in his own right and the founder of the Umayyad dynasty. A third group under command of Shurahbil b. Hasanah marched in the wake of Yazid, while a fourth force set out for Iraq under command of Khalid, the "Sword of Allah," who was to prove himself the most successful of these first Arab generals. Abu Bakr received an appeal for aid from Al-Muthanna ben-Haritha, the sheik of the Bakr tribe in northern Arabia. This man had once been a Christian but had accepted Islam when he learned about the success of the Riddah campaigns. But the raids he had undertaken on his own into Persia had provoked dangerous resistance, and he had begged Abu Bakr for help, whence Khalid's expedition.

Khalid appears to have gotten his troops on the march by the fall of 633, earlier than any of the other detachments. They left Mecca the following spring. As he moved forward the number of his forces steadily increased and may have approached 10,000 men by the time he entered Iraq. He contented himself at first with plundering villages and small communities until he reached the city of Anbar on the left bank of the Euphrates, which he forced to surrender. Here in Iraq, Khalid made the first acquisitions of territory for Islam outside Arabia. Being an exponent of aggressive warfare, he would have continued his penetration of this rich country but for instructions he now received from Abu Bakr that he cease his operations there and hurry to Syria, where a major confrontation with the Byzantine army seemed in the making.

Up to this point the Arab forces which had been operating in Syria had almost everything their own way. One circumstance which had enabled them to move about the region so freely and successfully was their use of the Saracens they found in the area who readily served them as guides. These men had either been expelled from Christian-held territory or belonged to those Arabic tribes who were no longer receiving their annual subsidy from Constantinople. Amr, who moved into Palestine, defeated a small detachment of Byzantine soldiers near Gaza under the command of the provincial governor, Sergius. The Romans fell back after this defeat and regrouped, only to suffer a second defeat in February 634, when Sergius was slain. One account says Sergius was not slain but taken captive. To punish him for having advised Emperor Heraclius to withhold further subsidies from the Arabs in the region, his captors skinned a camel, sewed him up in its hide, and left him to die a lingering death from suffocation as the hide dried in the sun.[9]

The death of Sergius and the destruction of his forces left Palestine open to Arab ravaging. Since the invaders lacked siege machines, however, they did not attempt to force the surrender of any large cities at this time. But the character of the fighting altered abruptly. Heraclius now realized that the number of Arab invaders together with their unbroken successes clearly showed he could not dismiss them as disorganized raiders similar to the smaller groups of plunderers who had periodically harried Syria and Palestine in the past. He hurriedly raised another army, although not so formidable a one as the situation demanded. What he knew of the undisciplined nature of desert nomads caused him to persist in underestimating the gravity of the threat. Because of his own poor health he placed the new army under command of his brother, Theodore.

In Mecca news of Arab successes had Abu Bakr reacting in an equally positive manner. In addition to sending more recruits up to Syria, he forwarded instructions to Khalid to move as quickly as possible into that province in order to assist the Arabs who were fighting there. How many troops of his army Khalid took with him across the Syrian desert remains in doubt. The conservative figure of about a thousand appears plausible, since even with that limited a number his feat of crossing long, waterless stretches of desert assumes the character of the incredible. The trek, which he accomplished in eighteen days, was made possible by using camels. The horses the riders took with them were kept alive with water taken from the paunches of old camels which were slaughtered on the way.

By means of this brilliant maneuver Khalid bypassed border fortresses which would otherwise have slowed his advance. Without interference he joined his fellow Arabs in the vicinity of Damascus, probably after the middle of June 634. Some weeks subsequent to this, in late July or early August, he fought and gained a clear victory at Ajnadain, some twenty miles west of Jerusalem, over the Byzantine army led by Theodore Trithurius, the imperial treasurer. Had Khalid's army of somewhat more than 15,000 men succeeded in destroying the 10,000 under Theodore, this battle might have ranked as the most decisive of the period rather than that which was shortly to follow on the Yarmuk River. It remains of major importance, nonetheless, even though Theodore was able to salvage the bulk of his army.

Abu Bakr died a few days after learning of the victory at Ajnadain and was succeeded by Omar, whom he had nominated as the new caliph. He could not have made a wiser choice. It was during the ten-year caliphate of Omar (646-656) that a solid foundation was given the burgeoning empire of Islam. The respect and devotion which Omar's deep faith, frugality, high sense of justice, and humaneness won him from his fellow Arabs served to keep the Muslim people united during this dangerous period of rapid expansion. A mark of his administrative talents was the policy of conciliation which he adopted toward the Riddah "rebels," whom he now invited to participate as "full citizens" in fighting the enemy. His modesty and his sincere attachment to the cause of the Prophet was illustrated by the title, commander of the faithful, that he selected for himself and that his successors continued to use until the end of the caliphate (1258).

For the moment Omar took no direct hand in the campaign in Syria, which was going well. Khalid, following his bloody victory at Ajnadain, moved on Busra and captured it without great difficulty. It is said the governor of Busra betrayed the city by revealing to the Arabs the existence of a secret underground passage that carried into the city beneath the walls. That he became a Muslim after the surrender of the city lends some credence to the story about the tunnel.

The Byzantine army, which had regrouped behind the marshes of Baysan following its defeat at Ajnadain, found itself obliged to cross the Jordan because of pressure from Khalid. The Muslim general who was now in supreme

command caught up with the Byzantine army shortly afterwards, sometime in January of 635, and defeated it a second
time. This defeat removed the final obstacle to laying siege
to Damascus. Since his army lacked siege engines, however,
and could expect none from Arabia, Khalid's only hope was
to cut the city off from supplies of food and force its surrender. Damascus could do little but hope that the appeals it
sent to Heraclius, who was at Emesa, would bring prompt
relief. Heraclius did fit out a cavalry force, but the Arabs
repulsed it when it reached the vicinity of Damascus, then
pursued it back to the outskirts of Emesa. There the Arabs
suffered a severe mauling and hurried back to Damascus.

This small victory before Emesa was the sole good fortune
that came the way of Heraclius during this dismal period.
When it became clear that Damascus could count on no real
aid, the city opened negotiations with the Arabs and
capitulated in early September. The city agreed to pay an annual tribute of 100,000 dinars, while the Arab conquerors
promised it protection against any form of pillage or property
expropriation. No doubt the generosity of the terms proved
an important factor in winning for the Arabs a majority of
the cities of Syria and Palestine without the expense of
costly sieges. According to the Moslem chronicler Al-
Baladhuri, the terms of surrender read as follows: "In the
name of Allah, the Compassionate, the Merciful. This is
what Khalid ibn-al-Walid would grant to the inhabitants of
Damascus if he enters therein: he promises them security
for their lives, property and churches. Their city wall shall
not be demolished, neither shall any Moslem be quartered in
their houses. Thereunto we give to them the pact of Allah
and the protection of his Prophet, the caliphs and the
believers. So long as they pay the poll tax, nothing but good
shall befall them."[10]

In the face of the continued advances of the Arabs, Heraclius moved his headquarters from Emesa to Antioch.
Despite the enemy's victories and his own poor health, he

had not given up hope. He set about raising a new army, which he hoped could contend successfully with Khalid. He drew men from the local militias, recruited volunteers where he could find them, and appealed to friendly Christian tribes and to the Armenians for mercenaries. About 10,000 Armenians under the command of their general, Vaanes, offered their services, and about the same number of Arabs from the Ghassan and Kalb tribes came forth under command of Djabalah ben-al-Hayyam, tribal leader of the Ghassanides. Since these mercenaries consisted generally of light-armed cavalry, they differed little in equipment and mobility from the Arab invaders.

According to Tabari, the overall size of the Byzantine army which the imperial treasurer, Theodore Trithurius, set out with from Antioch in the spring of 636 numbered some 250,000 men, which is palpably an absurd figure. Modern scholars suggest an army between 30,000 and 50,000. They argue that any larger force would not have been manageable given the hot climate of the region and the lack of food and water.

Scholars find it equally difficult to estimate the size of Khalid's army. Arab chroniclers who delight in exaggerating the number of men in the Byzantine army and in understating the number of Arabs speak of 25,000 and 35,000 for the latter, figures which modern writers are inclined to accept. These figures leave the Christian army a small advantage in numbers. But far offsetting this in importance was the unified command which the Arabs enjoyed under Khalid, the ablest general of the day, as against the confusion, if not suspicion, which prevailed among the leaders of the Byzantine army. The morale of the Byzantine army was also low, but that of the Arabs was high and tending to grow ever more fervid as reinforcements came from Arabia.

Both armies spent the months of the late spring and early summer of 636 moving cautiously about Syria and Palestine, each wary of the other, each fearful of being caught in a disadvantageous position, and each hopeful of maneuvering the other into a position whose drawbacks it might exploit. Of the two generals, Khalid had the clearer view of what he wanted to do and what he must avoid—he must not divide his troops in an effort to defend the large cities that had fallen to him. So, over the protests of their Christian inhabitants, he evacuated both Damascus and Emesa. He furthermore made every effort to cut the Byzantine army off from possible sources of aid from the north and west, while he enticed it to follow him toward the desert to the south. There the desert left the road open to Medina whence fresh reinforcements could come and where he could escape as well should he lose the approaching battle with the Byzantine army. And Khalid must also have reasoned that the closer he moved to the desert, the closer would conditions resemble those of dry, sandy Arabia where his warriors would be at their best.

Khalid may have learned of the low morale prevailing in the Byzantine army and the trouble its commander, Theodore Trithurius, was having with his Armenian and Ghassanide mercenaries. He sought to induce both Vaanes and Djabalah to abandon what he assured them was a losing cause. That he made such an effort and that he partially succeeded in his overtures leaves one wondering whether the situation for the Byzantine army may have deteriorated during the first half of 636. Had the reverse been the case and the prospects for a Byzantine victory bright, the Armenians would not have been receptive to Khalid's words.[11] After a skirmish between Khalid and a detachment of Byzantine troops on July 23, during which the latter were compelled to retreat, the Armenians cancelled their agreement with Heraclius and withdrew from the struggle.

The situation in which the Byzantine army now found itself was still not hopeless, and in three days of bitter fighting Theodore was able to repulse all of Khalid's efforts to cut his communications with Damascus. About the middle of August Khalid moved his army and headquarters southward to a point below the Yarmuk River. The Yarmuk is a small tributary of the Jordan that rises in the Harran range and flows westerly to the Jordan, which it enters just south of the Lake of Tiberias. Khalid counted on the deep ravines which traversed the area to protect his army from attack by the Byzantine host, which was positioned north of the river.

On the evening of August 19 a particularly hot wind began to blow from the south. While it beat against the backs of the Arabs, it blew clouds of dust directly into the faces of the imperial troops to the north. On August 20, as the Byzantine army began to pull back in order to avoid fighting under such savage conditions, its Christian Ghassanide allies defected and rode off.[12] At that very moment Khalid gave orders to attack. A fearful struggle followed, fought on an insufferably hot day and in what amounted to a veritable sandstorm. It is said that the wives of some of the Arab leaders removed the pegs of the camp tents and used these as clubs to drive back into the battle any Arabs who attempted to withdraw. The Christian resistance gradually began to crumble and within a short time a general massacre ensued. Some Byzantine troops fled into the deep ravines about the Yarmuk, where they were hunted down and slain. Others attempted flight in the deep sand, but the going was impossible, especially for the cataphracts with their heavy equipment. The Arabs cut them down without mercy. The battle ended in the near annihilation of the entire Byzantine army, with Theodore, the general, numbered among the dead.

After the fury of the battle had spent itself, a strange calm settled upon Syria. Khalid is said to have observed, "Syria sat as quiet as a camel." Heraclius made no further effort to retrieve the situation. He withdrew to the Taurus mountains to the north, which the Arabs did not dare penetrate, then returned to Constantinople. "Peace be with you, Syria," he said as he passed out of that country, "what a beautiful land you will be to the enemy."

Yarmuk sealed the fate of Syria and Palestine, and after them of Egypt. Emesa and Damascus opened their gates to the victor, as did most of the cities of the region. Jerusalem held out until the fall of 637. The Arabs lacked siege engines, so Sophronius, the patriarch, could wait, not so much for possible aid from Heraclius, but for better terms from the conqueror. It is said the patriarch insisted on negotiating with Omar in person. He had heard of Omar's benevolence and his integrity. As it happened, Omar was in Palestine. He had come to Syria as soon as he learned of the victory at the Yarmuk in order to supervise the organization of the newly conquered territories. The two men did meet. Omar owned but one shirt and one mantle, both by this time not only patched but deeply soiled from long wear. Omar first refused when Sophronius insisted that he change into the clean clothes he offered to furnish him, but finally relented, although he later returned to Sophronius the robes the patriarch had provided him. This tale may be true, as may also be that which has Sophronius reciting in the hearing of his attendants, when showing Omar the interior of the Church of the Resurrection, the words of Daniel the Prophet: "Truly this is the abomination of desolation spoken of by Daniel the Prophet as standing in the holy place."

Whatever the nature of Sophronius' demands, Omar would in all probability have come to Jerusalem anyway. Pious Muslim that he was, he would visit the sacred spot on the site of Solomon's temple whence Mohammed was believed to have made his ascent to heaven on a winged horse. Yet the so-called Mosque of Omar which continues to grace the city of Jerusalem does not owe its construction to this caliph. It is more properly known as the Dome of the Rock, the rock from where the Prophet made his ascent. Jerusalem itself has remained "The Holy [City]" to Moslems.

The battle of the Yarmuk was fought in the summer of 636. A year later the Arabs dealt the crumbling Persian empire a death blow with their crushing victory at Kadesiya near Ctesiphon. It was camels that had enabled Khalid to cross the Syrian desert and win his subsequent victory over the Byzantine army at the Yarmuk. At Kadesiya the Arabs trained their arrows at the eyes and trunks of the elephants the Persians had brought with them and, again with the help of a sandstorm, destroyed the Sassanid host. Within a few years Bukhara and Samarkand, the fabled cities of Turkestan, fell to the conquering Arabs, who then pushed forward across the Indus into the Punjab. By this time other Arabs had overrun Egypt, occupied the islands of Crete and Rhodes, and in 698 captured and destroyed Carthage. (This ancient city was one of the few that the Muslims razed in their march to world empire.) In 711 the Arabs, or better, the Moors, moved across the Straits of Gibraltar, then in 718 through passes in the Pyrenees into Gaul. What made possible these stupendous acquisitions of territory, what had held the key to the spectacular victories that intervened between the conclusion of the Riddah Wars and the hundredth anniversary of the Prophet's death in 732 was the bloody victory Khalid won in a sandstorm on the Yarmuk in August 636.[13]

4

THE BATTLE OF HASTINGS

GEOLOGISTS SAY THAT ENGLAND BECAME AN ISLAND SOME twenty-five thousand years ago toward the close of the glacial age, when the level of the earth's oceans was at its highest. The North Sea, which had been a marsh fed by the Rhine, became an ocean, and the Thames, until then a tributary of the Rhine, now became a river in its own right flowing directly into the sea. The "independence" won by the Thames, Britain's largest river, was shared by Britain itself as water moved into the low-lying region we know today as the English Channel and severed the land connection with the European continent.

No natural or human development has so affected the history of England as the fact of its being an island. Therefore one must reckon that phenomenon as the most decisive event in its history. Were one to employ the term "history" strictly in the sense of recorded events, nothing has proved more decisive in the history of England than the battle fought at Hastings on the southern edge of that island on October 14, 1066. Hastings was "one of the battles which at rare intervals have decided the fate of nations."[1]

The most significant consequence which followed upon the victory of William, duke of Normandy, and his Normans over the English at Hastings was the political connection it established between Britain and the Continent. What moorings England had maintained with Scandinavia—from 1016 to 1035 it had been part of the Scandinavian empire of Canute, king of England and Denmark—were now riven. Instead, the duke of Normandy became king of England and for centuries to come claimed to hold both honors of duke and monarch. Even after the English had been expelled from France they found it hard to forget that their king had once ruled Normandy. Even the uxorious Henry VIII found time to fit out two expeditions in attempt to recover territories across the Channel.

From 1066 until the close of the Middle Ages, French influences were strong in England. The language that the Normans brought with them continued to be the speech of the aristocracy and literate English people into the fifteenth century. Anglo-Saxon, which dropped out of use except among the illiterate lower classes, remained under a cloud until it regained acceptance in the late fourteenth century in the wake of Langland and Chaucer. Had it not been for the battle of Hastings and the introduction of French influences, the speech of the English and of people in the United States would today be much like that spoken in Holland and North Germany.

The victory of the Normans at Hastings brought about an almost immediate replacement of the Saxon aristocracy by a French ruling class and a somewhat slower although almost as complete substitution of a native hierarchy by French bishops and abbots. The coming of the Normans greatly expedited the introduction of feudal institutions and usages. Almost on the day of William's coronation as king of England royal directives went out to the abbeys of England with instructions to furnish the crown with mounted retainers, something they had never done before. After 1066 knights, which were new to England, would dominate the field of battle until the close of the Middle Ages.

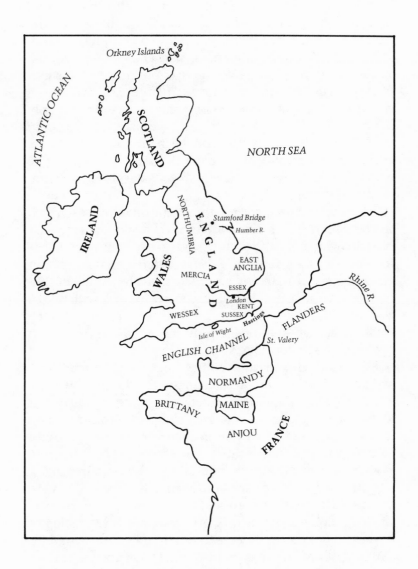

ATLANTIC OCEAN

Orkney Islands

SCOTLAND

IRELAND

NORTH SEA

NORTHUMBRIA

ENGLAND

Stamford Bridge
Humber R.

WALES

MERCIA

EAST
ANGLIA

ESSEX

London
KENT

WESSEX

SUSSEX

Hastings

Isle of Wight

FLANDERS

Rhine R.

St. Valery

ENGLISH CHANNEL

NORMANDY

BRITTANY

MAINE

ANJOU

FRANCE

83

Trade and industry received significant impetus because of the closer association with the Continent. (Thomas Becket's father came from Normandy to become a London merchant.) Norman influences, part cularly the Angevin which Henry II (1154–1189), duke of Normandy and count of Anjou, introduced, contributed to the growth of royal government and administration. England would certainly not have boasted the most efficient government in Europe in the late twelfth century had it not been for William's victory at Hastings. And, of course, but for William's triumph, there would not have been so lamentable a struggle as the Hundred Years' War.

Few battles have attracted the attention of more scholars than the battle of Hastings. Given its decisive character this is understandable, although there is something beyond the importance of a given battle which determines the amount of attention historians give it. There must be sufficient contemporary evidence at hand for scholars to work with. In the case of Hastings there remains a good measure of such evidence and, in addition, a sprinkling of "problems" which continue to stir controversy.

The most valuable source of contemporary information, and a most unique one to be sure, is the so-called Bayeux Tapestry. This is a strip of linen, two hundred thirty feet long and twenty inches wide, which has embroidered upon it in woolen thread and in seven colors what purports to be a pictorial narrative of the battle of Hastings. Special attention is given to the roles of its two principals, Harold, king of England, and William, duke of Normandy. Modern opinion assigns the tapestry to some dozen years after the battle and certainly no later than 1082. At that time Odo, bishop of Bayeux, who ordered its construction, fell out of favor with Duke William, his half-brother, and was imprisoned. A measure of Norman partisanship detracts from the complete reliability of the evidence presented, although the information the tapestry furnishes about eleventh-century dress, armor, weapons, methods of fighting, castle construction, transport of horses, and provisioning of ships is invaluable.

The most informative written source for the battle of Hastings is the chronicle of William of Poitiers, which apparently furnished the designers of the Bayeux Tapestry the substance of their narrative. William, who wrote his chronicle sometime between 1072 and 1074, got part of his information from survivors of the battle and part from William of Jumièges' history of the Norman dukes. Though William of Poitiers wrote an important chronicle, it is clear where his sympathies lay. To him Harold was "that stupid Englishman," a man "stained with vice, a cruel murderer," while William did only what was just in the eyes of God. William of Poitiers' lack of objectivity is characteristic of most of the written sources that deal with the battle, and no more frank. Henry of Huntington tells, for example, how William harangued his men so eloquently before the battle about the crimes of Harold and the splendid exploits of their brave Norman ancestors that they, "inflamed with rage, rushed on the enemy with indescribable impetuosity, and left the duke speaking to himself." The most reliable source, the *Anglo-Saxon Chronicle*, is unfortunately also the briefest, no doubt on the principle that the less said about that sorry business the better.

The battle of Hastings would never have been fought had Edward the Confessor (1042–1066) left a son. Edward was the son of Ethelred II, known somewhat inaccurately as Ethelred the Unready, and his wife, Emma. When Ethelred died in 1016, Canute, the king of Denmark, completed his conquest of England and then married Emma. Emma's two sons by Ethelred, Edward and Alfred, had found refuge in Normandy, where they enjoyed the protection of its duke. In 1041 Harthacanute, Emma's son by Canute, recalled Edward, who then succeeded to the throne the following year.

This came about, it seems, with the approval of both the Danes in England and the Anglo-Saxon earls. Chief among these was Godwin, the powerful earl of Wessex, whose daughter, Edith, married Edward. But Edward, to the woe of his land, sired no son, and the older he grew, the greater became the concern in England and in Normandy over who would succeed.

A number of circumstances brought the Normans into the problem of the succession to the English throne. None was compelling in itself, but their cumulative weight carried considerable impact, at least in Normandy. First in point of time was the fact that Edward's mother, Emma, was a sister of Richard II, duke of Normandy, and a grand-aunt of William the Conqueror. More significant was the fact that Edward had spent the years of his youth, from 1016 to 1041, in exile in Normandy, during the period when the Danish Canute and his sons were ruling in England. Edward had grown up more a Norman in his ways than an Anglo-Saxon and with great affinity for the manners of these "foreigners." When he became king in 1042 more Normans came to England than that land had ever seen, some to serve in Edward's court as clerks and servants, others to become bishops and abbots. The most important of these was Robert of Jumièges, who became bishop of London in 1044 and archbishop of Canterbury in 1051.

The year 1051 proved crucial to the question of who would succeed Edward to the English throne. If Edward the Confessor had hoped that William would fall heir to his crown, no overt evidence of any such hope comes to light prior to that year. During 1051 growing friction between Edward and the earl of Godwin boiled over—Edward blamed Godwin for the death of his brother Alfred. The upshot was that Godwin was forced into exile. Edward even packed his wife, Edith, Godwin's daughter, off to a convent. Then, with the Godwin faction momentarily powerless, he acted more freely in favoring Normans. The promotion of Robert of Jumièges came at this time. There is even some suggestion that William made a trip to England in 1051, and scholars generally accept the view that whether he came or not, Edward at this time made the duke some sort of promise to the throne.

How this arrangement stood up when Godwin returned from exile in 1052 continues to be a point of controversy. That Godwin and Edward did reach some kind of settlement is clear, but the nature of that settlement remains clouded. A number of Normans fled England or were expelled at this time, among them Robert of Jumièges, whose place at Canterbury was taken by the Saxon Stigand. And Edward took Edith back to his palace. This would suggest a complete break with Normandy and an end to what hopes William might have entertained of gaining the throne. Then, a few years later, either upon the Confessor's order or by his permission, Edward, the son of Edmund Ironside (a son of Ethelred II), returned from exile. As a grandson of Ethelred II, he had the clearest hereditary claim to the English throne.

Nonetheless, Edward the Confessor appears to have remained on friendly terms with William. In 1064 William of Poitiers and the Bayeux Tapestry have him sending Earl Harold, the son of Godwin, to Normandy in order to confirm the promise of the duke's succession. According to these sources, Harold promised on this visit to use his influence in England to advance the cause of William's succession once Edward died. He even agreed to turn over to the duke his castle at Dover and other castles which the duke might want him to build. There remains no question that the Normans were fully convinced that Harold had made these promises. So insists at least one modern scholar. He declares that "Harold actually took an oath which his enemies regarded as broken by his acceptance of the English crown is as certain as any fact in eleventh-century history."[2]

Other scholars and contemporary English chroniclers are less convinced. They agree that Harold found himself on the Channel some time in 1064, either on a fishing trip or an embassy to William (the Confessor had earlier sent him on an embassy to Flanders). They further agree that his ship ran aground, that he fell into the clutches of Guy, the count of Ponthieu, and that Ponthieu surrendered Harold to his overlord, William, having been suitably rewarded for doing so. These writers are silent about any promises Harold may have made to William, whether such promises accounted for his going to Normandy in the first place or whether William obliged him to make these pledges before permitting him to return to England.

There is another consideration which bears upon the problem of William's claim to the English throne, and that is the duke's ambition and power. A less ambitious man would not have made so pretentious a claim, and a less powerful one could not have entertained the hope of achieving it. As a boy William appreciated the fact that even though he was the only son of Robert, duke of Normandy, he was also illegitimate. As a bastard he must be both ambitious and wary if he hoped to succeed to the duchy. In 1035, when Robert died in Nicaea on his return from a pilgrimage to the Holy Land, William had double cause to be ambitious and wary. Not only was he a bastard but he was a minor as well, not more than seven or eight years of age. Given the general instability of western Europe in what is called the feudal age, the double curse of illegitimacy and minority might have proved too heavy for even so ambitious a young man as William. But his overlord, King Henry I of France, came to his assistance at the battle of Val-ès-Dune in 1047 and saved him his duchy against his rebellious vassals. Henry may have undertaken to help William because William's father, Robert, had earlier befriended him when Paris expelled him. William, for his part, never permitted a sense of gratitude to keep him from taking what he wanted or felt entitled to. In 1057 he defeated the same King Henry at the battle of Varaville, after which his position was so strong he could safely ignore whoever in Paris might happen to call himself king.

By the year 1057, William had so consolidated his position, both inside Normandy and in France that he could aspire to possessions in more distant lands. His first move toward strengthening his position once his own duchy was secure had been to marry Matilda, daughter of the powerful Count Baldwin V of Flanders. That he married the girl in the face of a formal injunction issued by Pope Leo IX says something about William's iron will. Although he was a man of considerable faith—according to one chronicler "He was gentle to the good men who loved God"—he would brook no interference from churchmen who got in his way. On precisely what grounds Leo chose to block the marriage is not clear. Consanguinity was the customary basis appealed to in the Middle Ages, but in the case of William and Matilda this cannot be established. More likely is the possibility that Henry I had asked the pope to forbid the marriage lest the marital alliance with Flanders leave his vassal too strong. In 1059, about eight or nine years after William and Matilda had wed, the papacy withdrew its objections and blessed the marriage, although it required the husband and wife to build two abbeys in Caen by way of penance for their sin. However much the modern Frenchman might puzzle over Leo's reasons for attempting to block the marriage, he remains grateful to the pope for the two stately abbeys, the *Abbaye-aux-Hommes* (S. Etienne) and *Abbaye-aux-Dames* (La Trinite) that continue to grace Caen. And all are pleased to know that after going to so much trouble to gain and keep Matilda as his wife, William remained attached to her throughout his life, a mark of spousal devotion not typical of many of his medieval successors.

William's efforts to enhance his position did not stop with his marriage to the daughter of the count of Flanders. Confident of his father-in-law's benevolent neutrality, he took possession of the county of Maine in 1063, an acquisition which served to protect his southern frontier against the ambitions of the count of Anjou. Some scholars say he sought approval in the imperial court in Germany for his projected acquisition of England, but this is questionable. William was a practical man. He would have known that Germany, during the period of factional strife which followed upon the death of Henry III in 1056, was incapable of effectively approving or disapproving of whatever he might choose to do. He could even afford to ignore Philip I. The new king of France was a minor and, more to the point, had as his regent none other than William's own father-in-law, the count of Flanders. And in 1060 Geoffrey, count of Anjou, died, leaving that province in turmoil.

The one person whose approval William appears to have been anxious to secure for his conquest of England was that of the pope, although one wonders whether it was less William and more his clerical adviser, Lanfranc, who was most concerned about the matter. After his own experience with papal injunctions, William must have been convinced that the pope could do little to advance or block his project, so Lanfranc probably pressed upon him the value of having the papal approval. The excommunicate Stigand still sat upon the archiepiscopal throne in Canterbury, which the exiled Robert of Jumièges had once occupied. This furnished the pope an easy motive for extending William his blessing, a token of which was a papal banner which William displayed among his other banners when he marched against Harold at Hastings. In return for the pope's blessing William was to remove Stigand, which he did in 1070 when he replaced Stigand with his counselor, Lanfranc. The request the pope later made, that William become his vassal for England, King William scarcely bothered to notice.

Of the three men who advanced claims to the English throne when Edward the Confessor died, William was the one who made good his claim, though the claimant who could present the strongest case was Harold, son of Godwin. He had become earl of Wessex in 1053 when his father died and since that time had won fame for himself by his martial exploits in Wales. In an age when the king must above all other considerations be a warrior, Harold's military prowess would itself have recommended him for the succession, since no one appeared more capable of thwarting the ambitions of some "foreign adventurer" who would be certain to put in a bid. So Edward the Confessor must have reasoned for on his deathbed he designated Harold to be his successor. For some years Edward had turned over to Harold the responsibility of maintaining the peace of the kingdom while he devoted his energies to the building of Westminster Abbey. In the words of the chronicler Florence of Worcester, Harold was the "under-king" during the closing years of Edward's reign. He officially became king on January 6, the day after Edward died, when he was crowned in Westminster Abbey. This followed upon his unanimous election by the witan, the Anglo-Saxon council composed of high ecclesiastics and magnates. Many of its members happened to be in London at the time for the dedication of Westminster Abbey.

The most important Saxon who sought to block Harold's succession was none other than his brother Tostig. Tostig appears to have been but slightly younger than Harold, a man of considerable experience in his own right and a favorite of Edward the Confessor. Since 1055 he had served as earl of Northumbria, the most extensive and probably the most important of the English earldoms. Had he still been earl in 1066, the history of England might have taken a different turn, since Edward may have preferred him to Harold. But in 1065, Tostig's thanes revolted over his harsh rule and forced him into exile. Edward urged Harold to go to his brother's assistance at the time, which Harold did in so ambiguous a manner, it seems, that he earned only Tostig's bitter hatred for his efforts.

Since Harold subsequently married the sister of the earl of Northumbria who had succeeded Tostig, one suspects Harold may have done more to block than to expedite Tostig's return to Northumbria. With Tostig out of the way, Harold's own ambitions to succeed to the throne would be materially advanced, and he could already count on the support of his younger brothers, Gyrth and Leofwine. Gyrth was the earl of East Anglia, Leofwine earl of a district which included London, the shires of Essex, Hartford, and Buckingham north and northeast of the city, and of Surrey and Kent to the south.

When Tostig was forced to flee England, he took himself to Flanders, whose count happened to be his wife's brother (father?). Later, with the aid of Flemish mercenaries and some Englishmen he had impressed in Sandwich, he set out to ravage the east coast of England. Copsi, a friend he had made while in Northumbria, came down from the Orkneys with seventeen ships to help him with his marauding, but to no avail. When the earls of Mercia and Northumbria showed themselves capable of beating off these raiders, most of Tostig's men and ships deserted him, whereupon he fled to Scotland. There he joined his hopes with those of Harald Hardrada, king of Norway, who stepped forward as a third claimant to the throne of England.

Harald Hardrada was one of the leading Viking adventurers of the century and probably the most illustrious warrior of his day. Early in his career he had turned his back on Norway and gone to Russia, where his exploits won him the esteem of Yaroslav the Wise and the hand of his daughter as well. Then he moved on to Constantinople where for a number of years he served as commander of the famous Varangian Guard. In 1047 he was back in Norway as king. Now in 1066 he came forward with a claim to Edward's throne which he based on a treaty that Canute's son, Harthacanute, had made with King Magnus of Norway, his predecessor and kinsman.

Too late Harold became aware of the seriousness of the threat from the north. In a belated move to wean Tostig away from Hardrada, he offered him Northumbria. When Tostig asked Harold what Hardrada would receive as his part in any settlement, only to be told "seven feet of earth, perhaps more, seeing that he is a tall man," he spurned Harold's offer.

Never before had so formidable a host invaded England from the north as that which Hardrada brought with him. By the time he reached the mouth of the Tyne, where Tostig and his friends joined him, his fleet had grown in excess of three hundred ships as it made its way from Bergen through the Shetlands and Orkneys. In early September Hardrada and Tostig started south, ravaged the coast of Yorkshire as they went. They continued on to the Humber River, sailed up the Humber to the Ouse, a tributary, then followed the Ouse as far as Riccall. On September 20, about two miles south of York at Gate Fulford, they defeated the English army under command of the earls of Mercia and Northumbria. The English "fled with great loss," writes the chronicler, "and many more of them were drowned in the river [Ouse] than slain in the fight." Hardrada moved to York, which surrendered, then established his camp nine miles south of the city at Stamford Bridge to await the arrival of hostages promised from the northern shires.

Harold, in the meantime, had been busy shoring up his uneasy throne. In April he traveled north to York where he married Ealdgyth, the sister of Edwin, earl of Mercia, and Morcar, earl of Northumbria, a step intended to assure him the cooperation of these northern earls. The month of May found him dealing with Tostig's raids along the southeast coast, raids which he feared were but preliminary to an invasion by William, duke of Normandy, who had been ex-tending Tostig his encouragement. Once Tostig had been driven north, Harold returned to London to begin in earnest his preparations for William's arrival. Of William's intent he had no doubt; William had charged him with perjury once he had learned Harold had accepted the crown, and warned that he could come in person to deprive Harold of its unlawful possession.

Little is known about Harold's preparations other than that he ordered up the fyrd, a militia of freemen, in the sum-mer to guard the coasts of Sussex and Kent which lay across from Normandy. He himself took command of the Saxon fleet, which was based on the Isle of Wight. On September 8 he disbanded the fyrd, then started his ships eastward on their way to London. What prompted him to take these steps at precisely this time is not clear. It may have been the result of two circumstances. First there is the possibility that the two months of service required of the members of the fyrd had expired and their money and provisions had been ex-hausted. The chronicler writes: "no man could keep them there any longer." Second, the winds which had been blow-ing out of the north during the month of August and had been making passage from Normandy impossible had not only continued into September but had taken on gale velo-cities. (Both Harold on the English coast and William across the Channel in Normandy lost ships to this gale.) Every day that the winds blew they diminished the threat of invasion, since approaching autumn and bad weather reduced the probability of William's coming. It would have been a diffi-cult task for William to campaign in an unfriendly country even during the summer months. Harold could, indeed, be excused for assuming the duke would not undertake so late in the year the conquest of a foreign land the size of England with its great resources of manpower and wealth.

Scarcely had Harold reached London than he learned that Harald Hardrada had landed in the north and had defeated the English earls at Fulford (September 20). He wasted no time. Riding day and night, he hurried north with his house-carls and what fyrd-men he could gather on his way. Harold was known for his impetuosity, but his experience in fighting the Welsh must also have taught him the importance of surprise. It may have been this element of surprise which provided him a critical advantage when on September 25 he came upon Hardrada's forces unexpectedly at Stamford Bridge. The chronicles say little about the battle other than to note the enormity of the slaughter and the death in the battle of both Hardrada and Tostig. Twenty-four ships sufficed to take the Norwegian survivors away—more than three hundred had brought them in—and fifty years later great heaps of bones still marked the battlefield, "memorials of the prodigious numbers which fell on both sides."

Stamford Bridge was Harold's greatest hour, but he had little time to enjoy it. Even while seated at a banquet in York celebrating his victory, according to one story, a messenger brought him the news that William had landed in Sussex. The winds that had blown from the north for weeks had finally shifted to the south, and despite the lateness of the season William had ferried his army across. William was no adventurer, quite the reverse; he had confidence in his army. Above all, he knew that Harold would have two invading armies to fight, his own in the south and Hardrada's in the north. So on September 27, two days after the battle of Stamford Bridge, he sailed from Normandy. He had of course no knowledge of what had transpired in the north.

That William was no gambler is clear from the nature of the preparations he had made for this invasion. He had assembled a host of about 10,000 men, an army the size of which even kings of that period would have been pressed to muster. Included in this number were many noncombatants —men needed to feed the soldiers, to sail the boats, to set up the camp once they reached the English shore, to assemble the castles, and to garrison them. While William was the most powerful lord in France and a wealthy one by the standards of the day, his own resources would never have sufficed to put so mighty a force into operation. The greater number of the men and amount of money required for the invasion came from his vassals and friends, from men who believed in his destiny and who were willing to stake their fortunes on his. His projected invasion had assumed the nature of a joint enterprise. His vassals had been under no firm compulsion to assist him. This was partly because the act constituted an invasion of a foreign land which posed no threat to Normandy, and partly because feudal practice had not yet jelled to the point at which vassals were required to give their lords a specified number of knights for a set period of time. William's vassals joined him on his promise to reward them with lands and booty.

What proportion of William's Norman vassals joined him in this invasion remains conjectural. Some of his friends sought to dissuade him from an undertaking they judged foolhardy, and of these friends prudence must have kept a number at home. Still, the core of William's army—the horsemen who would bear the brunt of the fighting and win him the victory—were Normans, so one must assume that the response in Normandy to his projected invasion was good. Many knights came from Brittany, a poor country at best, which had little to hold ambitious young men at home. They could do worse than try to improve their fortunes in England. A sprinkling of knights may have come from Flanders and from Maine, a few possibly even from southern Italy, where many Normans had settled earlier that century. Still the Worcester chronicler was indulging in rhetorical exaggeration when he wrote that William had help "from all parts of France."

Most of William's men were foot soldiers, and these had been principally his responsibility to recruit. While some of his vassals surely supplied small contingents of archers and spearmen, it is likely that the services of the bulk of the mercenaries who fought at Hastings had been procured by William. Their price was not high. In the second half of the eleventh century foot soldiers were almost expendable, and this was especially true on the Continent, where the knight had pretty well appropriated the battlefield for himself. Some of these men were unemployed soldiers, others simply unemployed—vagrants, ruffians, and adventurers—more eager for loot than work. Those who lacked weapons had these supplied by William, and the Bayeux Tapestry shows stores of spears, bows and arrows, and knives being gathered in preparation for the part these foot soldiers would play in the coming invasion.

That William suffered no great trouble from his foot soldiers is a tribute to his insistence upon discipline. These men were the most difficult to keep in line during intervals of inactivity and the first to flee should the battle go poorly. Since they lived as much by booty as by pay, they might fire a town regardless of the wishes of their commander should such action expedite their looting. Because William had a reputation for winning battles and capturing castles as well as employing "scorched earth" tactics against the enemy's towns and villages, it is possible mercenaries were eager to take service with him.

The most novel problem which William faced in preparing for his invasion was finding the means to transport his army across the Channel to England. Water-borne expeditions were strange to the age. The Vikings and their Scandinavian descendants had a long history of seafaring, and their military campaigns had generally involved ships. At the other corner of Europe, in Byzantium, the transport of troops by water was also not unusual. For centuries Constantinople had found it easier to supply its bases in mountainous Greece and Asia Minor, and even in Italy, by water than by land. But the peoples of western Europe were landlubbers, and this included even the Normans themselves who had forgotten the ways of their forefathers. It was William's good fortune that by the second half of the eleventh century western Europe was giving positive signs of a revival of trade. Had a similar invasion of England been attempted from France a century earlier the shipping could not have been found, surely not if the invading force was the size and character William had under his command.

William required sufficient ships to transport an army of about 10,000 men. Beyond the men, there were in excess of 2,000 horses, the mounts his knights would be needing in England. There were the materials for the two or three castles to be assembled once across, the huge supply of weapons and defensive armor, and the provisions which the army would require before moving into the country. How many ships William gathered for the invasion remains a question. One modern authority places the figure at 1,500, another at fewer than 500. Whatever the actual number, William secured some by requisition and some from his vassals, while others he had his men construct on the beaches of Normandy. However many ships William managed to assemble, the crossing of the Channel posed the most critical single obstacle to the success of his project.

By August 12 William was ready to cross the Channel. He had entrusted the management of affairs in Normandy to a regency headed by his wife, Matilda, and Roger of Beaumont while he assembled his army round the estuary of the Dives. There he waited as days passed, then weeks, and still the wind continued to blow out of the north. Until the wind shifted directions or stopped blowing altogether, there would be no crossing of the Channel. But the wind did neither. William of Poitiers speaks of a morale problem with which William had to deal as the weeks of waiting caused his men to grow restive. Still, if William cursed the weather, there was much for which he had reason to be grateful, for no major epidemic of dysentery struck his army. In the end the foul weather proved the single most important factor in making him king of England. Had he come earlier, before Hardrada appeared in the north, a waiting Harold would have defeated him.

On September 12 William moved his army up the coast to a new base in the estuary of St. Valery. The chroniclers give no explanation for this action. A westerly gale may have driven his ships to the east, or he may have decided that the shorter passage across the Channel at St. Valery offered advantages over Dives, even though his army would find a narrower beach in England on which to maneuver. The fact that he lost some ships and men in the move makes the agency of the gale the more likely explanation. It must have been a severe storm since it also cost Harold some ships across the Channel.

Whatever the virtues of the new base at St. Valery, the wind continued to blow out of the north, and for two more weeks William fumed while his army waited. In desperation he had the body of St. Valery brought from the church and carried in solemn procession through the town. Finally, on September 27, the wind shifted to the south. William gave immediate orders to cross, and at midnight the armada got under way, the duke's own ship in the lead with a lantern fastened to its mast. About nine the next morning, Thursday, September 28, William and his army debarked on the English shore at Pevensey Bay. The following day he moved his army to Hastings, eleven miles to the east. There he set

up a castle—he may have left a castle and garrison at
Pevensey—and settled down to wait.[3]

As soon as Harold received the news of William's landing,
which he did probably on October 2 or 3, he left York and
hurried the nearly one hundred fifty miles south to London.
He reached London on October 6, where he spent the following days gathering what soldiers he could round up. He may
have hoped the northern earls would catch up with him during this interval with their housecarls and foot soldiers.
After the heavy losses they had sustained at Gate Fulford,
Harold's hope could at best have been a slight one. It is more
probable he delayed in London in order to alert his own men
in Wessex, while giving his brothers Gyrth and Leofwine
time to summon theirs.

On October 11 he started his army toward Hastings,
which lay about fifty-eight miles to the south, and on the
evening of October 13 made camp about seven miles northwest of the town. He hoped no doubt that his march from
York and London had been so expeditious that he would
catch William off guard, as he had the Danes at Stamford
Bridge. If the Worcester chronicler is correct in saying that
"one half of his [Harold's] troops were not yet assembled"
when he reached Hastings, he would have had to depend on
something like surprise or luck to win a victory.

As is the case with William's army, there remain un-
answered questions concerning the size and composition of
Harold's. How large was it? It must have approximated
William's in size, but whether it was appreciably larger or
smaller it is impossible to say. Modern writers generally
place its number at about 5,000, although a recent historian
has reduced that figure to 3,000. Hastings in any case clearly
promised to be a smaller affair than Stamford Bridge.

The core of Harold's army consisted of housecarls. These
were professional soldiers whom he, his brothers, and the
more prosperous thanes brought with them to Hastings.

These soldiers might live with their employers, either in their homes or on lands provided by them. They served as a sort of bodyguard for their lord but also constituted a ready force at hand to put down any disturbance of the peace. They were not unlike the feudal retainers on the Continent but with one significant difference—they fought on foot, their horses serving merely as a means of transport.

Less a military class but possessing some training and experience were the thanes. They represented roughly the more prosperous landowners and owed personal military service of an order somewhat above that of the ordinary peasant who served in the fyrd. In times of war they led members of the local fyrd under command of the earl. Because conditions in England were more stable than on the Continent, these thanes devoted more time to administering their lands and participating in the business of the shire and hundred courts and less to fighting than their fellows in France. Such experience made them solid, responsible citizens, although probably not the equal in fighting ability to the knights who joined their counts and dukes to help William at Hastings.

The most numerous element in Harold's army was that of the peasants who made up the fyrd. At one time, centuries earlier, when the need arose it had been the duty of every able-bodied man to bear arms. Changes which began with Alfred the Great had gradually transformed the fyrd into a more select body, and here in the reign of Edward the Confessor probably no more than one of every five men was expected to put in a period of service. By this time it had also become the custom for peasant households which occupied five hides—a hide, 120 acres, theoretically sufficed for the maintenance of a single household—to send one of their number and to provide for his needs. It is possible these farmers selected the ablest of their members to so represent them, if he were willing. Should no one be willing to serve,

they might even have hired an outsider to perform the
service.

While our modern age with its obsession over specializa-
tion and training may wonder how effectively such raw
recruits might perform on the field of battle, this was a time
when muscle, dexterity, and motivation were the virtues
which counted the most in warfare. William's foot soldiers
were probably no better equipped nor more skillful at the
task of fighting than Harold's, and since many of them were
mercenaries and therefore not fighting for home and country, one may suspect they were not the equal of the Saxons.
It is worth noting that William as king of England did not
suppress the fyrd even though there was nothing like it in
Normandy. Along with the shire court and other Anglo-
Saxon institutions which he retained, he felt the fyrd
possessed real merit. He was proved correct when the fyrd
helped put down a rebellion in 1075. Of course, it was the
fyrd that had helped destroy the Norwegian army at Stamford Bridge.

One of the striking facts which a history of the art of war
reveals is the remarkable similarity in weapons and methods
of fighting employed by opposing contestants in any given
battle. Even the proud Romans who long refused to train
cavalry of their own found it prudent to call on their allies or
on mercenaries to fill that need when they encountered a foe
who fought on horseback. In terms of weapons and defensive
armor Hastings was no exception. The most formidable warrior on both sides wore a mail shirt composed of iron rings
that reached to the elbows and knees, called a byrnie by the
English, a hauberk by the French. Soldiers of both countries
wore mail hoods or conical helmets, with an extension
riveted to the rim to protect the nose. A few wore mail leg-
gings. For weapons they might carry a lance, javelin, axe,
mace, and a heavy sword with double-edged blade. They
protected themselves with kite-shaped shields—leather

stretched over a framework of iron, bronze, or wood—which in the case of the English might be rounded at the top. If the shields bore decorative markings, these had not as yet become heraldic in character and were not necessarily peculiar to any individual or family. In a class all by himself, as far as weapons was concerned, was Odo, bishop of Bayeux, who is said to have galloped about the field at Hastings armed with a club rather than sword or axe, since churchmen were forbidden to shed blood.

Despite the general similarity in weapons and armor used and worn by the best Norman and English warriors, two distinct differences call for comment. The most important of these was the role of the horse. The English used their mounts to get to the field of battle. There they dismounted and fought on foot. The Normans followed the practice that was becoming universal on the Continent and fought on horseback. The greater mobility and endurance this afforded them constituted less an advantage, however, than one might assume, since their horses lacked protective armor. William had three horses killed under him. The other significant difference between the Norman and English warrior was the long-handled Danish battle-ax which the Saxons used. The Vikings had once employed this weapon on their plundering expeditions. It still proved a devastating weapon when wielded by a robust Saxon against a Norman knight and his mount.

The foot soldier on both sides carried bow and arrow if an archer or javelin if a spearman, along with a knife and dagger. Chroniclers speak of crossbowmen although none appear in the Bayeux Tapestry. Some of the foot soldiers brought weapons of their own—they may have made them—while others had these furnished them as the tapestry suggests. Whatever their origin, these weapons lacked the uniformity of construction and workmanship which characterizes modern devices. The same lack of uniformity applied to

other aspects of medieval warfare of the eleventh century. If
the foot soldier was fortunate he might wear a helmet or
hauberk that he had happened upon, although most fighters
depended on their leather doublet, often padded, for protection against arrows. William's army boasted more archers
than Harold's, a significant plus for the Normans in the judgment of some analysts.

The battle of Hastings was fought in a relative wilderness.
The *Anglo-Saxon Chronicle* identifies the site simply as
marked by a "grey appletree," on a rise in the downs some
six miles north of Hastings. It was not the place Harold had
selected to force the issue with William. It just happened to
be the spot where the late evening of October 13 had found
him and his men, tired and worn from their hurried march
from London. He may have planned to rest that night, then
make a surprise attack on William's camp the following day.
The speed with which he covered the distance to Hastings
has most writers suggesting that he hoped to surprise
William the way he had the Norwegians at Stamford Bridge.
There is the possibility, however, that his hurry southward
was intended to discourage William in his ravaging of the
region, much of which was Harold's own estates. Harold's
scouts may have warned him of the dangerous size of
William's army, and Harold might indeed have planned to
do what all writers charge him with not doing, namely, to
wait for reinforcements.

One point is crystal clear—Harold did not take the offensive at Hastings. The *Anglo-Saxon Chronicle* even says that
the Normans caught the English by surprise before they were
fully awake, although this is scarcely reasonable. Harold had
scouts and friends who lived in the area who kept him in-
formed and, furthermore, if William had appeared unexpectedly, where would Harold's men have found the time to
bring up tree trunks, planks, sheep hurdles, door frames, and
similar physical impediments to bolster the shield wall with

which they confronted William and his army the morning of October 14? And there was no denying the strength of Harold's position. He was on an opening in the woods near the brow of a hill some six hundred yards in width and protected on either side by near ravines. He could look forward down the hill which the Norman army would have to ascend from its position two hundred yards away.

Contemporary writers say nothing about the manner in which Harold arranged his men beyond the shield wall that they formed, that is, shield to shield, shoulder to shoulder. William's army, on the other hand, appears to have divided itself into the three conventional parts: a center composed of Normans, a left made up of Bretons, and a right referred to simply as the "French" wing. Each of these apparently included a vanguard of archers and pikemen followed by more heavily armed foot soldiers, with knights on horseback bringing up the rear.

William started his vanguard up the slope about nine in the morning. Once his light-armed foot soldiers had reached a point in their march up the hill where they felt their arrows might be effective, they let fly. Against an enemy largely concealed behind shields and other protective devices, these arrows did little damage, and little more was worked on by the pikemen and spearmen with their missiles. By this time the English had begun to retaliate with everything they could throw or shoot—axes, javelins, stones tied to sticks, arrows—and they did this with such abandon that the Bretons to William's left broke in disorder and turned back down the hill. The panic of the Bretons prompted some of the English to hurry down the hill after them in the hope of decimating them in their confused flight. William sensed the critical nature of the situation and quickly moved in his horsemen to block the English in their pursuit, a maneuver which not only saved the Bretons from disaster but also caught a good number of English in a trap from which none escaped. A number of William's knights who had penetrated the Anglo-Saxon formation, including the famed bard Taillefer, were slain.

This incident is one of the few details about the battle which the chroniclers describe. Although the fighting went on for eight or nine hours, that is, until dusk, and at a furious pace, the reader is left to guess what precisely transpired. It appears probable that the combat assumed the character of a melee—a general, confused, hand-to-hand struggle between groups and individuals—the greater part of the battle taking place on the slope in front of the shield wall through which the Saxon warriors pushed to close with the enemy below. We are told that both Harold's brothers fell early in the battle. William was himself so hotly engaged that he had three horses killed under him. At one point in the fighting the cry went up that the duke had been slain, a development which would have brought a quick end to Norman resistance, for the tapestry shows William raising his helmet and shouting to his men that he was still very much alive.

The French chroniclers, possibly in an effort to explain Norman retreats or even their eventual victory, say that on several occasions—three according to William of Poitiers—William employed the tactic of a feigned retreat. He then counterattacked with deadly effect when the English mistook the retreat for a defeat and advanced too far ahead of their defenses. Some analysts disagree. So experienced a warrior as Harold, they maintain, would not thrice have been duped by the same stratagem, especially since the English from their shield wall enjoyed a good view of the battlefield. The analysts also doubt the ability of William to conduct such a difficult maneuver. Others accept William of Poitiers' words at face value and insist that the Norman army was so well disciplined that it could have managed a feigned retreat. The slow, cautious advance of the Saxons in front of their protective shield wall would have provided

William and his knights sufficient time to regroup their "retreating" foot soldiers for an advance.

As the battle wore on without a decisive turn and dusk began to settle, William grew increasingly apprehensive. Unless he could win the battle before night fell, the following morning would find his tired army facing fresh Englishmen who would be coming up during the night. So, it is said, he gave the order for one last general assault and this succeeded. The shield wall crumbled and, worse, Harold was slain.[4] Even yet all the fighting was not over. As the English fell back and scattered into the darkening forest, some housecarls turned on their Norman pursuers and slew a good number of William's bravest men before he hurried up and drove off the last of them. In the end, as the *Anglo-Saxon Chronicle* aptly puts it, "the French had possession of the place of slaughter."[5]

Hastings decided the fate of Anglo-Saxon England. For the moment the English leaders did not quite know what to do. Harold's death had removed the one man most of them had been willing to accept. The earls of Mercia and Northumbria, and some members of the hierarchy including the two archbishops of Canterbury and York, declared for Edgar Aetheling, the grandnephew of Edward the Confessor, but they did so without enthusiasm. The young man lacked the years and experience to command much confidence.

For his part William demonstrated the shrewdness for which men knew him and the ruthlessness as well. He moved first to Romney and Dover in order to make sure of his communications with Normandy, then on to Canterbury which, fortunately, escaped his fury. As he went his men barbarously harried the land, slew men and animals, burned houses, stables, and implements, and left only desolation in their wake. After one of his columns had burned Southwark he marched his army to the west of London up the Thames to Wallingford where the Saxon Stigand made his submission. Then William crossed the Thames, and by the time he had reached Berkhamsted in his approach to London from the northwest other Saxon leaders, including Edgar, were ready to swear allegiance. On Christmas Day, almost exactly a year after Ealdred of York had crowned Harold in Westminster Abbey, that archbishop placed the crown on the head of William the Conqueror.

5

THE BATTLE OF HATTIN

WILLIAM, ARCHBISHOP OF TYRE, A LEADING HISTORIAN OF THE twelfth century, closed his history of the kingdom of Jerusalem on a gloomy note. For the Christians in Syria, he wrote in 1184, "the only subjects that present themselves are the disasters of a sorrowing country and its manifold misfortunes."[1] William had cause to be gloomy. There was no hiding either the growing factionalism that divided the few Christians who had made their home in Syria or the growing unity of the Muslim world under the inspiring leadership of Saladin. The Crusader states were in grave danger. Three years later, on July 4, 1187, the accuracy of William's melancholy foreboding proved true when Saladin and his Saracen army annihilated the Crusaders at Hattin. On October 2, Jerusalem surrendered to Saladin and the kingdom of Jerusalem was no more.

The situation for the Christians when William sounded his alarming note in 1184 was indeed serious although not irretrievable. Unless one credits the chronicler with the powers of a clairvoyant, more personal reasons for his pessimism might be found in his poor health—he died shortly after—and possibly in a lingering bitterness over the appointment four years earlier of the unworthy Heraclius to

the position of patriarch of Jerusalem, a post he himself had
wanted.

The Christians had experienced crises before 1184 and had
managed to survive. While the battle of Hattin was a disaster
of the first order, what made it all the greater tragedy was the
fact that it need never have been fought. But for a calamitous
instance of bad judgment on the part of Guy, king of Jerusalem, the Christians could have continued their generally
successful policy of avoiding major battles with the enemy
until the united front created by Saladin crumbled. The
world, in that event, might never have heard of Saladin or of
Richard the Lionhearted or of the Third Crusade, which
brought these men into prominence, or probably of any of
the subsequent Crusades. The impact which the Crusades
had upon western Europe would then have been im-
measurably reduced. It is these considerations which justify
ranking the battle of Hattin as the most decisive engagement
fought during the period of the Crusades.

This period had begun in the late summer of 1096 when
Christian knights gathered in Constantinople in response to
the appeal by Pope Urban II for a holy war against the
Muslims. Pope Urban had harangued his listeners over the
mistreatment of pilgrims to the Holy Land, now in the
hands of the Infidel, and had reminded them that the
Biblical land of "milk and honey" was there waiting to be
conquered. From Constantinople the Crusaders had fought
their way by slow, painful stages through Asia Minor and
Syria. After escaping near disaster on several occasions, they
finally attained their objective on July 14, 1099, when they
captured Jerusalem.

During this Crusade as many as 30,000 warriors had taken
up the cross (Latin *crux*, whence *Crusade*). Under the circumstances, that was a magnificent response. Western
Europe's population was small and the land itself still in the
feudal age. This was a time of relative confusion when a

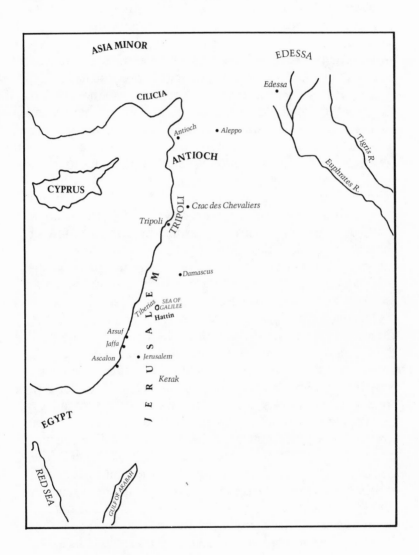

ASIA MINOR

EDESSA

CILICIA

Edessa

Antioch

Aleppo

ANTIOCH

CYPRUS

Tigris R.

Euphrates R.

TRIPOLI

Crac des Chevaliers

Tripoli

Damascus

J E R U S A L E M

Tiberias

SEA OF
GALILEE

Hattin

Arsuf

Jaffa

Ascalon

Jerusalem

Kerak

EGYPT

RED SEA

GULF OF AKABAH

powerful landed aristocracy concerned principally with its own aggrandizement dominated the area politically and economically. Except that the late eleventh century was alive with the spirit of religious reform and regeneration, Pope Urban's call would have stirred little enthusiasm.

Still, had twice the number of Christians responded to Urban's call, they would have been inadequate against the far greater number of warriors the Islamic world could have mustered had this world been united. It was not. The Muslims of Syria, who bore the brunt of the Christian attack, received no great assistance from the Muslims in Mesopotamia or from those in Egypt. The consequence was that by 1109 the Crusaders had carved out of the Islamic world four states for themselves along the eastern littoral of the Mediterranean, including the kingdom of Jerusalem to the south, the county of Tripoli and the principality of Antioch up the coast, and farthest north and almost touching Armenia, the county of Edessa.

Once Jerusalem was in Christian hands the majority of the Crusaders returned to their homes in Europe. Fortunately for the rulers of the four diminutive Christian states they left behind and for their tenuous hold on the edge of the vast Muslim world, Islam continued as divided as before. There were even occasions when Muslim chieftains made alliances with Christian lords against other Muslims, and times, too, which found Christians joining Muslims against other Christians. As an illustration of this lack of unity, the Crusader states could usually count on the neutrality, if not cooperation, of such Muslim principalities as Damascus and Aleppo, since these considered the caliph in Baghdad a greater threat to their autonomy than the Christians.

Following the failure of the Second Crusade (1147–49), even the less perceptive of the Christian lords, who may not have appreciated the weakness of their position, awoke to the necessity of making friends with the Infidel. The fall of the county of Edessa to the north had precipitated this

Crusade, and two armies, one led by Louis VII of France, the other by Conrad III of Germany, had undertaken to halt what western Christendom feared was the beginning of a Muslim offensive aimed at snuffing out all the Crusader states. Conrad lost his army in Asia Minor, where Louis' fared little better. Rather than write off the Crusade as a complete failure, Christian leaders undertook a mismanaged assault on "friendly" Damascus. The attack was both a mistake and a failure, although it did leave this salutary lesson with the Christians, namely, that the continued disunity of the Muslim world was their best hope of survival.

There existed factors other than the disunity of the Islamic world which furnished the Christian states hope of holding off Muslim pressure. Each year brought additional Crusaders from Europe. In the course of the year 1100–1101 three "armies" reached Constantinople on their way to Jerusalem. As it happened, none of these got beyond Anatolia where they foundered, but other companies of Crusaders did reach Syria, particularly when the Italian cities assumed the role of carriers and deposited them in Christian held cities along the coast. In 1101 a Genoese fleet arrived at Haifa with men and provisions. The following year two hundred ships came in from England with much needed manpower. When the situation happened to be critical, pilgrims who had come with no intention of fighting were pressed into service. Such an occasion presented itself in 1183, four years before the battle of Hattin, when Saladin made his first major assault on the kingdom of Jerusalem. Year after year back in Europe priests and monks kept reminding the faithful of their duty to assist the Crusade with men and money, and each year there were pilgrims and warriors who responded to these urgings.

The role of the Italian cities proved crucial to the survival of the Crusader states. These states lacked fleets of their own, and while Byzantine ships did come into the picture now and then, the emperor in Constantinople usually needed them elsewhere. It was to meet the Crusaders' need for ships that Italian cities came forward with their services. Most active were Venice, Genoa, and Pisa, which were also the most enterprising communities in advancing the expansion of trade which was slowly transforming the economy of western Europe. Although they had nothing to do with the establishment of the Crusader states, these Italian cities soon recognized the splendid opportunity this new development held for them in expanding their own commercial operations. True, they always acted as merchants and businessmen first and Crusaders second, but without their assistance the Crusaders could not have gained the territory they did nor held on to it for so long.

The ships which these Italian cities supplied enabled the Crusaders to bypass the dangerous overland route through Asia Minor where so many Christian armies had been destroyed. Their shipping simplified the enormous problem of supplying the Crusaders, once established in Syria, with armaments and siege equipment. The Italian ships proved indispensable in capturing Muslim held cities along the coast. Even the capture of the inland city of Jerusalem in 1099 was facilitated by the arrival of materials unloaded at Jaffa by a Genoese fleet. Following the disaster at Hattin, only the arrival of a Sicilian fleet prevented Saladin from sweeping up Tripoli and Antioch in his triumphant march through Syria.

The price that the Italian cities demanded for their services was high. In return for the use of their ships and their financial assistance, they received extensive trade concessions, including entire sections of cities which they then administered as their own. In 1123 Venice secured a quarter of every city in the kingdom of Jerusalem while Genoa and Pisa enjoyed similar concessions in other cities. These concessions hampered the rulers in governing their states, even in dealing with the enemy, since their aims and those of the Italian cities did not always jibe. The Italians were principally interested in trade, including trade with the enemy, and any policy which endangered the peace might find them opposed. As it happened, given the limited number of Christians in Syria, the peace policy that the Italian cities generally recommended was ordinarily the one prudence also recommended to the Crusader states.

Even in more personal ways did Italian gold affect the course of Crusade history. A curious illustration of this comes to view in the immediate background to the battle of Hattin. Raymond, the count of Tripoli, had promised Gerard of Ridefort, a knight errant in England, the hand of the next wealthy heiress who became available. When William Dorel, lord of Botron, died, Raymond gave his daughter not to Gerard, but to a rich Pisan, who, it is said, came forward and offered him the girl's weight in gold. If the story is true, Raymond never rued anything so much as breaking his word to Gerard, thus earning his undying hatred. Gerard left his service and later became master of the Templars. The night before the battle of Hattin he persuaded Guy, king of Jerusalem, to reject the sound strategy urged by Raymond and instead to attack Saladin, a move which ended tragically for the Christians and for Raymond.

It is doubtful whether any development proved of greater value to the Crusader states in their efforts to fight off the Muslims than the rise of the Templars and Hospitallers. Both these military orders had their origins with groups of religiously motivated men who wished to assist pilgrims on their visits to the Holy Land. These groups assumed in time the responsibility of protecting the pilgrims, a transformation which ceased only when these protectors had become full-fledged warriors. They proved, indeed, the doughtiest champions the Saracens ever faced, no longer concerned with protecting pilgrims but rather with fighting the Infidel at every turn and to the death. Saladin, who permitted his captives to ransom themselves or be ransomed, drew the line at the Templars and Hospitallers. Because their vows bound them to fight for the Christian God as long as they lived, he executed every Templar and Hospitaller who fell into his hands.

The members of these orders constituted the only standing army to which the rulers of the Christian states could turn in a crisis or who might be on hand to oppose some raiding party that was ravaging the countryside. Because of their dependence upon these military orders, it was only natural that the rulers of the Crusader states should turn over to the orders the powerful fortresses along the state frontiers. It is easy to understand how indispensable in time the orders came to be in the actual fighting in Syria. Unfortunately, like the Italian cities, bitter rivalry often turned them into enemies and thus impaired their value to the Crusader rulers. The military orders were also directly subject to the papacy and therefore took the field as allies, not as subjects, of the kings of Jerusalem. These rulers might have to bargain for their cooperation in much the same way they did for that of the Italian cities.

Mention of the Templars and Hospitallers brings to mind images of tremendous castles such as the Krak des Chevaliers, which they maintained and where they garrisoned their members. That this particular fortress contained a complement of 2,000 men suggests the vital importance these castles possessed during the period of the Crusades. This castle was located in northern Syria, where it controlled the movement of caravans from Hims and Hama to Mesopotamia. Unless a powerful force accompanied a Muslim caravan, it dared not pass by in time of war. The same held true of the mighty fortress of Kerak in Transjordan south of the Dead Sea, which might intercept any caravan moving between Damascus and Egypt.

This introduces one important role of the castles. Their presence at strategic points where they controlled the movement of goods encouraged the maintenance of peace between the two hostile communities. They also served as administrative centers in stabilizing Christian rule. By discouraging Saracen raiding parties, they advanced the colonization and economic exploitation of the area. Although their number was not sufficient nor the manpower they commanded great enough to thwart a major movement of the enemy, they did hamper the freedom with which smaller companies of Muslims might ravage the countryside. Even a larger army might hesitate to pass a powerful fortress lest it later find itself in difficulties and be obliged to retreat. Conversely, these castles provided Crusading groups a place of refuge when reverses forced them to fall back before an enemy attack.

In 1095 when Pope Urban made his appeal to the assembled clergy and aristocracy of France at Clermont for a Crusade against the Infidel, he did so in response to an appeal sent to him the year before by the Byzantine emperor, Alexius Comnenus. The emperor wanted warriors to help him in Anatolia against the Seljuk Turks, who had overrun the greater part of that country following their catastrophic victory over the Byzantine army at Manzikert in 1071. It was the pope who broadened what was essentially a modest request on the part of the emperor into a far-flung movement that was to include some seven or eight Crusades and to involve tens of thousands of warriors for almost two centuries before the Christians were ousted from the Levant. Alexius had never envisioned anything so ambitious. Neither he nor his successors were as concerned about Jerusalem and the Holy Land as they were about Anatolia and Antioch.

These Byzantine emperors nevertheless played a vital part in the success of the Crusades. Theirs was usually the most powerful fleet in that part of the Mediterranean, and though imperial interests normally kept their ships closer to home, they did cooperate at times with Crusader efforts as far south as Egypt. Had it not been for the Crusaders' deep-seated suspicion of the ultimate motives of Byzantium, as well as their own selfishness, the history of the Crusades would have counted many more pages of success for Christianity.

Constantinople had once ruled Syria as well as Egypt. Because western lords had succeeded in wresting the eastern littoral from Islam without the direct assistance of Byzantium, they had claimed these lands as their own, despite oaths they had made earlier to Alexius at Constantinople to recognize him as their overlord. For the moment Alexius could do nothing to enforce his claims. Later when the Crusader states encountered difficulty in maintaining themselves, they had no choice but seek Byzantine help. The consequence was that the principality of Antioch, the closest to Constantinople, was often held as a fief of the emperor.

More critical to the survival of the Crusader states was the presence of Byzantine power in Anatolia and in the area to the east of Cilicia. Until the annihilation of the Byzantine army at Myriocephalon in eastern Anatolia in 1176 by the Turks, a defeat which eliminated Byzantium as a major force in that area, the Muslims in Mosul and Mesopotamia had not felt free to concentrate their efforts on the capture of Aleppo and Damascus. These cities held the key to the control of northern Syria. So long as their Muslim governors succeeded in remaining independent, they served the Christians in Tripoli, Antioch, and the kingdom of Jerusalem as buffer states and protected them from direct attack from Mosul and Baghdad. Until the disaster at Myriocephalon the Byzantine army actually maintained a balance of power among the Crusader states, the autonomous Muslim cities of Aleppo and Damascus, and Mosul. The defeat sustained at Myriocephalon may therefore be considered as important a development as any other in tracing the story of the eventual fall of Jerusalem to Saladin.

What proved a constant factor in the history of the rise and fall of the fortunes of the four Crusader states was the ability of their particular rulers. This might appear surprising since the king or prince was a feudal lord and, as was the case in western Europe, administered a realm largely controlled by a semi-independent landed aristocracy. These barons possessed a consultative voice on almost all important issues, even the important matter of succession, but it would have been a foolhardy lord who would have adopted a policy that the majority of his vassals opposed. Given their tenuous position on the fringe of the Muslim world, these rulers were fortunate to enjoy more authority than their feudal cousins in western Europe. It was often a question of survival. For the aristocracy not to have cooperated with their overlord, at least during periods of crisis, would have invited destruction for all. Because of the larger size of his realm and the fact that it included Jerusalem, the king of Jerusalem exercised a kind of feudal suzerainty over the other Crusader states.

The first ruler of the kingdom of Jerusalem following the capture of the city in July 1099 was Godfrey of Bouillon. Godfrey's chief accomplishment was the defeat of an Egyptian army at Ascalon, which victory helped shore up his kingdom's southern frontier. Upon his death in 1104 he was succeeded by his brother Baldwin, the ruler of Edessa. Until then Jerusalem had been technically a state belonging to the church. Baldwin I proved himself as capable a ruler as his brother. He repelled Egyptian thrusts from the south, while to the north he maintained so strong a posture that the Muslim state of Aleppo paid him tribute. It was his son, Baldwin II (1118–31), who approved the establishment of the Templars and Hospitallers and encouraged them in their adopted role as warriors by entrusting them with fortresses along his eastern frontier.

The next king was Fulk, count of Anjou, who had married Baldwin's eldest daughter. Now the foreign policy of the kingdom took a significant turn. Up to this point both Egypt to the south and Aleppo and Damascus to the north had posed continuing threats to the kingdom's survival. After 1128 the threat to Jerusalem's survival grew more grave. That was the year Zengi, the atabeg or lieutenant of Mosul, captured Aleppo, then followed this the next year with the capture of Hama, another major city of northern Syria. Given Zengi's success, Jerusalem and Damascus could not afford to remain enemies, and in fact they generally pursued a policy of cooperation until the unfortunate Second Crusade. Not only did the Christian attack on Damascus at that time fail, but it threw that Muslim state into the waiting arms of Zengi's son and successor, Nur al-Din, thereby greatly aggravating the threat to Jerusalem from the north. The next king, Baldwin III, sought to counter this threat by negotiating an alliance with the emperor in Constantinople. This stood the kingdom of Jerusalem in good stead until Byzantium's disaster at Myriocephalon in 1176.

The death of Baldwin III in 1163 at the early age of thirty-three would have proved a tragic loss for the kingdom of Jerusalem had not his younger brother, Amalric (Amaury) I, showed himself as gifted a monarch as ever ruled Jerusalem. Among his nonpolitical accomplishments was the appointment of William of Tyre as court historian, without whose excellent chronicle we would know so much less about the kingdom of Jerusalem and the early Crusades. Amalric continued the policy of maintaining strong ties with the Byzantine empire, even to the extent of accepting the status of a protectorate for Jerusalem. A mistaken sense of power which this alliance sired led Amalric and the emperor to attempt the conquest of Egypt. Their notion of Egypt's enormous wealth was correct enough, but they misjudged the measure of that Muslim state's decadence. Their meddling only resulted in further weakening Egypt and opened the door to Nur al-Din's intervention and that of his lieutenant, Saladin, who shortly made himself master there.

Amalric's premature death in 1174 proved a tragic blow to the kingdom of Jerusalem. He left the throne to his thirteen-year-old son, Baldwin IV, who was not only a minor, but a leper as well. Questions of succession understandably plagued Baldwin's reign of twelve years, as did the matter of regency; for two years Baldwin was a minor and after that required a replacement during periods of extreme illness. His first regent, Raymond III, count of Tripoli, proved his wisest choice. While Raymond's career has drawn varying appraisals, he stands out among the Crusader leaders of the period as the one most ready to recognize the necessity of achieving some kind of accommodation with the Saracens. William of Tyre describes him as a "rather thin man, moderately tall, with eagle-like features, a swarthy complexion, smooth somewhat dark hair, sharp eyes and shoulders erect."

Two events of major importance marked the early years of Baldwin's reign. The first was the destruction of the Byzantine army in 1176 at Myriocephalon. This defeat removed Byzantine power as a factor in Syria and in so doing indirectly deprived the kingdom of Jerusalem of its principal ally. The other event came a year later, in 1177, when Saladin suffered a stinging defeat at Mont Gisard to the south and west of Jerusalem. Saladin, who by this time had gained possession of Damascus and northern Syria, sent his army, a large one, to ravage the defenseless countryside and villages between Jerusalem and the coast in the hope of luring the Crusaders into accepting battle. Fortunately for them Baldwin refused battle, but once Saladin's army had scattered in its foraying operations Baldwin gave orders to attack. The result was the destruction of the Saracen force and Saladin's precipitate flight to Egpyt. Had Saladin not found a swift camel to carry him back to Egypt, the entire history of the Crusades might have been altered. The Muslim world was producing few men like Saladin who were capable of securing the cooperation of its dissident rulers against the Christians.

Saladin's defeat at Mont Gisard was one of the few bright moments of Baldwin's sad reign. As his condition deteriorated with the advance of his malady, so did the political situation in the kingdom. To provide for the succession he had his oldest sister, Sibyl, marry Guy of Lusignan, a newcomer from France, who as count of Jaffa and Ascalon ranked as one of the most powerful vassals in the kingdom. In 1182 when Baldwin became blind, he appointed Guy regent, only to remove him a year later because of his incompetency and arrogance. He appointed Raymond of Tripoli in Guy's stead and then in a move to block Sibyl's succession, and through her that of Guy, he had Sibyl's son, Baldwin (V), by her first husband (William of Montferrat) crowned. But the boy died shortly after Baldwin IV's own death, whereupon Sibyl and Guy carried out a coup in collusion with Reginald of Chatillon, the masters of the military orders, and the patriarch Heraclius. They sealed off Jerusalem to the other barons, including Raymond of Tripoli, long enough to have Sibyl and Guy crowned king and queen. Raymond refused to do homage and instead went to Tiberias.

Saladin could not have hoped for a more propitious opportunity to strike at the kingdom of Jerusalem than this time of bitter dissension among the Christian leaders. He had been waiting for something like this and he was ready. He had carried to completion the resurgence of Islam which Zengi had initiated back in 1127–28 when he established a dynasty based upon control of Aleppo, Harran, and Mosul. Later in 1144 Zengi had forced Edessa to accept his authority, but assassination ended his career. Zengi's son, Nur al-Din, continued where his father left off. He seized Damascus, compelled the semi-independent Muslim princes of northern Syria to recognize his overlordship, and overran the parts of the principality of Antioch which lay east of the Orontes. Then when Shawar, an Egyptian vizier who was struggling for supremacy, appealed to Nur al-Din for assistance, he sent an army south under his Kurdish general, Shirkuh. Shirkuh was successful and appointed Shawar vizier, but shortly after had him murdered and assumed that office himself. Two months later he was dead and his nephew Saladin succeeded to office (March 1169).

Saladin, the most distinguished leader Islam produced during the twelfth century, had grown up in Baalbeck where Zengi appointed his father governor. He served in the household of Nur al-Din and later accompanied his uncle Shirkuh to Egypt. Once vizier of Egypt, he set about building up that country's military power and soon extended his authority over Arabia and Yemen. In 1171 he put an end to the inept Fatimid dynasty in Egypt and ordered prayers in all the mosques for the Abbasid caliph in Baghdad, thereby restoring the religious unity of Islam in Egypt and Asia under the one Sunnite dispensation. In 1174 he enjoyed a great stroke of good fortune when Nur al-Din died and left only an eleven-year-old son to succeed him. Saladin hurried north, married Nur al-Din's widow, and took control of Syria. By 1185 he had forced the caliph in Baghdad to recognize him as sultan of the Sunnite world. He was now ready to destroy the kingdom of Jerusalem together with the other Crusader states.

Before proceeding further with the fortunes of Saladin and the misfortunes of these Crusader states, both of which would reach their peak at the battle of Hattin, it will be useful to consider the respective military strengths and weaknesses of the two opponents. The principal problem which faced the Crusader states in their efforts to maintain themselves against Muslim pressure was lack of manpower. Few families other than members of the aristocracy had left Europe to make their homes in the east, and of these only a handful had come. These Christian newcomers remained a small minority among the large native population. The majority element was Muslim and Arabic. Under Christian rule they were passive for the most part, although their behavior might bear watching should a crisis develop. They certainly could not be expected to offer significant aid against any Muslim attack.

Not much more can be said for the Greek and Syrian Christians whose ancestors had been occupying these lands prior to the rise of Islam. They had been content under Muslim rule, had paid a light tax, and had practiced their religion without interference. Because their relations with their Muslim governors had been amicable, they had not welcomed with any great enthusiasm the coming of the westerners whom they considered culturally their inferiors and schismatics as well. They lent the Crusaders aid reluctantly. They would not lift a finger to prevent the Muslims from forcing out the Crusaders.

Under the circumstances, the Crusader states had chiefly themselves and visitors from the west to depend upon in meeting the threat from Islam. A major source of strength was that provided by the military orders. Other assistance came from the steady flow of warriors from Europe. Now and then pilgrims might lend a hand, and there were occasions when these states would not have survived without the cooperation of the Italian cities.

The most reliable source of warriors was that supplied by the feudal aristocracy which controlled the land. In the kingdom of Jerusalem the most important of these were the lords of the four great baronies into which the realm was divided. Each baron owed one hundred knights. Individual knights, those who held directly of the king, rendered personal service. Ecclesiastical and urban communities were held to a quota of sergeants who might serve as cavalry, more commonly as foot soldiers. In theory as many as 1,800 knights were available to the king of Jerusalem and approximately 10,000 foot soldiers. As Nur al-Din and Saladin in their advances whittled away at the eastern fringes of the kingdom or subjected it to devastating raids, even this theoretical figure was apt to drop.

To compensate for their lack of manpower, the Crusader states were obliged to use mercenaries. Just prior to the battle of Hattin in 1183, for instance, the king of Jerusalem imposed a levy to raise money for hiring stipendiary troops. In ordinary times he benefited from a steady trickle of money from the west contributed by members of the faithful who were not able to come in person but who wished to share in the special graces the church assured them would become theirs in this indirect fashion. A large sum became available in the 1180s, money Henry II had pledged as part of his penance for his share in the murder of Thomas Becket.

In a time of real emergency the Crusader princes as a last resort made appeal to the popular levy known as the *arrière-ban*. This was a service based upon the public obligation of every free man to help defend the community. Because men recruited by this method generally lacked both experience and equipment, the *arrière-ban* was an expedient employed only in desperate situations. The men so recruited might use their limited talents best in the defense of cities and fortresses, but even then their presence never eliminated completely the need to maintain sizeable professional garrisons. It was in measure the failure or inability of the Crusader states to maintain standing armies to meet the enemy in force, and at the same time provision adequate garrisons to defend their cities, which ultimately spelled their destruction.

By contrast the forces upon which Saladin could call appeared inexhaustible. They were not, of course, but Saladin's ability to draw on the manpower of both Egypt and Syria, and after 1185 of Mosul—which added some 6,000 horsemen to his army—never left him wanting. He might lose an army, as all but happened at Mont Gisard in 1177, and still be back menacing the Christians the year following. Since Saladin lacked administrative talents and was at the same time overly generous in his disposition of funds, he too had a financial problem, although not as grave as that of his Crusader foes. His chief problem remained gaining and holding the loyalty of the powerful emirs who ruled their provinces virtually as independent potentates. Each emir was under obligation to help in financing the war with the Christians and to supply a specified number of horsemen. Because of the great respect Saladin enjoyed for his genuinely deep faith and his high sense of honor, his emirs could be counted on to cooperate with him, at least as long as the future promised success.

While Saladin had access to larger manpower resources than the Christians, the size of his army in actual combat was generally about that of his foe. What limited the number of men he took with him on campaigns was usually less the availability of these men than the nature of the terrain and of the climate of Syria. The poverty of the land and especially the lack of water made the employment of larger armies impractical. This applied in particular to foot soldiers, who would prove a burden where trekking long distances might be necessary. For this reason Saracen armies were constituted almost exclusively of horsemen except in Egypt, where the bowmen fought on foot. In Syria and Palestine horse-archers replaced these bowmen.

The Crusader armies on the other hand, contained many foot soldiers for a number of reasons. For one thing they lacked the inexhaustible supply of horses available to the Saracens. For another, whenever the enemy put in an appearance in force, they had to press into service all men they could find, in particular the foot soldiers who were doing garrison duty in fortresses and cities. The main reason, however, for employing foot soldiers was that these proved indispensable as a defensive barrier between the heavy-armed Crusader knights and the enemy's light-armed, more mobile cavalry. Given the showers of arrows the Saracens could let fly, together with their harassing tactics, the Crusaders' horsemen would be destroyed before hand-to-hand combat could be achieved.

To look more closely at the types of opposing combatants who faced each other in Syria, the most formidable warrior of all was the Crusader knight. That distinction his counter-part enjoyed in western Europe, where conditions had produced this particular type of fighter. His superiority was also recognized in the Near East even though higher temperatures and the shortage of fodder and water frequently made fighting extremely difficult. This knight carried a lance and sword, and often a dagger as well. For protective gear he wore a shirt of chain mail that had sleeves and reached to his knees. Other metal protected his forearms, wrists, hands, legs, and even his feet. A cylindrical or conical helmet covered the upper part of his head, a mail coif guarded his neck and the greater part of his face. His heavy mount also carried protective armor, although not to the extent of its rider. Had its protective armor made the horse as invulnerable as the knight, the history of the Crusades would have taken a different course. When the din had quieted and dust settled after the battle of Hattin, scarcely a horse remained alive in the Christian army, which still counted hundreds of uninjured but unhorsed knights.

In order to provide themselves a light-armed cavalry which could support these powerful knights and carry out assignments suited to more mobile horsemen, the Crusader states fell back upon the native population and upon their allies. Such horsemen, commonly known as Turcopoles, fought after the fashion of their own country. The Turks employed bow and arrow and thus constituted a counterforce to the mounted archers of the enemy. They were also used for reconnaissance work. Their mobility served to reduce the freedom with which Saracen cavalry raided the countryside. When engaged in fighting a massed enemy in actual battle, they might be intermingled with the more heavily armed knights.

The foot soldiers who fought in the Crusader armies established themselves as vital partners to the heavily armed horsemen in all major operations. Their equipment and skills varied with their background. The professional soldiers among them came well armed and with experience. They might wear an iron cap, some body armor, usually a gambeson or cloak of heavy leather or quilted linen, and carry a shield, pike, bow, or crossbow. The crossbow was heavier than the ordinary bow and more difficult to load, but its missiles carried such crushing power that they could shatter armor and limbs at close range. Nothing so frightened the Turkish horse-archers into keeping their distance as the crossbowmen. By sheer mass of numbers, as well as the cruel arrows they fired, these foot soldiers served to hold off the enemy until the moment came for the knights to drive forward in a massive charge.

The Arab chronicler Boha-ed-din described the march that Richard the Lion-Hearted's army made fewer than ten years after the battle of Hattin toward Arsuf which was under continued harassment by Saladin's horsemen. He gives this picture of the role of the humble foot soldier.

"The enemy moved in order of battle: their infantry marched between us and their cavalry, keeping as level and firm as a wall. Each foot-soldier had a thick cassock of felt, and under it a mail-shirt so strong that our arrows made no impression on them. They, meanwhile, shot at us with crossbows, which struck down horse and man among the Moslems. I noted among them men who had from one to ten shafts sticking in their backs, yet trudged on at their ordinary pace and did not fall out of their ranks. The infantry were divided into two halves: one marched so as to cover the cavalry, the other moved along the beach and took no part in the fighting, but rested itself. When the first half was wearied, it changed places with the second and got its turn of repose. The cavalry marched between the two halves of the infantry, and only came out when it wished to charge."[2]

This page from a contemporary writer suggests the kind of tactics and precautionary measures the Christians normally employed against the Saracen enemy. Much of their knowledge about how to deal with the foe had come from hard experience, but some of it they had acquired from Byzantine military advisers in Constantinople. If some Crusaders were inclined to scoff at the warning these advisers had given them about the speedy Turkish cavalry they would be encountering, their near-annihilation at Dorylaeum in Asia Minor in the opening battle of the First Crusade would have been a sobering lesson. Later their own experience in Syria taught them other lessons they had to learn in order to survive, such as never to stray far from water, never to go off in pursuit of a fleeing army or disperse in search for booty, and never to ignore the danger of being encircled by the wily Saracen.

An especially difficult lesson that the Crusaders were obliged to learn was the importance of maintaining an organized, cohesive unit against an enemy whose prime objective was to shatter that unity. In France the knight had operated largely on his own. After the initial charge against the enemy, he might go off by himself to close with an individual opponent or, with several of his friends, to attack a group of the enemy. He might even ride away if he felt he had had enough fighting for one day. Not so here in Syria. He must stay with his army; he must coordinate his movements with that of the foot soldiers, whose presence was essential to the survival of the army. He must not allow gaps to appear in his ranks or permit his speedy foe to drive a wedge between himself and the infantry. He must, in short, learn discipline, a virtue almost entirely foreign to the character of the knight.

In an effort to achieve some measure of cohesiveness for the Crusader army against an enemy which sought to destroy this, it became customary to divide the striking force into small units. These operated under the direct instructions of a single commander, who in turn observed a prearranged strategy upon which the leaders had agreed. These units did not attack at the same time, but in successive waves and at different points in the enemy's line. The initial charge, a solid line of knights driving forward, was nothing new. But in France the need to maintain some cooperation following this charge had seldom been necessary, since the foe generally fought in the same loosely organized fashion. In Syria it would have been suicidal not to have retained some unity. The Templars attached such importance to the matter of keeping in rank that they incorporated this requirement into their statutes and severely punished any knight who left his place without permission.

Most critical to the Crusader armies in the matter of organization was the cooperation between cavalry and foot soldiers. The latter ordinarily were placed between the mounted warriors and the enemy, where they served as a protective screen against the arrows that would otherwise have wounded the knights' horses. Their mass also served to slow any direct attack the speedy Turks might have attempted against the flanks of a marching army. The knights in turn came to the assistance of the foot soldiers should the enemy cavalry press too heavily upon them. In offensive operations, once the moment had come for the knights to attack, the foot soldiers would open a path and permit the horsemen to charge through. Richard might have destroyed Saladin's entire army at Arsuf had not the Hospitallers disobeyed his instructions and attacked the enemy before the king had given the signal. Despite this mistake, the premature move of the Hospitallers forced the reluctant Richard to order his forces to attack. The infantry opened ranks and the resulting charge of the king's knights dealt Saladin one of the sharpest reverses of his career.

Here is the report of the Christian chronicler of this battle. Many of the circumstances were similar to those which attended the battle of Hattin fought a few years before. "All over the face of the land you could see the well-ordered bands of the Turks, myriads of parti-coloured banners, marshalled in troops and squadrons; of mailed men alone there appeared to be more than twenty thousand. With unswerving course, swifter than eagles, they swept down upon our line of march. The air was turned black by the dust of their hoofs cast up. Before the face of each emir went his musicians, making a horrid din with horns, trumpets, drums, cymbals, and all manner of brazen instruments, while the troops behind pressed on with howls and cries of war. For the Infidels think that the louder the noise, the bolder grows the spirit of the warrior. So did the cursed Turks beset us before, behind, and on the flank, and they pressed in so close that for two miles around there was not a spot of the bare earth visible; all was covered by the thick array of the enemy."

When Richard finally gave the order to attack, this is how the Muslim reporter describes what happened: "On a sudden we saw the cavalry of the enemy, who were now drawn together in three main masses, brandish their lances, raise their war cry, and dash out at us. The infantry suddenly opened up gaps in their line to let them pass through."

The mobility of the Saracen armies dictated the tactics they generally adopted against the more heavily armed Crusader host. Since they could move about and maneuver more quickly than their Christian foes, they could usually avoid battles they preferred not to fight. They could select the time and place to launch their attack. Should the fortunes of war appear to be unfavorable, they might turn after engaging the enemy and ride off. Then of a sudden they might reassemble and resume the fighting. This is precisely what the Christian chronicler describes them doing against Richard and the Crusaders as they marched toward Arsuf. "The Infidels, not weighed down with heavy armour like our knights, but always able to outstrip them in pace, were a constant trouble. When charged they are wont to fly, and their horses are more nimble than any others in the world; one may liken them to swallows for swiftness. When they see that you have ceased to pursue them, they no longer fly but return upon you; they are like tiresome flies which you can flap away for a moment, but which come back the instant you have stopped hitting at them; as long as you beat about they keep off: the moment you cease, they are on you again. So the Turk, when you wheel about after driving him off, follows you home without a second's delay, but will fly again if you turn on him.

Since the Saracens recognized the superiority of the Crusader knight with his heavier armor and weapons, they sought to wear him down as he marched by harassing attacks on his flanks. They also learned that sharp, prolonged pressure exerted on the rear of a marching army held the promise of throwing the entire host into confusion, even if it failed to destroy that vital part of the army. As they rode toward the enemy, they would let fly veritable showers of arrows from their arc bows, then close in when they felt they had the disconcerted foe off balance and attack with lance, sword, and sabre. Should the Crusading army succeed in repelling the assault, they would ride off or pretend to do so, only to resume the attack after a few hours, or even a few days, when they might catch the unsuspecting enemy off guard. On occasion the Saracen armies were able to trap the

Christians by getting them to follow a decoying force or simulating a retreat. This would have the Crusaders breaking rank in their eagerness to exploit a supposed victory, only to find the Saracens counterattacking with disastrous effectiveness. Two hundred years before Hattin, Otto II, king of Germany, was one of a fortunate few who managed to escape when the Saracens caught his army in such a trap in southern Italy.

Because of the mobility of the Muslim forces and their greater number, and the manifest fact that the Christians held but a foothold on the edge of an Islamic world, the Crusading princes almost from the beginning accepted the necessity of adopting and holding to a defensive strategy against the enemy. They tried to avoid battle at all cost. Their precious knights were too few in number and too difficult to replace. Even the satisfaction of a victory would be short lived, since the enemy with his enormous resources could return shortly and again offer battle. Only when victory was reasonably certain, only when a conflict could not be avoided without serious consequences, did the Christians do battle. The destruction of their army would be catastrophic since they had no resources to fall back on. Once the Crusader army was destroyed, that would be the end of the kingdom of Jerusalem. For this reason, so the Muslim chronicler Usamah observed, "Of all men, the Franks [Crusaders] are the most cautious in warfare."

That this sort of defensive strategy worked as well and as long as it did is a tribute to the sagacity of the Crusader princes. Yet there is no escaping the fact that had the Muslim world been united under as able a caliph as Omar,[3] no amount of defensive strategy would have sufficed for the Crusaders. It would not have succeeded even during the generation or two prior to the battle of Hattin except for the seasonal nature of the fighting in Syria. The majority of the Saracen soldiers were not professionals. They served for a number of months, after which they grew restive and insisted on returning to their homes and families. Equally anxious to return whence they had come were the men who fought principally for loot. After five or six months of campaigning they would have collected all they could physically carry back with them, so why continue to fight. In any event, the rains and cold weather that came in late fall normally put an end to fighting. By the following spring, a man like Saladin would be facing the perennial problems of persuading his emirs to come forward with their new recruits and welding them into a cohesive fighting force able to destroy the Crusaders before the fall rains would again terminate the fighting.

Let us return to the events which led immediately to the catastrophe at Hattin. The man who merits principal responsibility for setting these events in motion was Reginald of Chatillon, the brave but irresponsible lord of Kerak. It was a dark day for the kingdom of Jerusalem when Reginald, who had joined Louis VII on the Second Crusade, decided to remain in Syria and seek his fortune there. Reginald seems to have been very much the traditional knight-errant. He was reckless, brave, and handsome, but he was lacking in prudence and self-discipline. His looks and dashing manner caught the fancy of Constance, the widowed ruler of Antioch, who persuaded Baldwin III in a moment of weakness to permit her to marry Reginald. In 1160 the Saracens did the Christians a great favor when they captured Reginald and for sixteen years held him a prisoner in Aleppo. No one moved a finger to ransom him. Upon his release he married Stephanie, the heiress of the important lordship of Transjordan. This domain boasted the mighty fortress of Kerak, the Stone of the Desert, as it was known, whose location on a high point south of the Dead Sea gave it command of the caravan route between Damascus to the north and Egypt and Mecca to the south.

In the summer of 1181, during a period of truce, Reginald intercepted a caravan on its way to Mecca. The following year he built a squadron of galleys on the shore of the Dead Sea and transported them in sections to the Gulf of Akaba, where he assembled them and proceeded to attack Muslim shipping on the Red Sea as far south as the ports serving Mecca and Medina. There was even talk that Reginald contemplated an assault on the holy cities of Mecca and Medina themselves. Saladin was infuriated. Early in 1187 when Reginald again pounced on a caravan during a period of truce and refused to make restitution, although begged to do so by King Guy of Jerusalem, Saladin proclaimed a holy war (*jihad*) and swore to kill Reginald by his own hand. By June 24 he and his emirs had gathered some 20,000 warriors just east of the Lake of Tiberias near the borders of the Holy Land. Two days later, on Friday, June 26, the holy day of worship for Muslims, Saladin crossed the Jordan and the war was on.

Meantime King Guy and his magnates were making feverish preparations to meet Saladin's attack. This threatened to be the most dangerous campaign the Muslim chieftain had ever organized against them. Despite their fear and hatred of Raymond, the situation was so serious that they sent a delegation to beg his cooperation. This might ordinarily have been difficult to secure. Not only had relations between Saladin and Raymond been friendly since each man respected the other, but Raymond was still bitter over the arrogant manner Guy and his friends had maneuvered his accession to the throne. But the situation was so desperate Raymond swallowed his pride and promised his help. He knew that once the kingdom of Jerusalem was lost to the Christians, his Tripoli would be the next to go.

Never before had the Christians assembled so large a host. To an appeal for help, Bohemond of Antioch sent his son, Raymond, with fifty knights. Cities and fortresses emptied themselves of their garrisons. The king published the *arrière-ban* to secure the last resources of manpower. The gold recently sent by Henry II was expended on mercenaries, and as a final and mightily inspiring ally, the relic of the True Cross was brought from Jerusalem. All told perhaps some 18,000 men—1,200 heavy-armed knights, 4,000 light cavalry, and the rest foot soldiers—gathered at Saffuriya, a small town in the lordship of Tiberias about four miles northwest of Nazareth.

There at Saffuriya, on July 2, King Guy and his magnates met in grave conference. The crisis had come to a head. Saladin had forced the issue and a decision must be made. When his other moves to lure the Christian army into fighting had failed, he had attacked the town of Tiberias, overrun the community, and was laying siege to the citadel where Eschiva, wife of Raymond of Tripoli, had taken refuge. It was Eschiva's urgent appeal for help which precipitated Guy's summoning his magnates. The question was, should the Crusader army march to Tiberias and relieve the citadel, a step which would lead to a major battle with Saladin, or should it remain at Saffuriya and wait Saladin's next move?

Upon this question, a relatively simple one at first glance, hinged not only the fate of the Crusader army but of the kingdom of Jerusalem as well. This fact the assembled magnates seemed to have appreciated, and the discussion went on heatedly for several hours. The spokesman for those magnates who favored remaining where they were at Saffuriya was none other than Eschiva's husband, Raymond. Raymond had had long experience with all aspects of fighting in Syria and with Saladin's tactics in particular. He warned the other leaders that the Saracen leader's attack on Tiberias was nothing more than a trap deliberately set in the hope of causing the Christian army to leave Saffuriya. Their position at Saffuriya was a strong one. The nature of the terrain protected them from encirclement, their proximity to their fortresses and to friendly villages assured them protection and food, and the large spring just south of Saffuriya supplied them all the water they needed.

If Saladin wanted a fight, Raymond pointed out, he would have to march against them in July, the hottest and driest month of the year, over rocky, parched earth, conditions, in short, which should dissuade any prudent commander from attacking. By the same token, it would be suicide for the Christians to attempt the march of some fifteen or sixteen miles to Tiberias under those same terrible conditions, without the promise of water along the march and under constant attack by Saladin's swarming horsemen. Raymond urged them to wait, since time was on the side of the Christians. Avoid battle with Saladin for a few months, and his army would melt away and with it the crisis.

There were men who hotly disputed Raymond's arguments, chief among them Gerard of Ridefort, master of the Templars, and Reginald of Chatillon. For the moment Raymond's arguments gained acceptance by the majority of the magnates, and when the meeting broke up about midnight and the barons retired to their tents, it was with the understanding that the Christian army would remain at Saffuriya. Later than night, Gerard, and probably Reginald, went to Guy's tent in a last effort to persuade him to change his mind. Reginald was never one to avoid a risky undertaking, while Ridefort's continuing ill will toward Raymond may have led him to discover weaknesses in a strategy which his personal enemy had recommended.

There may have been a more immediate cause for Ridefort's bitterness toward Raymond. Some scholars accept the authenticity of the Muslim chronicler's story that Raymond, upon the request of Saladin, had two months previously permitted Saladin's son to cross through his lordship of Tiberias in order to raid Christian territory. This was in retaliation for Reginald's seizure of the caravan near Kerak. Raymond had given his consent to this strange request only in order to retain Saladin's good will, and he had insisted that the raiding party enter the area after sunrise and leave before sunset. In order to protect the Christians from severe losses, he sent them warning to remain in their villages where they would not be molested. The raiders apparently did little damage, but on their return encountered a company of Templars and other knights near Nazareth and decimated them, leaving sixty Templars dead on the field. Ridefort was one of the few who escaped the slaughter. If the incident did take place, it would have inclined Raymond to make his peace with Guy in order to cover his questionable conduct; it would also have furnished Ridefort further cause for questioning Raymond's reliability.

It was the question of Raymond's loyalty which Ridefort is believed to have pressed in his conversation with Guy. Raymond, he argued, was not a man to be trusted. He had once refused Guy homage, and everyone knew him to be a friend of Saladin. Might he not have urged remaining in Saffuriya simply to protect his friend Saladin from defeat? Ridefort may also have warned Guy that to fail to fight Saladin now would leave him open to the charge of cowardice. He had been so charged some years earlier in 1183 when he had refused to do battle with Saladin, who had then proceeded to ravage the country about Tubania. Ridefort must also have reminded Guy that as feudal suzerain it was the king's first duty to go to the aid of Eschiva, his vassal, who had appealed to him for help. Above all, he must have convinced Guy that, despite the heat and the lack of water and the damage Saladin might do them on the march, the army should undertake to reach Tiberias. He and his Templars would be guarding the rear where the Saracens would most likely mount their most furious attack, and he could guarantee the king that that part of the army would do its duty.

Whatever the arguments Ridefort and Reginald pressed, Guy changed his mind, and in the early hours of the morning of July 3 the troubled Christian army broke camp. In the front rode Raymond, while Guy commanded the center and the Templars and Ridefort brought up the rear. The feeling of foreboding with which many Crusaders started their march deepened as the day grew hotter and the thirst of man and beast greater, while the speedy horse-archers of Saladin's army spewed arrows at them from every side. The situation gradually became intolerable.

About noon Ridefort sent word forward to Guy that his men could go no farther. They were exhausted. Because of the heat, the lack of water, and the furious attacks which the enemy horsemen had been making without letup on the rear, his men could not possibly keep up the pace. Unless Guy called a halt, the enemy would drive a wedge between Ridefort's men and the rest of the army, a development which would lead ultimately to the destruction of all. Even though it was a most critical decision to make, Guy felt he had no choice under the circumstances. He issued the order to halt and make camp there in the midst of the desert with the howling enemy swarming about them, still only halfway to Tiberias and many hours from water. To Raymond and several of the other leaders Guy's decision to halt appeared calamitous. When he learned of Guy's order, the chronicler has Raymond exclaiming: "Alas! alas Lord God! The war is over; we are dead men."

The Crusader army bivouacked at a place called Marescallia near the village of Hattin, on the lower slope of a dark, rocky hillock which rose about a thousand feet above the valley. Natives referred to the two low hummocks on the crest of the hill as the Horns of Hattin; tradition had it that it was on this height that Christ had preached the Sermon on the Mount. For the Christians, that night proved a veritable hell. There was no slaking their thirst. If the dust settled, there was now a choking smoke to suffocate them from the scrub brush which the Saracens had fired. So tight was the encirclement which the enemy had thrown about them that not even a cat could have gotten through, so the chronicler wrote. Adding to the despair of the Christians were the exultant cries of the enemy all about them: "Allah is great! There is no god but Allah!" The demoralization of the Christian army, brought on by extreme physical exhaustion and fear, was complete. There was no fight, no hope left in them.

The next morning, July 4, the bedraggled Crusader army resumed its weary march. Until about noon the men kept moving, by which time the will to resist had completely gone out of the foot soldiers. They had borne the worst of the previous day's hardships and they now refused to keep up with the cavalry any longer. In a huddled mass they moved up the side of a hill, probably one of the Horns of Hattin, and there they remained despite the pleas of their commanders and the admonitions of the bishops whom Guy had sent to exhort them. And there the Saracens found them. Those they did not slaughter or hurl down the precipice, they dragged off to be sold as slaves.

The situation now became truly desperate. Without the protection of the foot soldiers, the horsemen were open to the direct fire of the Saracen horse-archers. Raymond and his followers cut their way through the encirclement and escaped. A few others were equally fortunate. There is mention of six knights who deserted. They may have brought Saladin word of the critical plight of the Christian army, who then ordered a final charge.

The fiercest fighting centered on the top of one of the Horns, possibly the one which had witnessed the slaughter of the foot soldiers earlier in the day. According to the testimony of Saladin's son, the Christian knights "made a tremendous charge against our troops and drove them back to my father. I looked at him and noticed that he had become sad and pale, and was holding his beard in his hand." Then upon Saladin's urging, the Moslems counterattacked with the Christians retreating only to come down the hill a second time and once more drive back the Muslims. But a second counterattack succeeded. Once Saladin had seen that the king's banner was down, he sprang off his horse and threw himself on the ground to thank God. He knew the victory was finally won.

The carnage was immense, and a great number of Christians were captured. Saladin is said to have slain Reginald with his own hand. He permitted Guy, the other magnates, and anyone else who could produce the necessary gold to ransom themselves, all except the Templars and Hospitallers. These were publicly executed. Only Ridefort was spared, to live out the rest of his life with the memory of the catastrophe he had been largely responsible for causing. What happened to the True Cross nobody knows.

The consequences of Hattin were overwhelming, immediate, and permanent. Since the garrisons throughout the kingdom of Jerusalem had been depleted in order to meet the manpower needs of the enemy, cities and fortresses surrendered almost without resistance. An Arab chronicler lists fifty-two places which were captured in short order. On July 10 Acre fell and on September 4, Ascalon. Jerusalem opened its gates to Saladin on October 2, and the kingdom of Jerusalem ceased to exist. With the coastal cities Saladin had more difficulty, since they received aid from the sea. Tripoli, Antioch, and Tyre remained in Christian hands. Yet the loss of so much in so short a time galvanized western Europe into immediate action. By January following the fall of Jerusalem, Richard of England and Philip Augustus of France were already discussing plans for the Third Crusade.

Had the Christian leaders heeded Raymond's advice and not left Saffuriya in an effort to relieve Tiberias, there would have been no Hattin, no Third Crusade, and perhaps no further need or opportunity for Europe to send major armies to Syria. After Hattin, Saladin's prestige and influence began to ebb, and the Islamic world never produced another leader of his stature to continue the war against Christendom. As for western Europe, from the last quarter of the thirteenth century onward, its kings usually had more practical objectives to engage their attention than that of fighting another Crusade.

6

THE BATTLE OF BOUVINES

HENRY II OF ENGLAND AND LOUIS VII OF FRANCE WERE
frequently at odds. Louis was uncomfortable over the large
number of fiefs that Henry held in France, including such
important ones as Normandy and Anjou. There was also
Toulouse in southern France over which both kings pressed
claims. Henry's rights were those he acquired when he married Eleanor of Aquitaine, who had earlier been Louis' wife.
Louis divorced her for her inability to give him a son. She
gave Henry five![1] The two kings also disagreed over Thomas
Becket, the archbishop of Canterbury. The harsh measures
Henry took to destroy Becket led that prelate to flee to
France, where Louis had given him haven. And, finally,
Louis had been encouraging Henry's unruly sons in their
ambitions to assume control of the fiefs their father held in
France.

Yet such rivalry was the nature of medieval kings who
were neighbors. Neither man bore the other any ill will. The
fact that both men had experienced the wifely firmness of
the high-spirited Eleanor might indeed have made them feel
as comrades. In any event, in 1179 Henry welcomed his
cousin-king at Dover, whence he conducted him to the
shrine of the illustrious martyr Thomas Becket at Canterbury. Louis had come to gain the saint's intercession for his

sickly son, Philip, who appeared to be close to death, and Henry joined him in his prayers. Had Henry been able to see into the future he would not have prayed with Louis, and in fact might not have permitted him to come to Canterbury to implore the mighty saint's intercession. For the boy Philip recovered his health, and during his subsequent reign as Philip Augustus (1180–1223) did more than any other French king for France. This at the expense of England and of Henry's achievement there. And it was at Bouvines, one of the most decisive battles of the Middle Ages, that Philip placed the capstone on this achievement.

Philip II, better known in history as Philip Augustus, gave little promise of making himself medieval France's greatest monarch. One of his eyes was blind, and this might cause men to joke. But there was nothing frivolous about the man himself. Few rulers possessed a greater measure of practical wisdom or the energy and persistence to stay with objectives until they had been attained. Not all such persistence was necessary of course, surely not that which Philip displayed in the case of his wife, Ingeborg. He repudiated her the day after their wedding, then finally brought her back into his palace after twenty years of quarreling with the papacy, which had come to her defense and had fought her battle.

As it happened, Philip's problems with Ingeborg furnish another illustration of his persistence. He married Ingeborg, sister of the king of Denmark, in 1193 in order to have the assistance of the Danish fleet for an invasion of England. In 1213 he took her back into his home in order to lead a papal crusade against England when Pope Innocent III wanted King John deposed. This was the one obsession Philip lived with his entire life. He would not be content with depriving the king of England of all the fiefs he held in France, something he almost accomplished. His ultimate goal was to one day actually unite the crowns of England and France in his own person or in that of his son.

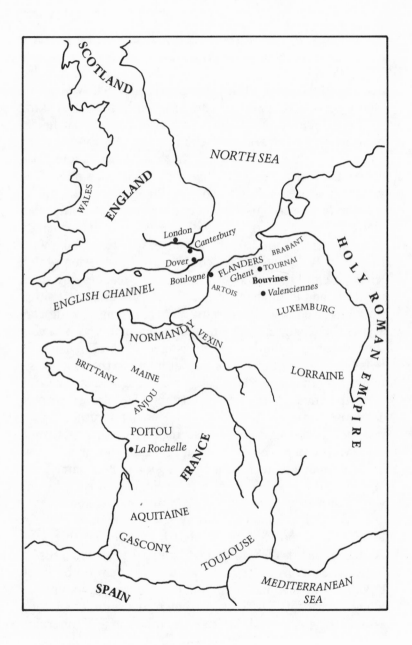

From his boyhood years Philip had learned to view England as the enemy. Even a less precocious boy would have taken this view since Henry, king of England, ruled more of France than Philip's own father, Louis. What lands Henry possessed in France he held as feudal fiefs of the king of France, and for these he rendered homage. That feudal relationshp did not obscure the fact that Henry exercised greater influence and authority in these provinces and collected more revenues there than did Louis. Louis might live with that situation, but his son, Philip, found it intolerable.

Henry's possessions included a chain of fiefs which ran along the entire length of the Atlantic coast from Normandy in the north to Aquitaine in the south. No French king with the means to do otherwise could accept a situation which left a foreign king to rule such extensive reaches of French territory, and Philip bent his whole effort to undo that situation. He gave most of his attention to Normandy, which lay across the Channel from England and which was probably the richest and the best administered of the English-held fiefs. He paid least attention to Aquitaine to the southwest, which was the largest but least governable, and at the same time the most distant from England. He almost ignored Toulouse to the south and the Albigensian Crusade which was being fought there. These regions to the south and southwest could wait. Philip's most dangerous enemy was England. Once he had gained possession of Normandy, not only would he be safe from further English threats, but he would himself be in a position to threaten England.

Except for England Philip was most concerned over Flanders. The position of Flanders just to the northwest of France and across from England lent that province unusual importance. A lively trade in wool had developed between England and Flanders with English raw wool moving to Flanders in return for Flemish woolen goods. Philip's father, Louis, had appreciated the strategic importance of the region to the defense of France and the threat this thriving woolen trade posed for the future. He betrothed his son to the heiress of the region which bordered Flanders to the south, a land later known as Artois. Philip married the girl. When in Syria on the Third Crusade, Phillip learned of the death of his father-in-law. He left Richard the Lion-Hearted and the war with Saladin to return home to make good his succession to that critical region, Artois.

By the time Philip took his abrupt leave from Syria, he and Richard had neither love nor trust for the other. They earlier had been friends, confederates in a contest with Henry II, Richard's father. Philip, the younger of the two men but shrewder than his muscular cousin, had nurtured Richard's good will in the hope of using him against his father. He had encouraged the undutiful Richard in his ambition to take over control of Henry's fiefs in France, an ambition which not only would turn father against son, but might leave Richard in possession, a man Philip felt confident he could handle. These fiefs constituted the most populous, richest part of Henry's empire, an empire which he had worked long and hard to establish. Even though it was an extensive realm, Henry was not ready to relinquish control of any part of it, less out of selfishness than the fear his sons would bungle the job of administering it and thus permit some to fall to Philip. In the end all of Henry's sons turned against him. Just before Henry died in July 1189, Richard, who was in nominal possession of Normandy and Anjou, had renounced his loyalty to his father and paid homage to Philip.

If Philip believed Richard would prove an easier foe than Henry II, he was mistaken. Richard compensated for his lack of diplomatic and administrative talents with a knowledge of warfare and a degree of personal prowess that offset Philip's superior knowledge of statecraft. During the interval that Richard tarried in Syria to fight Saladin, Philip had marched into Normandy with the connivance of John,

Richard's traitorous brother, whom Philip had abetted in his designs upon the English throne. When Richard returned from the Crusade and from imprisonment in Germany, he quickly recovered what territories Philip had seized. Then, in the hope of reaching a permanent settlement with Philip, Richard surrendered to him the region known as Vexin, a small triangular bit of territory wedged between Normandy and Anjou, which held the key to Normandy. In order to block French approaches to Normandy, he next constructed on an island in the Seine the Chateau Gaillard, the most formidable castle yet seen in western Europe. Philip had met his match in Richard. Had an infection from an arrow-wound[2] not ended Richard's life in April 1199, the course of French and English history would have been altered. There would have been no Bouvines, or if there had been a battle fought there, it would not have ended in victory for Philip.

In John, Richard's brother, Philip found an easier adversary. Only in the matter of degree do scholars differ in their evaluation of John's deficiencies. In the main they speak of him as treacherous, cruel, phlegmatic, shrewd, and crafty, loyal only to his mother, Eleanor, the one friend he had. Yet this must be said for John, he would have left a more favorable record for historians to scrutinize but for the hostile monastic chroniclers who feared him and for the serious problems which confronted him. Several of these problems were of his own making. Such was his protracted dispute with Pope Innocent III over Stephen Langton, the pope's choice for the office of archbishop of Canterbury, but a man John would not accept. In this contest John could argue that his royal predecessors had all placed the man of their choice in that important see. Yet his stubborn refusal to accept Stephen, a stand which brought an interdict and much grief to England, can be laid only to his obstinacy and to his need for the church revenues he continued to confiscate during the duration of the interdict.

Another difficulty John brought on himself was his precipitate marriage to Isabella of Angoulême. It may have been infatuation that inspired John to marry when he met her in Aquitaine on his way to Castile, where he was to complete arrangements for his marriage to the heiress of Portugal. That John's aged but still sharp-witted mother, Eleanor, appears to have approved of the marriage, however, would seem to rule out romance. Isabella was the heiress of Angoulême, a province that had a long history of opposition to English rule in Aquitaine. She had been betrothed to Hugh the Brown of the house of Lusignan, also a family hostile to English rule. The projected marriage between Isabella and Hugh would accordingly have united these two families in a powerful alliance that would have jeopardized any English hope of controlling Aquitaine. It would likewise have severed the land connection between Aquitaine to the south and the other English-held fiefs to the north.

While John's hasty marriage may be rationalized on diplomatic grounds, it did furnish Philip Augustus the legal pretext for declaring John's fiefs forfeit when the English king failed to appear in Paris to hear the judgment of a feudal court. Hugh and the Lusignans had appealed to Philip upon John's refusal to pay them the damages they demanded. That Philip had projected himself into the quarrel was quite proper under the circumstances, since he was the feudal suzerain of both John and the Lusignans. No one could deny his joy over John's failure to placate the Lusignans. Philip had already been planning the invasion of Normandy. Had John's contumacy in refusing to appear not provided him an excuse for declaring that province forfeit, he would have discovered some other justification for his invasion.

Philip would have encountered difficulty in carrying out the judgment of his court in Paris except for further mistakes on John's part. Normandy was not happy under John's arrogant rule and particularly outraged over the depredations

committed by his mercenaries. The province might nevertheless have persisted in its resistance to Philip had it not
been for John's treatment of Arthur. Arthur, a young man of
fifteen, was John's nephew, the son of John's older brother,
Geoffrey, count of Brittany. Geoffrey was dead. Had strict
principles of heredity been established, Arthur would have
succeeded to the English throne when Richard died, and so
Philip would have wished. But Richard gave his nod to John,
as did Eleanor, because neither one felt Arthur capable of
thwarting the wily Philip in his plan to take over Normandy
and the other English-held fiefs. For a time Philip indulged
the hope that Arthur might succeed to the throne, but finally
in 1200 he recognized John as the legitimate ruler of all these
fiefs in France.

Then came the judgment of the court in Paris, which
changed all of this. Philip promptly recognized Arthur as
ruler of Brittany, Maine, Anjou, and Aquitaine, but not of
Normandy, which was to pass directly under his control.
The situation looked bad for John. Arthur, the Lusignans,
and their friends were to move south into Aquitaine, while
Philip would march into Normandy. So quickly did Arthur's
company strike that they captured the town of Mirebeau
where John's mother, Eleanor, happened to be staying. She
managed to escape to the town's citadel from where she sent
an urgent plea to John for help. For once in his life, John
showed real alacrity. He came so swiftly to his mother's
rescue that he captured the unsuspecting Arthur and the
Lusignans while they were still asleep in their beds.

With Arthur in John's hands, all of Philip's dream-castles
threatened to evaporate into thin air, and they would have
had John not committed the greatest blunder of his career.
When Arthur disappeared, it was rumored that John killed
him in a drunken rage. John's real or suspected crime caused
the resistance to Philip in Normandy and the other northern
provinces to melt away. In December 1203, John abandoned

all of France with the exception of the Aquitaine, although Chateau Gaillard held out until the following March. By the end of 1206 all of the English-held possessions in France, with the exception of Aquitaine, had passed under Philip's control.

Had John accepted the loss of these provinces, the course of events in western Europe during the decade following would have been radically altered. In England there would probably have come no confrontation at Runnymede between John and his barons and no *Magna Charta*, since it was the harsh measures John employed to raise money and men in his efforts to recover these lost provinces in France that led his barons to rebel. There would clearly have been no battle of Bouvines, since this engagement was fought in order to determine finally whether John would recover these territories or not. (And as will be discussed later, Frederick, the young king of Sicily, would not have become Frederick II, king of Germany, since it was Philip's fear of John, the ally of Otto IV, the reigning king of Germany, that led Philip to support Frederick in the latter's ambition to replace Otto.)

Even if John's store of deficiencies included obstinacy, he can scarcely be faulted for making the recovery of these provinces the major objective of his reign. The first obligation of any monarch was that of holding on to what possessions he had inherited. Normandy, the most valuable of the lost possessions, had been under English rule since 1066, when its duke, William, had made himself king of England. Most of the other possessions had come with John's father, Henry II, who had been count of Anjou, count of Brittany, and through his marriage to Eleanor, duke of Aquitaine.

Aquitaine, the only one remaining to John, was in no danger of slipping away. The king of France had never exercised direct authority over the region; its powerful aristocracy, furthermore, actually preferred the pretensions of the

distant English king to rule there than those of the French
monarch who was closer by. As long as the English king did
not attempt to reduce their autonomy, they would remain
loyal. During the period of English rule a flourishing wine
trade had sprung up between England and Gascony, the
most southerly province of Aquitaine. The good will which
this trade engendered carried more weight with the people of
southwestern France than did national consciousness in an
age when men felt little of that sentiment.

John had his father's appreciation of the power of money.
Nothing could quite take the place of money, surely not in
the matter of winning men and battles. But where Henry
had shown moderation in raising revenues, John did not.
Henry introduced the payment of scutage, a fee his vassals
might prefer to pay in lieu of the military service they owed
their king, but he had imposed this sparingly. Not so John.
He demanded scutage every year until 1206, then annually
again from 1209, until his barons revolted. Still, the financial demands he made upon his barons would probably not
have precipitated a revolt but for other circumstances, chief
among these the defeat of his allies at Bouvines (but more of
this later). For the moment John found a more submissive
victim for his financial tyranny in the English church. From
1208 until 1213, the period of the interdict, his officials se-
questered all ecclesiastical revenues and left the clergy barely enough to live on. With the enormous sums thus confis-
cated—considerably more than the 10,000 marks he was
willing to settle for with Pope Innocent in 1213—he hired
mercenaries to do his fighting while he sent his agents with
bags of gold to buy friends among the aristocracy of the Low
Countries and Germany.

For John, hoping to recover the provinces he had lost to
Philip, needed allies as badly as he needed mercenaries. The
critical region was Flanders and the principalities along the
lower Rhine, and here John's agents expected to open many

doors with money. Philip was aware of this danger. Most crucial for him was the friendship of Flanders. In 1212 he arranged the marriage of its heiress to Ferrand, son of Sancho I of Portugal, and even had the pair married in the royal chapel in Paris. This might have guaranteed Philip the loyalty of the young groom had not Louis, Philip's son, with his father's permission, detached several towns from Flanders, among these the prosperous community of Saint-Omer. The angry Ferrand forthwith joined the growing number of John's allies. Boulogne, a county on the southern border of Flanders, also threw in its lot with John. In May 1212, Count Renaud of Dammartin, never one to prize honor above money, accepted a money fief from John. When the suspicious Philip drove Renaud from Boulogne, the count became John's most zealous agent in the organization of an Anglo-German alliance against the king of France.

What made the threat of such a northern alliance so dangerous to Philip was the likely adherence to it of none other than Otto IV, king of Germany and Holy Roman emperor. As events transpired, Germany did become a partner to the alliance not only because of the contest between John and Philip but also because the throne of Germany had itself become involved in this dispute. For the background to the situation in Germany, it is necessary to go back to 1197, the year Henry VI, king of Germany and Holy Roman emperor, died. His early death at the age of thirty-one had brought confusion and woe to Germany, since he left only his son, Frederick, not yet three years old, to rule his far-flung dominions. Frederick's mother, Constance, was the daughter of an earlier king of Sicily, a country which Henry VI's empire had come to include. She hoped at least to salvage that island for her son and succeeded in doing so. Henry VI's brother Philip (of Swabia) had been first inclined to press for the young Frederick's succession in Germany, but when it became clear that the German princes would not

accept a boy-king, he made himself a candidate for the
throne. A majority of the princes opted for Philip, although a
sizeable group accepted money from Richard of England and
gave their support to his nephew, Otto of Brunswick.

There now followed for Germany fifteen years of desul-
tory though devastating civil war, that ended only with the
decision reached on the battlefield of Bouvines. Despite
their traditional divisiveness the German princes might
have succeeded in electing a king had they been left to themselves, but their lack of unity invited foreign interference.
Foremost among these foreigners were the kings of England
and France and Pope Innocent III.

Richard advanced the candidature of Otto, who was his
favorite nephew. Otto had grown up under Richard's tute-
lage at the Anglo-Norman court, where his physical prowess
and bravery gained him his uncle's affection. Otto also
represented the so-called Welf interests in Germany. These
had been traditionally anti-imperialistic, which meant that
a Welf monarch would presumably be content to leave the
states along the North Sea and the lower Rhine pretty much
to themselves where English influences could then hope to
grow correspondingly stronger. Given England's powerful
support, Otto might eventually have succeeded in uniting
Germany but for his own weaknesses of character. The
chronicler describes him as "haughty, stupid, but brave."

Since Richard and then his successor, John, supported
Otto in the contest over the German crown, it was axiom-
atic that Philip Augustus, king of France, should oppose him
and endorse the candidature of Philip of Swabia.

Philip was a member of the Hohenstaufen family, the
most illustrious dynasty in the history of medieval Germany. This family dominated Germany during the second
half of the twelfth century. In the person of Frederick Barbarossa (1159–90) it had boasted Europe's greatest monarch
and Crusader. The Hohenstaufen interests centered in

Swabia and southern Germany, regions in which Philip had little interest. The reverse was true of the Welfs and the petty princes along the middle and lower Rhine, whose domains fronted Philip's country on the east.

Historians have generally designated Innocent III, whose pontificate covered this critical period, as the most powerful and ambitious of the popes of the Middle Ages. Among Innocent's prime objectives was that of reforming the church, an aim which might have occasioned kings little concern had Innocent not judged the influence which kings exercised in the selection of bishops to be a major obstacle to reform. In order to reduce if not eliminate that influence, he accepted a long, bitter struggle with John of England, who refused to recognize Stephen Langton as archbishop of Canterbury. In the case of Philip, with whom Innocent also tangled, the issue was a more personal one. Ingeborg, Philip's wife, had appealed to the papacy to restore her rights as Philip's legitimate wife, and this Innocent set out to do. In this instance he had no axe to grind other than that of convincing kings that in the moral order they enjoyed no special prerogatives above those of any peasant.

A special circumstance complicated Innocent's relations with Germany beyond the dominant position the German king had long maintained in the affairs of the German church. This was the influence the king of Germany enjoyed in Italy by virtue of his office as Holy Roman emperor. Under this title the king of Germany might aspire to exercise authority not only in Germany, but in Italy as well, and this included the pope's own city of Rome. Because the kings of Germany and Holy Roman emperors since 1152 had been Hohenstaufens, all had claimed wide jurisdictional powers for themselves in Italy. Therefore, Pope Innocent from the beginning of the dispute in Germany over the succession had favored the cause of Otto of Brunswick as promising the least interference in Italy. He and his legal advisers did all they could to justify the "rights" of Otto to the German throne.

The contest over the succession in Germany got under way as soon as Henry VI died in 1197. Year followed upon year of confusion and strife, but no king emerged from out of all the distress. In time a majority of the princes swung around to Philip of Swabia, Henry's brother, rather than Otto of Brunswick. Their preference had no doubt been affected by John's loss of Normandy and the drying up of English money. In 1206 Otto's position in Germany had so deteriorated that he was obliged to leave that country, whereupon Innocent, realizing that time was running out and hoping to salvage what he could, reached an agreement with Philip regarding their respective rights in Italy. Then in 1208 when the election of Philip seemed about to bring peace to Germany, the dagger of a personal enemy cut down the new king. So harassed had the German princes grown over the question of succession that they closed their minds to other alternatives and promptly chose Otto.

Innocent had but a short time in which to enjoy this unexpected windfall, that is, the election of the candidate he had wanted. Within a few months Otto was advancing the same claims to territories and imperial rights in Italy as the Hohenstaufen emperors had pressed. Had Otto stopped with pretensions, Innocent could have tolerated him. It was a different matter when Otto marched into Italy, crossed papal territories into southern Italy, and made preparations to take his army to Sicily. In deep anguish Innocent announced that he had no choice but to repudiate Otto and then accept as king of Germany and Holy Roman emperor the only viable candidate available. This was none other than young Frederick of the house of Hohenstaufen, the son of Henry VI, who had ruled both Germany and Italy. Innocent did secure Frederick's promise that he would leave Sicily to his son Henry, while he would himself remain in Germany north of the Alps.

At this sudden turn in their fortunes, both Otto and Frederick hurried up the Italian peninsula to Germany, Otto to retain his hold on that country, Frederick to gain acceptance there. The young man's fortunes, which hung by a thread, slowly improved. The Hohenstaufen name attracted some nobles, especially in southern Germany. Other nobles Frederick managed to win over by his diplomacy and with the money Philip Augustus advanced him. Otto's rough ways, on the other hand, together with his lack of statesmanship and his clearly revealed aim of ruling Germany, not just reigning there, cost him some friends. Still, as long as King John's money kept coming, his position in central and north Germany promised to remain secure.

The year 1213 opened, accordingly, with western Europe divided into two imposing alliances. The one alliance counted Otto, still king of Germany to many, King John of England, and the count of Flanders, along with a majority of the princes of the Low Countries and the middle and lower Rhine. The opposing alliance included Frederick, who was contesting Otto's claim to the throne of Germany, and Philip Augustus of France. Much was at stake for the major contestants. A victory for John would enable him to recover Normandy and Anjou; a defeat might cost him Aquitaine and surely lead to trouble back home from his barons. To Philip Augustus a victory would insure his hold on Normandy and a bright future for the royal ambitions of the Capetian dynasty. If Otto and his allies gained the victory, Otto's crown in Germany would be secure; defeat would mean oblivion. If Philip Augustus won, so would Frederick, who would then rule Germany as king and Holy Roman emperor. If Philip lost, Frederick would be fortunate to retain possession of Sicily.

And where did Pope Innocent stand in the coming conflict? He was himself not entirely sure, and it was his good fortune that he had nothing more overt than prayers to offer, for he must have puzzled over which alliance to favor. Christians

should, of course, be fighting the Infidels who held Jerusalem, not other Christians. Of the two kings of Germany,
Frederick and Otto, the one a Hohenstaufen and the other
as ambitious as any Hohenstaufen, Innocent could scarcely
make up his mind as to which was the more dangerous.
John and Philip left him in a similar quandary. Philip was
again in his good graces now that he had taken back Ingeborg. John, too, was no longer an enemy. The prospect of
John's restive barons joining in a papal crusade which Philip
would lead across the Channel to dethrone him had led that
stubborn monarch to capitulate to Innocent's demands. He
accepted Stephen Langton; then in a clever maneuver
which he hoped would immobilize his enemies, he turned
England over to Innocent and received it back as a fief. His
new character as the pope's vassal would hopefully provide
him immunity from Philip's attack and from a baronial
revolt as well.

    Some fighting had begun by the late spring of 1213. It
came in the wake of Philip's preparations to invade England
as the leader of a papal crusade against John. Philip gathered
his fleet and forces at Boulogne in April, then in May moved
to Gravelines on the Flemish border. No sooner had he
reached that embarking point than papal legates confronted
him with an injunction to halt all hostile measures against
the now repentant John. Philip, who had a long history of ig-
noring papal injunctions, ignored this one as well. He proceeded with the occupation of a number of Flemish cities including Bruges and Ghent, then abandoned all thought of invading England when an English fleet under John's half-
brother, the earl of Salisbury, surprised and destroyed the
greater part of his own fleet. To add to Philip's chagrin, the
counts of Boulogne, Flanders, and Holland chose this moment to join John's alliance.

    Never had John's hopes of destroying Philip and recover-
ing Normandy looked brighter. Late in July 1213 he sent an

embassy to Germany to finalize matters of strategy. Otto, together with his Rhenish and Flemish allies, was to invade France from the northeast, while John and what friends he could recruit in Aquitaine would move up across the Loire toward Paris. As it happened, neither army was ready to move. John was set to march, but not his barons. They argued that since this was to be an expedition outside the English realm, no military service was owing their lord. They would not have reasoned in this fashion against Henry II, John's father. Henry was too popular with the English and too strong to have accepted such defiance. Equally important, many more English barons had held fiefs in Normandy in Henry's day than in John's. They would have had something to gain from an invasion. Now few barons retained lands in Normandy, while there were far too many at home challenging John for him to dare to punish them. In bitter frustration he postponed his campaign.

By February 1214 circumstances had altered, and John was once again ready to move. He had succeeded in raising an army, principally of stipendiary troops. They landed at La Rochelle on the fifteenth. All went well for the moment as many Aquitainian nobles joined him in what was John's immediate objective, the recovery of the county of Poitou to the north of Aquitaine. So rapidly did John drive northward that Philip, who had been watching the movements of the northern allies, marched southward by way of Saumur and Chinon in an effort to catch up with John and cut off his retreat to Aquitaine. Had John's northern allies been ready to strike at this precise moment, that might have been the end of Philip. Unfortunately for John, they were not ready, although Philip thought it unwise to commit his entire army to watching John. He turned half of his troops over to his son Louis and returned to the north.

John, who at Philip's approach had retreated south of the Loire, now recrossed that river and on June 19 invested the strong fortress of La Roche-au-Moine, his last hurdle before Paris. When Louis came with his army, however, John lifted his siege and again withdrew to the south. His Poitevin allies had left him no choice; they simply refused to do battle with the son of their overlord, Philip, the king of France. All John could do was fall back toward La Rochelle to wait his fate, which was in the hands of the dilatory Otto and his allies in the north.

There at long last Otto had gotten his allies into line. Given his lack of skill in dealing with his aristocratic fellows, it would have been an even longer matter but for John's agents, who greased the wheels of diplomacy with English money. The work of these agents and Otto's own efforts finally wove together a formidable alliance consisting of the dukes of Brabant, Lorraine, and Limburg, the counts of Flanders, Boulogne, and Holland, and scattered French noblemen who feared Philip or whom he had dispossessed. Most notable of these was the count of Nevers. There was, finally, an English contingent under command of the earl of Salisbury. These allied forces gathered in Hainaut in the vicinity of Valenciennes. Only a few miles away at Peronne were Philip and his army. The fateful day for many lords, for four kings, and for their possessions had come.

Despite the singular importance of the coming battle there remains less firm information concerning the number of men who fought on each side than one might expect. It is not that careful studies are lacking. The problem is the dubious character of the statistics contemporary writers have left modern scholars to analyze. Contemporaries wrote for an audience less interested in exact numbers than in dramatic appeal. Why not fire their interest by padding numbers as does Richard of Sens who states Otto had an army of more than 100,000 men including 25,000 knights. Precise figures were difficult to come by, so even the more responsible chronicles felt justified in suggesting figures commensurate with the importance of the battle.

Oman, the most distinguished English scholar to write on the art of war, pares the figures given by contemporary sources down to something like 2,500 knights, 25,000 foot soldiers, and 4,000 light cavalry for Philip. To Otto and his allies he allots some 1,300 knights and 40,000 foot soldiers. Delbruck, a leading German scholar, believes Philip had somewhat more than the 1,500 knights he assigns to Otto, while he reduces the number of foot soldiers on both sides, on the argument that they performed no significant role in the battle. Beeler, an American scholar, suggests a French army of 1,200 knights,[3] 3,000 mounted sergeants, and possibly 10,000 foot soldiers. Because Philip had earlier detached some 10,000 of his own troops to serve under his son, Louis, against John, Beeler concludes that at Bouvines his army must have been somewhat smaller than Otto's. Ferdinand Lot, the French historian, feels Otto's army was slightly larger than Philip's, which he believes counted 1,200 knights and 10,000 foot soldiers. What weighed heaviest in the fortunes of battles were knights, however, and here Philip clearly held the advantage, not only in quantity but in quality. French knights were probably the best in the world, a superiority that can be traced to their extensive experience in the Crusades and to the fairly constant warfare which troubled France throughout much of the twelfth century.

Some question remains about the role the infantry played in the battle of Bouvines. The foot soldier comes in for little mention, a circumstance which leads most writers to conclude that he had little to do with the outcome. This may appear strange since by this time the foot soldier had proved himself an indispensable partner to the knight when battling the Muslims in Syria. Still, the situation in northern France was unlike that in Syria. In the arid Near East the Christian foot soldiers served as a buffer in protecting the slower, more heavily armed knights from the sharp attacks of the swift Saracen cavalry. In western Europe the infantry enjoyed no such role, and sometimes they were left behind, as was done at the battles of Tagliacozzo (1268) and Marchfield (1278).

The most effective company of foot soldiers at Bouvines was probably the Saxon. In the gradual shift from fighting on foot to fighting on horseback, the Germans were slower in making the change than the English and French. At Bouvines many Saxons were still fighting much as their Anglo-Saxon cousins had at Hastings a hundred-fifty years earlier. They carried pikes, some with hooks to drag knights off their horses, and three-edged daggers to jab for weak spots in a knight's armor. It must have been the presence of these Saxons that led Philip Augustus to make the encouraging statement he is supposed to have addressed to his soldiers just before the battle, namely, that "the Germans will fight on foot, you Gallicans always on horseback."

The role of the foot soldiers in 1214 at the battle of Bouvines, other than that of the Saxons, was principally that of supporting the knight. In this capacity some carried a sword and spear, others crossbows, while all who could so equip themselves wore mail shirts and steel caps. While they might serve to slow an attack by the opposing knights or hold them off until their own knights were ready to charge, the foot soldiers' responsibilities were generally limited to furnishing additional mounts for knights who had lost theirs, stabbing the horses of the enemy when these came too close, and slaying or capturing any unhorsed rider they might stumble across. About a hundred years after Bouvines the foot soldiers did gain a spectacular victory for the Flemish against Philip IV of France at Courtrai (1302), although it remained for the Hussites and the Swiss in the fifteenth century to demonstrate that the foot soldier could undertake offensive action on his own.

The character of the armor which the knight wore at Bouvines and the weapons he carried had undergone only moderate change since the battle of Hastings. The sleeves of his mail shirt had grown longer with the lower part now split into leg coverings which extended down the calf of the leg. In place of the earlier conical steel cap, he now wore a pot helm, a sort of cylindrical steel helmet which had slits for the eyes. As armor grew thicker and more extensive in its coverage, the size of the knight's shield shrunk in size. His heavier armor necessitated the use of additional mounts, and he might ride one horse to battle, then transfer to a fresh one on which to do battle. The knight had also adopted a different method of handling his lance. Rather than throw it as a javelin at the enemy or use it as a kind of elongated dagger, he now kept it braced against his upper arm and shoulder, from which position he found he could deliver a heavier blow against his opponent.

What had always been a weak link in the knight's armament, his unprotected horse, became more an object of the enemy's attack as his own body became the better protected. From the middle of the twelfth century, some effort had been given to protecting the horse, but the horse remained by far more vulnerable than the rider. In 1266 at the battle of Beneventum, for instance, Charles of Anjou instructed his men to concentrate their attacks on horses, not their riders. Once a knight was unhorsed, he became almost helpless. Such was the fate of the valiant Renaud, count of Boulogne, at the battle of Bouvines, who found his leg pinned beneath his horse when the beast was stabbed. A foot soldier was about to kill him, and had already struck him in the face, when he was rescued by the four knights who had been arguing about which of them had legal possession of so valuable a prisoner.

Of greater significance than modifications in armaments or methods of fighting since the battle of Hastings were the

means employed by John, Philip, and Otto for recruiting
their armies. The traditional knightly service that men holding of feudal lords were required to pay over a period of forty
days each year had gradually given way to a fee, called
scutage, which the individual knight had the option of paying in lieu of personal service. Of the two, personal service or
scutage, many men preferred the latter although the
baronage generally chose to come leading their own men,
possibly because of the glory they hoped to win, more probably in order to keep in the good graces of their sovereign.
Town and ecclesiastical institutions preferred to pay the fee,
even though Amiens, Beauvais, Compiègne, and Arras sent
their own men to fight at Bouvines. The major advantage
scutage held for the king was that it enabled him to recruit
an army of mercenaries and to staff this with captains of his
own choice. That Philip could muster as many as 27,000
men and divide these into two field armies signalled a basic
departure in methods of recruitment since Harold the Anglo-
Saxon and William of Normandy had brought their armies to
Hastings.

A distinct advantage which Philip enjoyed over his foes at
Bouvines, apart from the larger number of knights he had
brought with him, was the fact that he had sole command of
his forces. (He appointed Bishop Guerin, a former Hospitaller, to serve as supreme tactical commander.) The reverse
was true of Otto. If one may suggest the lack of cohesiveness
as the most glaring weakness in the feudal armies of the
period, that lack was particularly marked in an army such as
Otto's, which was composed of contingents from a number
of different states. Otto and his allied leaders might agree on
some sort of concerted action, but their armies always remained separate units under individual commanders, who
might reserve the right to depart from any planned strategy
should they feel it was in their best interest to do so. How
serious such divided commands could be was revealed at

Bouvines when the duke of Brabant's order to his men to leave the battlefield apparently led to the collapse of the entire allied army.

Otto and his allies first assembled their forces at Nivelles to the south of Brussels, then on July 23 moved to Valenciennes in Hainaut. That same day Philip took his army from Peronne to Tournai, perhaps with the intention of preventing Otto from reaching the Channel. In any event, neither army was certain of the whereabouts of the other, which explains why they passed each other by and why the French found themselves as a consequence to the north of the allied army. Once Philip discovered the location of Otto's army, he quickly turned about and moved south in the direction of Lille, where he expected the terrain to have fewer marshes and swamps. It was of vital importance to him to fight on solid ground, since he placed all his hopes in his knights. By the morning of July 27 he had reached Bouvines, but as the ground still remained swampy, he ordered his foot soldiers to march on to the west over the one bridge that crossed the river Marcq at that point. These men had already proceeded some four kilometers beyond the bridge when they received urgent orders to return to Bouvines. Word had reached Philip that Otto's army was approaching and that some of the imperial troops were in fact engaging his rear guard. Otto had clearly moved up faster than Philip had expected. Otto may have hoped to cut off Philip's retreat toward Paris, which would have left the king of France isolated in hostile Flanders.

One might suppose that of the two armies—Otto's moving forward toward the west in an effort to catch Philip, Philip's facing about toward the east, his foot soldiers forced to scurry back over the river Marcq—that Otto's would be more ready for action once the battle was joined. The opposite appears to have been the case. Even though Philip had to reverse the movement of his army, so disciplined were his men that the turnabout occasioned little confusion. When the battle broke, the foot soldiers had taken their proper station in front of the knights. Otto's army, on the other hand, not only moved forward on a narrow front and was strung out to a distance of several miles, but in its anxiety to catch the French advanced at a pace that threatened its cohesiveness. Verbruggen writes: "It seems likely that the hasty march of his [Otto's] troops was largely the cause of their defeat."[4]

Philip seems to have been completely confident of defeating the enemy. Had he harbored misgivings, he might have avoided battle by continuing the movement of his army to the west across the Marcq. He surely had sufficient time to pursue with this action since the foot soldiers who had proceeded four kilometers beyond the river not only had returned but had managed to take their place in front of the knights facing the east. That Philip chose to fight Otto with his back to this river and a single bridge to furnish him a means of escape bespeaks his optimism. Otto is said to have been surprised to find Philip's entire army ready to meet him at Bouvines, not just the part that had remained east of the Marcq. Renaud, count of Boulogne, sensed the danger in the situation and cautioned Otto against fighting, a counsel the emperor dismissed.

As the two armies took their positions for the coming battle, Philip, who was in the center of the French line facing toward the east, found himself in front of Otto, who was supported by the knights of Lorraine and the Westphalian Saxon infantry. To Otto's left was the count of Flanders, to his right, Renaud of Boulogne, the count of Salisbury, and the Brabantine foot soldiers. It was under a scorching sun, shortly after midday on Sunday July 15, when the French crossbowmen began firing their missiles, and the battle was joined.

The French right moved forward under the immediate command of Bishop Guérin, and after heavy fighting pushed back the Flemish and captured their Count Ferrand. Philip and his center fared less well. Such was the ferocity of the charge which the Saxon foot soldiers launched that they shattered the ranks of infantry from the French communes. Philip found himself dragged from his horse and would have been slain but for the heroism of Pierre Tristan, who covered Philip's body with his own and shielded it from any lethal blow until French knights came to the rescue. Otto suffered a similar experience. After several attempts had failed to bring down the magnificent horse that he rode, a foot soldier did finally stab the beast. Otto managed to escape capture on a horse given him by his squire, Bernhard of Hortsmar.

The fiercest and what may have proved the most critical fighting took place between the French left and the Brabantine infantry. When the duke of Brabant finally gave orders to fall back, a general disintegration of Otto's entire army quickly followed. There is some suggestion that the duke had been bought by Philip. A number of formations, including contingents from Brabant, Limbourg, Bruges, and Ghent, which came up late, decided not to fight when they learned how the fortunes of the battle were going. This meant in effect that while the allied army of Otto was larger than Philip's on paper, it was not in fact, since a significant number of men who had promised to fight failed to do so.

Oman says the battle lasted for three hours, Verbruggen says it lasted even longer, but other scholars question this. They point to the small number of prominent men who were listed among the casualties as ruling out a long struggle. The chronicle of Melrose, for example, gives the names of but three French knights among the slain at Bouvines. Fewer than a hundred knights of the imperial army, perhaps only seventy, were counted among the slain, although more than two hundred were captured.[5] Philip's most prized prisoners were the count of Flanders and the count of Boulogne. He left the latter to die in prison thirteen years later. The count of Flanders spent the same number of years in the newly erected prison of the Louvre before Philip permitted the much chastened nobleman to return to his province.

Bouvines proved a magnificent victory for Philip. Lot speaks of it as a medieval Austerlitz. Flanders and Boulogne to the north were now in his hands, and there remained no longer any question that Normandy, Anjou, and the other provinces above the Loire would continue under the rule of the French king. The Capetian house was in Paris and on the French throne to stay. Bouvines destroyed John's last hope of regaining the provinces in France that his father, Henry II, had once held. And worse was to come. Scarcely had the news of Bouvines reached England than his barons began to organize their attack on his "tyranny." Without the defeat at Bouvines in all likelihood there would have been no *Magna Charta*.

For Otto, Bouvines meant the end of the road. He led a harassed existence until 1218 when he died in the Harzburg, a castle located in Brunswick, the small patrimonial state to which he had managed to cling. Frederick II emerged the winner in Germany even though he had taken no part in the battle of Bouvines. He owed Philip his crown, also the wagon with the imperial eagle and dragon which the fleeing Otto had left behind. He now proudly assumed unquestioned possession of the titles king of Germany and Holy Roman emperor, even though neither title evoked the esteem they had called forth during the reign of his Hohenstaufen grandfather, Frederick Barbarossa. Only by virtue of the victory Philip and the French army had won at Bouvines had these titles come into his possession. A new era had dawned for western Europe. France had replaced Germany as its leading power. From this time forward, lamented the Lauterberg chronicle, "the fame of the Germans ever sank lower among foreigners."

7

THE BATTLE OF CRECY

THERE WOULD PROBABLY HAVE BEEN NO HUNDRED YEARS' WAR and therefore no battle of Crecy had Louis IX of France been less of a saint than he was. King Henry III of England, Louis' brother-in-law across the Channel, had twice abetted rebellious nobles in France in their efforts to unseat Louis, so ample justification was present for pushing Henry and the English out of France. (They were still holding on to Gascony in southwestern France.) And Louis was quite capable of expelling the English. Under the leadership of the virtuous but weak Henry, England was no match for France. But Louis had no stomach for fighting other Christians, to say nothing of brothers-in-law. Christian princes should live together in amity and pool their resources in the never-ending struggle with the Infidel in Syria. (Louis led the last two Crusades.)

Louis not only permitted the English to retain Gascony but by the Treaty of Paris (1259) confirmed Henry's possession of that province and even turned over to him several adjoining territories that he hoped would leave Henry and the English content. Henry for his part formally renounced English claims to Normandy, Anjou, and the other provinces north of the Loire River, which his grandfather Henry II had held but which Philip Augustus had taken from John,

Henry's father. Since there existed not the remotest chance of ever recovering these provinces, Henry had indeed surrendered little in 1259, and it was with complete willingness that he consented to do homage to Louis for Gascony. For this reason England continued to govern that part of France and was so doing at the outbreak of the Hundred Years' War. All of which underscores the point made above, namely that Louis' patience with Henry in permitting him to retain Gascony led ultimately to the Hundred Years' War, since by the early fourteenth century when the conflict opened, the French had come to view the continued presence of the English in southwestern France as no longer tolerable.

History records no longer hostility between two peoples than that of the French and English from 1066 when William the duke of Normandy defeated Harold the Anglo-Saxon at Hastings, until 1904, when the fear of Germany led France and England to become allies. William's victory in 1066 left him both king of England and duke of Normandy, the latter province perhaps the most important in France at the time. Western Europe in the feudal age was quite willing to accept a situation in which a foreign king ruled a large province in another king's realm. It even acquiesced when Henry II of England ruled Anjou, Aquitaine, Brittany, and other provinces as vassal of the French king and in fact administered more French territory in the late twelfth century than did the king of France himself.

Philip Augustus could not agree, and his victory over the allied army at Bouvines in 1214 confirmed him in his conquest of Normandy and Anjou and of all English-held lands north of the Loire. The feudal age was already on the wane in Philip Augustus' day, and it was all but spent in the early fourteenth century. What had been accepted as proper in 1066 and as not particularly irregular during the lifetime of Henry II, the fourteenth century could no longer tolerate. The control of a large portion of southwestern France by the

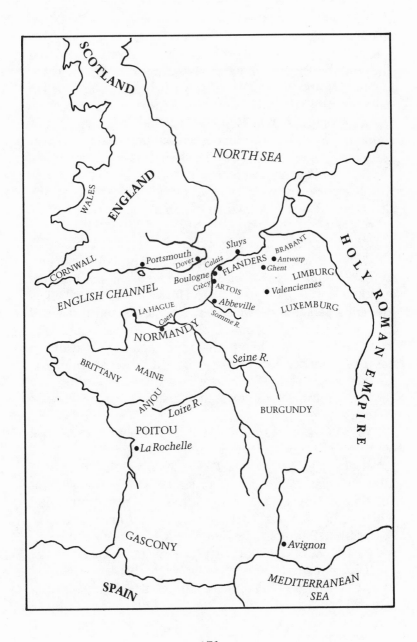

alien king of England remains the basic cause for the Hundred Years' War.

Kings of a different sort than Edward III of England and Philip VI of France who were reigning in 1337 when the Hundred Years' War got under way might have continued to live with the situation in Gascony. True, the situation there was a bad one, and in 1304 Edward I and Philip IV had almost come to blows. The boundaries of Gascony were as unclear as the rights of petty lords in their privileged enclaves. Disputes and quarrels were frequent and so were the appeals which aggrieved vassals brought to the king's court in Paris against officials of the English crown in Gascony.

Still, war had not come under Edward I and Philip IV nor with their immediate successors; it did break out under Edward III and Philip VI. One reason was Edward III's desire for military renown. He has been compared to his famous great granduncle, Richard the Lion-Hearted. Edward lacked Richard's personal prowess, but shared his ability to lead men on the battlefield and his skill as a tactician. Both men loved nothing more than to ride with their barons against a foe they were confident of besting. Since war provided the quickest road to honor and glory, Edward had little difficulty convincing himself of its being justified in the case of Gascony.

Philip VI was Edward's equal in personal bravery and love of chivalry. (He instituted the Order of the Star; Edward, the Order of the Garter.) He lacked Edward's ability to inspire men, however, and was a poor strategist. He was also indecisive at times, permitting others to control him, and when he lost his temper, he was apt to act rashly. Neither Edward nor Philip showed much interest in good government. This was less a liability in Edward's case since the English court was superior to begin with, thanks to the solid work of Henry II (1154–89). Philip's court was less centralized and constantly hampered in its action by the existence of the four great independent fiefs of Gascony, Brittany, Flanders, and Burgundy. Edward might have accommodated himself to a consistent policy on the part of the French court regarding his rights and responsibilities in Gascony, but Philip VI was not the kind of king capable of forcing the French court to furnish this.

The signal for war came in May 1337 when Philip ordered the confiscation of Gascony, the third such confiscation in a little more than forty years. If any war is inevitable, this one between Philip VI and Edward III might have claimed to be so. Kings in the fourteenth century were becoming more persistent in their efforts to control their vassals. Philip's ambition to force his vassals in Gascony to accept closer regulation was bound to precipitate a dangerous situation, and this for two reasons. First, Gascony's ducal ruler was the king of England, who would not readily submit to the bullying tactics that French officials employed in their efforts to reduce the autonomy of the king's vassals. Second, Gascony furnished the English king a valuable bridgehead in France should he wish to exploit it, for which reason the French monarch was especially anxious to insist upon Edward's acknowledging the full implications of his position as vassal.

In the years following Philip's coronation in 1328, Edward's sensitivity to his "inferior" position in Gascony increased. Isabella, wife of the dethroned Edward II, and her paramour, Roger Mortimer, were in control of England at the time of Philip's coronation, so the absence of the English vassal to do homage for Gascony on this occasion provoked no crisis. Once Edward III had executed Mortimer, sent his mother off to a distant castle, and assumed control in his own right, the French court reminded him of his feudal obligations. There followed some hesitation on Edward's part and a threat of confiscation on the part of the French, but he eventually agreed to tender his homage. He crossed the Channel and in July 1329 at Amiens formally paid his oath of homage.

If Edward thought this settled that matter he was mistaken. The year following he received a brusque order from the French court to signify beyond the shadow of a doubt that the homage he had sworn at Amiens was not the simple but the more binding liege homage, which pledged personal service to Philip. Edward's ire rose over the French court's order, which he interpreted simply as a maneuver on the part of Philip to justify his confiscating Gascony, but war did not come. In the end Philip excused Edward from performing another act of homage and agreed to be satisfied with Edward's written statement that the homage he had performed at Amiens had indeed been liege. When Edward went to France in April 1331 to confirm in person what he had written, the air cleared so completely that the two kings, in an outburst of cordiality, turned their backs on Gascony and in great friendliness discussed a joint Crusade against the Infidel. They even reached an agreement whereby they would embark from Mediterranean ports in the spring of 1335. The two kings might have been in earnest, so personal was government action in the Middle Ages and so spasmodic much of the enthusiasm over Crusades, but within a year trouble broke out on the Tweed along the Scottish border and all thought of a Crusade was dismissed.

The intrusion of the Scots supplies another facet to the background of the Hundred Years' War. That the Scots should have forced themselves into the picture was to be expected. Relations between England and Scotland had long been strained, and their common border was the scene of frequent disputes. English kings had claimed suzerainty over Scotland since Henry II had captured King Malcolm and forced him to swear homage. It was on the basis of his position as overlord that Edward I, in 1290, when the Scottish royal line became extinct, insisted upon his right to choose a king among the different aspirants to the Scottish throne and gave the nod to John Balliol. In 1295, when Edward made demands on Balliol which the latter considered unreasonable, the Scots turned to the French for support. Since that time, Scotland and France viewed England as a common enemy and had remained formal or informal allies.

Edward had been keeping a wary eye on Scotland. While he made no direct attack on the country, he did give encouragement by means of money and men to Edward Balliol, son of John Balliol, in his efforts to dethrone David II, Scotland's reigning monarch. When Edward learned that Philip had been subsidizing David, he advanced to the north, took Berwick, and on July 11, 1333, won a great victory over the Scots at Halidon Hill. Had Edward stopped with that victory, the developing crisis between himself and Philip might have abated and war would not have been carried over to the Continent. But Edward continued his advance into Scotland, and in the summer of 1336 Philip ordered his ships, which had assembled at Marseilles preparatory to going on a Crusade, to sail instead to Norman ports whence they might move on to Scotland. Philip's action led Edward to abandon his conquest of Scotland, since it convinced him that this would be impossible so long as France was able to intervene. He decided to force the issue of Gascony with Philip, and in the fall of 1336 Parliament obliged with subsidies for the fleet and for the defenses along the coast. Philip, in turn, sent troops to the borders of Gascony, where they laid siege to several forts. Finally, on May 24, 1337, after charging Edward with having been derelict in honoring his obligations in that province, Philip declared it forfeit. At this point neither pope nor good fortune could have halted the coming of war.

French interference in Scotland helped precipitate the war between Edward and Philip over Gascony. English intrigue in Flanders worked toward the same end. Flanders, a large, rich province lying along the northwestern frontier of France and fronting on the North Sea, was one of the most industrialized regions in Europe. It boasted such thriving cities as Bruges, Ghent, and Ypres. In the early twelfth century the kings of France began to stake out claims to the territory, and Philip Augustus (1180–1223) managed to take over several southern districts including Artois and Vermandois. When a century later in 1302 Philip IV attempted to establish direct control over the entire province, his army of knights suffered a bloody defeat at the hands of the burgher foot soldiers at Courtrai. Any thought that the French threat to Flanders' independence was gone for good, however, ended abruptly in 1328 when Philip VI gained a smashing victory over the Flemish at Cassel, a battle that wiped out all memory of Courtrai and much of the province's autonomy as well. The victory at Cassel enabled the king of France to exercise considerable influence in Flemish affairs through the count of Flanders, who had to rely on the support of the French crown in order to hold his position. Officials of the king of France regularly interfered in the municipal affairs of the Flemish cities and enforced the circulation of the royal currency.

The count of Flanders did enjoy some support within his province. For example, wealthy merchants counted on French royal influence to help maintain their dominant position in the industrial exploitation of the province against the resentment of the artisans and the merchants in the smaller communities. These artisans and small merchants had developed economic ties with England, since it was from England that the bulk of the raw wool that fed their looms came. The English were also among the heaviest purchasers of their woolen textiles. This lively trade in wool and woolen goods between Flanders and England quite naturally brought the English king into the picture. He welcomed the establishment of friendly ties with a country on

France's northern flank and, more importantly, he had come to depend on export duties on wool for a significant part of his revenue. Since Edward did not want this flow of revenue interrupted, he opposed any attempt by the king of France to bring the province under his direct rule. In this event Philip might be able to disrupt the trade at his pleasure. Since the count and the wealthier merchants had thrown in their lot with the French king, Edward gave his sympathetic encouragement to the artisans and the smaller merchants.

In August 1336, in a move to induce the Flemish to break with Philip and join him, Edward placed an embargo on the shipment of English wool to Flanders. He then transferred the staple[1] to Brabant, where the towns of Antwerp, Brussels, and Malines were willing to pledge Edward their friendship in return for English wool with which to build up their own cloth-making industry. To win over the remaining states in the Low Countries, Edward used money, which his agents dispensed freely from their headquarters in Valenciennes. Gelderland, Hainaut, Berg, Juliers, Cleves, Marck, and Limburg all joined the anti-French alliance. Edward's biggest prize came in August 1337, when the Holy Roman emperor, Louis of Bavaria, brother-in-law of the English queen, joined ranks with the growing company of Edward's allies. Louis promised 2,000 men-at-arms, for whose services Edward guaranteed the princely sum of 300,000 florins.

A man who proved himself especially helpful to Edward in negotiating these alliances was Robert of Artois, a brother-in-law of Philip VI. Philip banished Robert in 1332 because of the vicious means Robert employed in his efforts to gain control of Artois. Edward was happy to give asylum to so important a noble as Robert, whatever his virtues or lack thereof, and it was Robert who pressed Edward to buy more friends in the Low Countries and the Rhineland and to get on with his war against Philip. Robert's activities had not gone

unnoticed, especially by Pope Benedict XII, who was working anxiously to prevent the outbreak of this war. He urged
Edward to expel Robert in the interest of peace, since Philip
had announced he would attack any country which gave
haven to his brother-in-law.

Unfortunately for Edward all these alliances cost money,
and as Pope Benedict had warned him, once his money ran
out so would his newly bought friends on the Continent.
The landing which Edward had planned for the fall of 1337
had to be abandoned for lack of funds. Prospects grew
brighter by the following September, when Emperor Louis
invested Edward with the insignia of vicar-general of the empire. The office invested Edward, in theory at least, with
authority over the princes whom he had been subsidizing.
This appointment warranted in turn a series of festive but
expensive ceremonies at which the princes of the Low
Countries swore their undying loyalty. So pressed did Edward find himself for funds after these celebrations that he
was obliged to pawn the magnificent crown he had ordered
to grace his early coronation as joint king of England and
France.

All of Edward's fortunes, so he must have been convinced,
depended upon what happened in Flanders, and there the
situation looked encouraging. As the looms shut down in
Ghent, Bruges, and the other towns of Flanders for lack of
English wool, rising unemployment led to demonstrations
and then to rioting. Resentment built up against the king of
France, against the count, and against the wealthy merchants, whom English agents said were responsible for the
plight of the workers. Early in 1338 a rebellion in Ghent put
an end to the authority of the count of Flanders in favor of
James van Arteveld, a wealthy merchant who had himself
elected "captain" by the citizenry. Other cities joined the
anti-French movement until the larger part of Flanders stood
in defiance of the count. In February 1339, after a vain at-

tempt to force Ghent and Bruges into submission, the count fled the country, which then declared its independence under the presidency of Arteveld.

Edward expected Flanders to join his alliance without delay, but Arteveld demurred. Only a flow of English wool could right the situation in Flanders, Arteveld argued, so something must be done about the wool which had been going to the cities of Brabant and building up a rival cloth-making industry there. Only after prolonged negotiations was Edward able to secure a promise of an alliance from Flanders and then only on his assurance that he would transfer the staple from Antwerp to Bruges and that he would send a fleet and men-at-arms to help the Flemish in the event Philip should attack the province.

Edward made a second promise to Arteveld and the Flemish—that he would assume the title of king of France for himself. Following their defeat at the battle of Cassel in 1328, the Flemish had bound themselves by a bond of two million florins never again to rebel against their French suzerain. The money had been deposited as a bond with the papacy at Avignon, where it would go forfeit should the Flemish now defy the king of France. A simple means of circumventing that misfortune would be for Edward to assume the crown of France for himself.

As it happened, Edward was quite willing to make this claim; he had in fact been pressing his right to the French throne for some years. The basis for his claim grew out of the inability of the three sons of Philip IV to sire sons. Louis X (1314–16) had failed,[2] and so had Philip V (1316–22) and Charles IV (1322–28). What made this inability seem especially curious was the phenomenal success of the Capetian ancestors of these kings to father sons, which they had done in unbroken sequence for more than three hundred years, ever since 987 when Hugh Capet had founded the dynasty.

When Charles IV died in 1328 and left no sons, the French had little difficulty deciding that Philip of Valois, a cousin of the deceased, should be their king. Edward had a better claim, since he was a nephew of Charles, his mother Isabella being Charles' sister. But French lawyers argued that a woman could not succeed to so noble a position as that of king; neither could a woman transmit such a right to her son. Edward was barely sixteen at the time, a circumstance which did not improve his case. The fact that his profligate mother and Roger Mortimer were in control of England at the time was sufficient cause to remove him from serious consideration. Isabella did protest the accession of Philip V in the name of her son, but no one paid her much attention, and in 1329 Edward went to France and did homage to Philip VI for Gascony.

Edward formally claimed to be the rightful sovereign of both England and France, but his financial problems remained as acute as ever. History provides an odd reminder of Edward's insolvency. So desperate had his financial condition grown by February 1340 that he received permission from his Dutch creditors in Ghent to return to England to raise money only if he left his pregnant wife and his young children as hostages for the payment of his debts. His third son, baptized John, is known in history as John of Gaunt (Ghent), since he was born during his father's absence.

While the year 1340 opened on this dismal note, Edward did experience some real satisfaction that summer when his ships engaged a French fleet at Sluys on its way to Flanders and destroyed it. The French fleet was superior to the English in numbers—"their masts seemed to be like a great wood" wrote Froissart. In fact, there were too many ships in too small a space and too little cooperation between the French ships and those that had come up from Castile and Genoa to help. The victory afforded the discouraged English some cheer, and for the next few years it gave the English freedom to use the Channel at will. An early attempt by the English to exploit this victory nevertheless went awry. Edward moved a strong army of some 25,000 men including the Flemish militia to Tournai, but there they remained mired in the marshes. Edward lacked the necessary siege equipment to take the city, while the French army in the vicinity refused to do battle and contented itself rather with harassing Edward's communications. By September both the French and English armies had expended their supplies of fodder, so they readily accepted papal mediation and agreed to a truce which was to run to the following June.

Of the two confrontations in the year 1340, at Sluys and Tournai, England's allies must have judged Edward's inability to take Tournai the more significant, since that autumn saw the collapse of his expensive system of alliances in the Low Countries. In January 1341, Emperor Louis revoked Edward's appointment as vicar of the empire and announced the termination of his own alliance. No doubt French money shared responsibility with Edward's lack of funds for this sad turn in his fortunes.

In 1342 the persistent Edward was back on French soil, this time because of something fortuitous. In April 1341 the duke of Brittany died. He left no son, and what was worse, two claimants to the duchy. John, count of Montfort, the man with the poorer claim to the duchy, felt his only hope of making good that claim would be to defy the French king and openly ally himself with Edward. John's maneuver brought Edward to Brittany in the fall of 1342 with an army of some 12,000 men. With this army and some good fortune he was able, by the end of 1345, to gain control of the larger part of Brittany. Possession of Brittany was of course valuable in itself, but more important to Edward were the Breton ports which he sorely needed to provide him a bridgehead in northwestern France. The assassination of Arteveld earlier that year and the collapse of his Flemish alliance had deprived him of Flemish harbors.

Meanwhile, truces arranged by papal emissaries had reduced the fighting in Brittany and Gascony to relatively minor operations. However high papal hopes of mediating a final settlement between Edward and Philip might have been, Edward never relinquished his objective of gaining full sovereignty over southwestern France. By the summer of 1346 he felt the time had come to make another major effort in this direction. He assembled an army at Portsmouth and may initially have planned to bring them to Gascony in order to assist his troops against Philip's lieutenants, who were seeking to dislodge them. But the winds which were to take him southward decided otherwise and blew his ships instead toward Cornwall. Upon this misadventure, it is said, Edward announced that he would now go wherever they might blow him. Whether the story is true, the winds shortly did an about-face and drove his ships conveniently to the coast of Normandy and La Hogue, whose lord had declared for Edward after having been dispossessed by Philip. There at La Hogue Edward put in on July 12 and during the days following disembarked an army that counted some 8,000 cavalry and several thousand foot soldiers.

The area proved poorly defended, and Edward had no difficulty moving forward. On July 26 he captured and plundered the beautiful town of Caen. He did not wait to take the citadel. From Caen he pushed on toward Paris along the south bank of the Seine, having nothing more ambitious in mind apparently than to do as much damage to the countryside as possible. When he reached the vicinity of Paris he learned that Philip was moving up with a large army to intercept him. Prudence advised Edward to hurry back to England, but his fleet had already gone. Some of his ships had gone on his orders to transfer wounded men and the plunder taken at Caen to England, but the remaining ships had mutinied. The situation looked critical for Edward; he was in hostile country with a superior army moving up to engage him and no ships at hand to provide him escape. He turned his army towards Flanders in the hope of finding either allies there or ships which would take him back to England. His first obstacle and a formidable one was the Seine, because all the bridges had either been destroyed or were too strongly defended. Since he could not afford the time to make an assault, it was most fortunate that he found a weakly held bridge at Poissy, and on August 16 hurriedly led his army across and toward the Somme.

By this time Philip and his army had come dangerously near, and the French king had high hopes of catching up with the retreating Edward and defeating him. Though Edward managed to cross the Seine, there still remained a good possibility of pinning him down between that river and the Somme. Edward was aware of the danger of being trapped, and it was only good fortune that saved him from disaster. A native of the village of Acheux, in return for a handsome reward, disclosed the location of a place ten miles below Abbeville where the Somme could be forded at low tide. Edward succeeded in crossing on August 24 just as the French advance guard was about to catch up, only to find himself blocked by the rising tide. Edward realized his tired infantry could not long keep ahead of the French cavalry, so he looked about for a favorable site to make a stand. For the battle which would decide his fate he selected a position on a small hill just east of the village of Crecy.

Before describing what was about to happen at Crecy, the first and greatest battle of the Hundred Years' War, it will be useful to consider the comparative strength of the two armies and the resources upon which each king had to draw. As for manpower and wealth, England might at first glance be likened to a pygmy about to close with a giant. To

France's some 16 million people, 12 million of these on the royal domain and under Philip's direct rule, England could count somewhat in excess of 2 million. France's industrial development was also far beyond that of England's. Indeed France's population and wealth left her unquestionably the leading country of western Europe, while England could scarcely rate a poor fourth.

In the medieval world of the fourteenth century, however, neither population nor industrial development carried anything approaching the weight they do in modern warfare. What did count, then as now, was money. Generally speaking, the more money the ruler had at his disposal with which to acquire men-at-arms, mercenaries, and allies, the stronger the army he could pit against his adversary. Given Edward's earlier feverish and expensive efforts to make friends, it comes as a surprise to learn that he had none to help him at Crecy. In this respect Philip probably fared slightly better than Edward. While no formal ally came to his aid, there were a few knights-errant such as John of Luxemburg, the blind king of Bohemia, who came with his retinue of knights. Both monarchs used money to raise the bulk of their warriors.

Both armies were on the move: Edward's army on a gigantic raiding expedition; Philip's mustered in short order to give chase. Each army maintained itself on the march after the manner generally accepted up to this time, that is, they lived off the countryside. This necessity limited the size of armies more effectively than the actual pool of manpower which might have been available to either king. As for the amount of money each king could spend on the coming encounter, neither had found their respective tax-voting assemblies overly generous. The English king was fighting battles in what most Englishmen considered a foreign land, so Edward found parliament unresponsive. France was still too disunited and provincial to have developed a sense of national consciousness, a sentiment which might have moved the estates to a more liberal response to the king's appeal for funds. It would require the lapse of another century, the continued presence of the hated English during much of that time, and the appearance of the heroic Joan of Arc before the French king could hope his appeals would evoke something like a united effort against the foreigner. It is quite probable that England, the poorer country, furnished its king greater financial assistance than France did for Philip.

The French army in 1346 under Philip VI revealed no basic change from that which had fought at Bouvines under Philip Augustus in 1214. Significant change would come three-quarters of a century later, during the closing years of the Hundred Years' War. What was judged to constitute the real strength of his army still remained the mounted nobility and the heavy-armed knights who accompanied them. The accouterments and weapons of these warriors had changed little since Bouvines. Armor was somewhat heavier and more expensive, helmets were equipped with visors, and horses carried a greater amount of protective armor. The increased cost of armor tended to reduce the number of heavy-armed knights while increasing the number of those wearing less protective gear. These were the light-armed cavalry, identified usually as mounted sergeants or squires. They might find themselves organized into companies called *routes*, and they came under command of experienced captains who sold their services for a price. Members of the lower nobility along with ambitious young men took up this kind of armed service, since it furnished them the surest and quickest way to excitement and fortune. It was only after the disaster at Poitiers ten years after Crecy, when the French throne was tottering on the brink of collapse, that the name *routier* acquired its infamous connotation for the pillaging and rapine these soldiers committed over the French countryside.

The fortunes of war would be decided by the heavy-armed cavalry, both the English and French believed. Individual knights on both sides might win distinction for their unusual prowess, but it was the number of knights that in the last analysis would determine the outcome. For this reason Philip felt confident of victory, since he enjoyed a preponderance in this category. Edward, because he was lacking in heavy-armed cavalry, was on the defensive and presumably fleeing with what some scholars believe to have been the numerically larger army. It is probable that the French superiority in the number of knights led ironically to their overconfidence, which proved as fatal to French fortunes as did the defensive measures which Edward's lack of knights forced him to adopt.

Philip did have some foot soldiers under his command at Crecy, principally the militia of towns which he recruited as he passed through on his way to Crecy. These men carried pikes only. As pikemen in the coming battle their role was to block a charge by the opposing horsemen and to be available should fighting reach the hand-to-hand level. Philip and his advisors did not anticipate that kind of fighting, so the cavalry might have ridden on in advance of the foot soldiers had it not been for the Genoese crossbowmen. The missiles of these bowmen would be needed to offset the impact of the large number of archers Edward was known to be bringing with him. The French had never interested themselves in archery, either as a sport or as an arm of the military. They had no choice but to hire foreign crossbowmen. They did this in a limited way, since these men were not only expensive but apt to turn to pillaging if not kept under close control. (Edward had the services of some crossbowmen from Gascony.)

While the French army had remained essentially the feudal institution of a century earlier, with its strength centered in heavy-armed horsemen, the English army had adopted a significant change or two. These had come into use not because of any superior talent the English might have possessed in their knowledge of the art of war, but simply as a result of the hard experience they had gained in their battles with the Welsh and Scots. Neither the poor Welsh nor equally poor Scots could afford armies of heavy-armed knights. Even had this been possible, the mountainous character of both countries discouraged the use of horses. It was when fighting the Welsh that the English first discovered how painfully effective arrows could be when shot from longbows by archers hidden behind boulders and crags. Edward I in his first attempt to conquer Wales had relied on an infantry armed with pikes, but he soon learned the superiority of the longbow and adopted it. His Statute of Winchester (1285) defined an earlier requirement laid upon all freeholders of property worth forty shillings that they equip themselves with bow and arrows. By Edward III's day the English free peasantry, commonly identified as the yeoman class, constituted a reservoir of archer militia upon which the king could draw in fighting the French. These archers were both relatively cheap and effective. The French had nothing to compare with them.

The bow which these yeomen used was six feet long, whence the name longbow. Being longer than the conventional bow it shot arrows a longer distance and with greater accuracy. At two hundred yards its arrows could pierce two layers of mail armor, though accuracy at that range would be limited. But when fired by a large body of archers into an advancing mass of horsemen, these weapons could be devastating. Even if few missiles proved immediately fatal, they would leave many men wounded while more would be thrown by their terrified, rearing mounts. The result could be a confused and demoralized mass of men and horses.

The longer fire range of the longbow gave it a significant advantage over the more cumbersome and harder to fire crossbow. A more important advantage was the fact that an expert archer could shoot six or seven arrows a minute to the two bolts fired by an experienced crossbowman. Edward had learned how best to use these archers. He placed them in the

front line where they rained arrows on the opposing spearmen. Once these spearmen had been thrown into disorder,
the archers would step aside and permit the English horsemen to charge forward. Should the opposing horsemen
charge without an escort of pikemen, Edward would have
his archers stationed to the right and left of center, whence
they could shoot their deadly arrows into the flanks of the
advancing enemy.

A body of knights did accompany Edward to Crecy
although not so numerous a group as that which went with
Philip; neither was it so prestigious. Dukes and counts still
occupied a conspicuous place in the French army of the fourteenth century, probably because traditional notions of
chivalry remained stronger there than in any other country
of western Europe. It was also on French territory where the
fighting was to take place and in some instances in regions
directly menaced by the English. As for the English nobility,
the majority of its members remained at home since the
fighting was to be on foreign soil where they had no interest
and could expect little for their efforts. Edward was willing
that the bulk of his nobles stay at home—experience had
shown them a difficult class to manage—provided parliament voted him sufficient money to recruit companies of
knights whom he then placed under his own lieutenants.
Edward also used parliament's subsidies to recruit archers
and pikemen. About the only warriors who did not represent
a drain on his treasury were the few earls and barons who
stood close to the crown and who came with their own
retinues of horsemen.

The historian has less difficulty identifying the different
kinds of warriors at Crecy and the variety of weapons they
used than in determining the actual number who took part
in the battle. Figures supplied by contemporary chroniclers
are unreliable. These writers were as much concerned with

piquing the interest of their readers as they were in reporting accurately, even if they had had the means of securing accurate figures. The only reliable records are the few extant administrative documents, which may supply reasonably firm information on matters of recruitment and supply. Even with the assistance of these records, considerable variation remains among the overall figures given by modern scholars.

Lot accepts the figures of the English historian Ramsay, who has Edward's army approaching 10,000 men, 1,200 knights, and the remainder archers and spearmen, several thousand of these being mounted (hobelers). Delbruck suggests a number between 14,000 and 20,000 on the basis of what are judged to be fairly reliable figures for the size of the besieging army with which Edward invested Calais shortly after the battle of Crecy. Oman's figures run slightly less. He proposes an army of 2,400 horsemen and about 10,000 foot soldiers. Both Delbrück and Lot believe the French army may have been the smaller of the two, Delbrück attributing Philip's confidence to the clear preponderance he enjoyed in heavy-armed knights and to the fact that Edward was apparently seeking to avoid battle.

Edward halted his army just east of Crecy, not directly on the road he expected the French would be taking from Abbeville, but on a rise paralleling that road on the left. A woods and small stream provided some protection for his right flank on that side. To further protect that wing Edward had ditches dug to prevent a charge by horsemen. Edward also reasoned that if the French kept their march to the road, it would be difficult for any but the most disciplined knights not to break rank once they had come abreast of the first English troops. He hoped for that kind of precipitate, unorganized attack; it was only that kind of attack that he felt able to defeat. If the first French soldiers held their attack until the entire army had taken its position opposite the English line, prospects for an English victory would surely fade.

Edward drew up his army in three divisions or "battles," each division composed of a core of pikemen and dismounted knights and each flanked on either side by a screen of archers. Edward ordered his knights to dismount and mingle with the foot soldiers, since there were too few of them to operate as a unit. Their presence among the pikemen would also reassure these foot soldiers that the horsemen were committed to fight it out and that they would not be riding off should the battle take a bad turn. Edward stationed two of the divisions to the left of and facing the road. The third he kept in the rear near a windmill which he used as a lookout tower. Once his men were in their assigned positions, they ate their midday meal and awaited developments.

Philip spent the night at Abbeville, two-and-a-half miles south of Crecy. In the morning after he had heard mass in honor of his saintly ancestor, Louis IX, he set out to find the English. Valuable time was lost in locating the enemy. It was learned that Edward was near Crecy, while the road on which the French were moving would have taken them to the west of that village. The subsequent haste to correct the movement of the army caused considerable delay and confusion. Because of the time lost in correcting the direction of their march, the French did not catch up with the English until the late afternoon, probably around four o'clock. Prudence recommended that before forcing a battle, Philip should permit his tired, hungry men to rest and that is what he and his advisors decided to do. Word to that effect was sent forward to the count of Alençon, who was in command of the forward division. (The French army was also organized in three "battles.")

For the moment all went as ordered. Alençon and the front line halted their advance as instructed, which by this time must have left them almost abreast of the right flank of Edward's army, but the men to the rear continued to press forward. They had either not been properly instructed about the matter of halting or, given their disorganized state, that order could not be carried out. Confusion reigned as the men in back pushed forward and crowded themselves among those who had already halted. It may have been to relieve this situation which promised to get worse, it may have been Philip's impetuosity which got the better of his judgment, or it may have been the realization that he could not hold back his knights once they were moving directly in front of the enemy—whatever the explanation, the French king gave orders to attack.

Froissart speaks of a heavy shower falling at the beginning of the battle, then the clouds cleared and a bright sun emerged to shine directly into the eyes of the attacking Frenchmen. Not only did the English have the sun at their backs, but they also enjoyed the psychological and physical advantages of being on higher ground and having a clear view of the enemy.

The Genoese crossbowmen opened the battle. After three loud shouts which they may have hoped would intimidate the English archers, they raised their crossbows and let fly their bolts. Most of these fell harmlessly in front of the English.[3] It has been suggested that the rain dampened the leather thongs of the crossbows and seriously reduced their efficiency. Then the English archers took a step forward and discharged their arrows in such quantity, according to Froissart, that it appeared to be snowing. When the Genoese crossbowmen, already disconcerted over the failure of their attack, turned about to escape the deadly English arrows, they found their way blocked by ranks of advancing horsemen. Philip, who may have attributed the retreat of his crossbowmen to cowardice or treason, ordered his knights to drive forward, riding and cutting down any crossbowmen who got in their way. "Kill me those scoundrels," he shouted, "for they stop up our road without any reason."

This first attack by the French knights may have been the most furious. In all fifteen or sixteen charges are said to have been made, the last one late in the night. (Froissart says the last came about evensong.) One of the charges against the English right wing proved so savage that Edward felt it necessary to send thirty knights to succor the hard-pressed prince of Wales who was in command. But generally all went badly for the French. Most damaging was the withering fire of the longbowmen. Then there were the charges of English pikemen with their sharp, long knives which they used to disembowel horses and cut the throats of any Frenchmen they could find. Even Edward, so Froissart reports, was chagrined over the ruthless ardor of his pikemen. Among "the Englishmen there were certain rascals," the chronicler wrote, "who went on foot with great knives, and they went in among the men of arms and slew and murdered many as they lay on the ground, both earls, barons, knights, and squires, whereof the king of England was afterwards displeased, for he had rather they had been taken prisoners." A dead count did Edward little good. The handsome ransoms which he could collect from a score of counts for their release might cover the cost of the war!

The French historian Perroy describes the battle as one that gave the English victory but did them little honor. He writes: "In fact, Edward owed his triumph, strange as it may seem, to his numerical inferiority. To have awaited the enemy in the open, to have sought a hand-to-hand fight between the knights, that is, to have waged war according to the rules which he himself respected and his vassals certainly wanted to observe, would have been unpardonable folly. He had to resort to improvised ruses, of which in his heart of hearts, he was somewhat ashamed.... Fences and hedges concealed the despised infantry. First the Welsh archers were ordered, by very rapid fire, to decimate the horses and unhorse the knights. Even a few cannon, still reserved solely for siege warfare, were perhaps used to create panic at the right moment. When the melee began it was a frightful butchery."[4] The following morning, the earl of Salisbury cut to pieces newly arrived foot soldiers sent by several towns but who had been late in reaching Crecy.

French losses were staggering. Proof of the bitterness of the battle and the enormity of the disaster suffered by the French was the long list of great nobles who had lost their lives. These included the duke of Lorraine, the counts of Flanders, Alençon, Auxerre, Harcourt, Sancerre, Blois, Grandpré, Salm, Blamont, and Forez, and the blind king of Bohemia. All told some 1,500 knights and squires are said to have been slain. Philip suffered an arrow wound in the neck and had his horse killed under him. There was clearly no lack of heroism on the part of the French. English losses were light. The name of not one great noble appears among the slain; of course, most English noblemen had remained in England.

Of major importance in contributing to the victory of the English was the defensive position Edward had selected and which he was able to hold throughout the fighting. On July 19, 1333, he had defeated the Scots at Halidon Hill, where he had his army of archers and dismounted knights fighting from a similarly strong defensive position. It is also a tribute to Edward's sagacity that he was able to hold his army to fighting a wholly defensive battle. Even after the battle, he gave strict orders against conducting any kind of pursuit. Had a band of Englishmen ridden off to follow up their victory with looting, for instance, they might have found themselves quickly overwhelmed by French knights who either had not taken part in the battle or, having dispersed, were anxious to resume it. The inability of the French knights to break Edward's defensive position may be traced to the failure of the crossbowmen to do their job, then to the lack of discipline on the part of the French knights. They should never have engaged the enemy until they had all reached a position in front of the English, when they could have attacked all along the line.

The role of the longbowmen was probably decisive. Philip's personal mishaps—his neck wound and his slain horse—were the work of archers. This point is nonetheless worth pondering, namely, that contemporary students of warfare did not feel the longbow had worked any basic change in the art of war. In highland country, where knights were at a disadvantage and could not fight at top efficiency, it unquestionably had its place. At Crecy Edward would gladly have exchanged his archers for an equal number of knights. Throughout the Hundred Years' War, while the English continued to use archers in their battles with the French, both they and the French were convinced that the heavy-armed cavalry constituted the fighting force *par excellence* of the period.

Edward must have been surprised at the ease of his victory, surely at its magnitude. Since he appears to have contemplated nothing beyond making a destructive raid into French territory and since the summer was coming to a close, he gave no thought to exploiting his victory. In this he again showed his prudence. France was still intact, and a few weeks might bring together a new French army equally as large as the one he had defeated and perhaps sobered by the mistakes committed at Crecy.

Edward simply wanted to return to England. He needed a port for embarkation, however, and one that might also serve as a bridgehead for future expeditions to the Continent. So he moved his army to Calais, in the county of

Boulogne, which bordered Flanders to the south. Calais, the best port along the entire seacoast between Brittany and Flanders, would be a difficult city to capture. Wide ditches and a double wall left it impregnable to direct assault. Edward knew he would have to starve it into submission and for this reason encircled the city with an embankment to cut off supplies by land while he had his ships block all access by sea. All during the long winter and spring, he and his army of more than 15,000 men watched the city. Philip did bring up an army the following July and challenged Edward to come out from behind his barricades and fight, but Edward refused. He knew time was on his side, and it was. On August 4, 1347, Calais surrendered. Edward left a garrison in the city and in October returned to England.

What precisely did Edward's spectacular victory at Crecy mean for England and for France? The most immediate consequences of Edward's victory, the capture of Calais, proved of signal importance. As long as the English held this port (until 1558), they had no great fear of a French invasion. Calais also provided them a bridgehead across the straits from Dover that was superior to any in Flanders or faraway Gascony. After the Hundred Years' War, during the period of the so-called Wars of the Roses (1455-85), it was Edward of York's possession of Calais which assured him his ultimate victory over the Lancastrians.

Crecy represented the first major victory which England gained on the Continent as a "national" state. After Crecy, French, German, and other continental states were less inclined to dismiss the English and England as being of little consequence. At the beginning of the Hundred Years' War, England would have been content to hold Gascony as a fief of the French crown provided French officials ceased their efforts to build up the crown's authority in that province. After Crecy the English judged it their right to keep Gascony as their own and to claim what other parts of France the fortunes of war might bring. In short, Edward's victory at Crecy assured the continuation of the conflict known as the Hundred Years' War. That victory, followed by another at Poitiers in 1356 and a third at Agincourt in 1415, kept the English convinced that, despite their marked inferiority in population and resources, they were quite able to hold as much of France as the French themselves did.

8

THE BATTLE OF ANGORA

"His name was Timur.... The birthplace of this deceiver was a village of a lord named Ilgar in the territory of Kesh—may Allah remove him from the garden of Paradise!...Kesh is one of the cities of Transoxiana, about two days distant from Samarkand.... [Timur] and his father were shepherds.... [Some] say that his father was a poor smith, but that he himself from his youth excelled in keenness of intellect and strength; but because of poverty began to commit acts of brigandage and in the course of these exploits was wounded and mutilated; for when he wanted to carry off a sheep which he had stolen one night, the shepherd cleft his shoulder with an arrow and maimed it, and shooting a second arrow at his hip, damaged the hip. So mutilation was added to his poverty and a blemish to his wickedness and fury, with which he went about with his hand against every man."[1]

So wrote Arabshah, who was taken to Samarkand with his mother and brothers, together with thousands of other unfortunates, when the great metropolis of Damascus fell to Timur in 1401 A.D. By this time Timur had made Samarkand the largest, most beautiful, and most successful trading center of middle Asia. Though Arabshah came to Samarkand as a slave, fortune must have smiled on him. He received his education in Samarkand, traveled widely, and eventually served as secretary of Sultan Ahmed Jalayir of Baghdad. If Arabshah retained from his boyhood any bitterness toward Timur for enslaving his family, this was further aggravated in 1401 when Timur captured Baghdad and forced Ahmed Jalayir to flee to Bayazid, the sultan of Ottoman Turkey, for haven. It was against Bayazid that Timur fought the battle of Angora.

Clearly Arabshah is not a sympathetic source of information about Timur's life, yet scholars have accepted as true much of what he wrote of the man. Thus it is generally believed that Timur came from humble origins, probably those of a shepherd, that he was born in 1336 near Kesh (modern Shahrisabz), fifty miles south of Samarkand in Transoxiana, that he turned to brigandage in his youth, and that somewhere during his turbulent career he received wounds which left him crippled in his right arm and leg. He might indeed have received these wounds from an angry shepherd. The noted Arab historian Ibn Khaldun, who visited Timur in his angry camp outside Damascus, declares Timur made this admission to him.[2] This lameness gave Timur the name Tamerlane (from the Persian Timur-Leng or Timur the Lame) and was confirmed in 1914 when his tomb in Samarkand was opened. Finally, that Timur "went about with his hand against every man," as Arabshah charged, is almost true. Probably the only man prior to modern times who caused the slaughter of more people and greater destruction in the course of his empire-building than Timur was his Mongol[3] predecessor, Genghis-khan.

Westerners had little knowledge of the land where Timur was born. Alexander the Great ventured into this unknown region in 329 B.C. before moving southward toward India. Beginning in the twelfth century Nestorian missionaries began to penetrate the curtain which hid these lands from Europe. The man who forced the Christian world to take

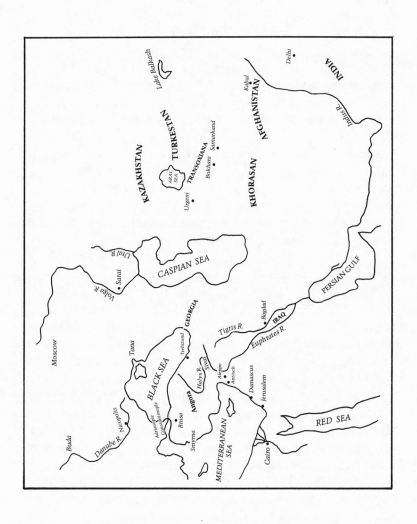

notice was Genghis-khan, the most famous of the Mongol conquerors. The empire he created during his lifetime, and which his sons and grandsons extended, included China, central Asia, Persia, Mesopotamia, part of Poland and Hungary, and the larger part of Russia. While the Mongol empire remained intact only for a short time and tended to disintegrate from the close of the thirteenth century, the fiction of a single Mongol state lived on. There was the tradition that all local chieftains exercised their authority through the higher power bestowed upon them by a descendant of Genghis. Only a Genghisite could be a khan. The local lords (emirs) who were scattered about the Mongol world ruled their tribes and fought their neighbors all presumably as representatives of a titular khan whom they might keep in relative seclusion.

This was the situation in Transoxiana when Timur was born. His family traced its descent from Mongol ancestors and had become Turkicized by the time Timur was born, although Timur always expressed the greatest reverence for the memory of Genghis-khan. Timur early took to the life of a warrior, for which there was ample opportunity in a land as unstable, rich, and fertile as Transoxiana. Thriving cities such as Samarkand and Bokhara graced the land. Long caravans constantly traversed along the Old Silk Road between western Asia and China. In time Timur took service with the emir and so ingratiated himself that he was given the emir's granddaughter as his wife. The next years saw him cooperating with his brother-in-law, Husayn, in establishing their authority over Transoxiana. A major step in his career came when he slew Husayn, married his wife, who was related to Genghis-khan—the only connection Timur ever claimed with the family of the illustrious khan—and in 1370 was elected by the emirs as the heir of Chaghatay (second son of Genghis-khan) and ruler of Transoxiana.

Timur spent the next years consolidating his hold on Transoxiana and extending his authority over the khans of Turkestan and Khorasan. Most of this region once comprised the empire which Genghis had given to Chaghatay, whose successor Timur considered himself to be. This empire lay roughly to the south of Lake Aral and Lake Balkash. Once Timur had brought this huge steppe country under his rule, he made the mistake of his life, according to Arnold Toynbee.[4] Instead of devoting himself to the re-establishment of the Eurasian empire of Genghis-khan and to the hard task of imposing peace on the different hordes of nomads who roamed this enormous region, he turned his attention to the west and to the south, to Russia, the Caucasus, Iran, India, even Syria, where he wasted himself in appallingly destructive campaigns and territorial gains that evaporated almost the minute he died.

Timur led his army north of the Aral Sea in order to force the Turks of Kazakhstan to accept his rule. By moving into this area he invited conflict with the khans of the Golden and White Hordes, whose domains extended westward to Russia and beyond. The first Horde Timur met was the nearest, the White, and Timur found the opportunity to intrude himself when a royal noble, Tokhtamish, fled to him for sanctuary. For several years Timur supplied Tokhtamish with armies with which to fight the khan of the White Horde. Only after a number of unsuccessful attempts, the loss of three armies, and more patience than Timur was accustomed to display did Tokhtamish finally defeat the khan and declare himself ruler of the White Horde (1378). Three years later Tokhtamish defeated the khan of the Golden Horde, took Moscow by treachery, and proclaimed himself khan of both the Golden and White Hordes.

Tokhtamish's success led him to forget who his patron and suzerain had been. In his ambition to erect an even larger empire he opened negotiations with the sultan of Egypt about a possible alliance against Timur. Soon Timur and Tokhtamish were at war, first over the border provinces of Khorasan and Transcaucasia, then over Transoxiana itself. Tokhtamish's most daring venture carried him all the way to Bokhara, but he found the city too strongly fortified to capture. The two men fought several bitter but indecisive battles, the last in April 1395 in the Caucasus. Timur prevailed and destroyed his opponent's army.

Timur now moved into Russia to take Moscow. With Tokhtamish eliminated, the strongest man in Russia was the grand duke of Moscow, who had extended his rule over the neighboring principalities and Novgorod to the north. On Timur's approach the city of Moscow readied itself feverishly for its defense and even sent to the cathedral at Vladimir for the miraculous Icon of Our Lady in order to recruit heaven's assistance. Perhaps by coincidence, the day the icon reached Moscow Timur turned his army about and started back to Samarkand. He left the impression, however, that he had captured Moscow and conquered Russia, and several modern scholars have accepted his propaganda at face value. Timur probably could have taken Moscow, but only after a long siege and heavy losses. He apparently had a high regard for the courage and fighting qualities of the Russian warriors and their allies. No doubt he had learned that it was only by means of treachery that Tokhtamish had earlier taken the city.

Timur turned back toward Transoxiana in any event, plundering and pillaging as he went. All the great trading centers of southern Russia—Saray, Azov (Tana), Astrakhan —were leveled. So completely did he devastate Saray that nothing remained but ruins. As a consequence Timur's campaign in Russia struck a fatal blow at the economic life of the khanate of the Golden Horde. The trade routes which had formerly passed above the Caspian Sea to China and India now shifted southward through Transoxiana. The Golden Horde never recovered the dominant position it had once held in Russia and slowly declined, for which good fortune the Russians could thank the dread Timur.

The course of Timur's campaigns against Tokhtamish had taken him far on his way to becoming a world conqueror—Edgar Allan Poe has Timur musing, "A cottager, I marked a throne of half the world as all my own."[5] By 1395 when he had destroyed Tokhtamish, he had conquered Afghanistan, Moghulistan—this enormous region comprised the country of the Jats and extended south of Lake Balkash to the frontiers of China—Khorasan, Georgia, and Iraq. He had moved into Iraq in 1393. Upon his approach, Ahmed Jalayir, sultan of Baghdad, fled without offering resistance to take refuge with Barquq, the sultan of Egypt. When Timur sent his envoys to Cairo to demand Ahmed's surrender, Barquq not only refused to deliver up his refugee but had one of Timur's envoys executed. He followed up this act of defiance by reaching some kind of understanding with Bayazid, the Turkish sultan, for a united front against Timur. Clearly both Egypt and Ottoman Turkey remained to be dealt with, but their turn would come later.

In the spring of 1398 Timur led his army not against the Ottoman Turks or the sultan of Egypt, his principal foes, but to India. Since India posed no threat to his empire, the only explanation for his going there was the enormous amount of loot he and his army expected to find. For many years Mongol princes had been making raids into northern India. That region, which was dotted with rich cities, lacked political unity. This, together with its warm climate and lush river valleys, made it especially attractive to Timur and his Mongols. By August Timur had reached Kabul in Afghanistan, where envoys sent by anxious rulers from the surrounding states hurried to assure him of their masters' submission. In September he reached the Indus River and by

December was laying siege to the great city of Delhi. The more than 100,000 male captives he had taken on his march southward he slaughtered lest they prove troublesome during the coming siege.

Timur could have taken the city without great difficulty, but its weak ruler expedited the matter for him by taking his army outside the walls and confronting Timur there. Timur, who knew his army would be meeting elephants, had bundles of dried grass tied to the backs of camels and buffaloes, set these on fire, then drove the animals toward the elephants, which stampeded. So the capture of Delhi, the leading city of northwest India, came easier than anticipated, and with it probably the greatest store of booty ever taken by the Mongols at any one time. "The wealth accumulated by generations of sultans disappeared in a few days into the hands of the Tatar."[6] Delhi itself was subjected to three days of pitiless pillaging, after which, as a warning to any who might dare question Timur's will, towers of skulls were erected from the bodies of the slaughtered.

In May 1399 Timur returned to Samarkand from India. He had reached his sixty-third year. Considering his age, the lameness which occasionally necessitated his being transported in a litter, and various maladies which troubled him, one might have expected him to remain in his beautiful capital. But Timur was a hard-bitten nomad who had never liked cities, not even his own Samarkand. There still remained at least two empires that needed humbling, Egypt and Ottoman Turkey. Since the ruling dynasties in both countries together with a good part of their armies hailed from the same stock as Timur's own warriors, these two empires promised to furnish him the greatest test of his career.

By this time Timur had revealed a degree of ruthlessness few men in history have approached. He would permit nothing to get in the way of his ambitions, not even his brother-in-law, Husayn, with whose help he had been able to win control of Transoxiana. Once Husayn had served his purpose, Timur had him removed. Timur encouraged the same ruthlessness in his men. After artisans, scholars, girls, and similarly "useful" people had been separated from a captured city's inhabitants to be sent back to Samarkand, he had his soldiers slaughter the men, women, and children who remained as having no greater worth than chickens. Since enemy cities were of no use to Timur and his nomads, few were left standing. To mind comes the harsh judgment the ancient historian Tacitus, in his *Agricola*, passed on Rome's conquest of Britain: "They create a desolation and call it peace."[7]

Timur's ruthlessness was one of the weapons he employed against his enemies. He let people whose land he coveted know what was in store for those who resisted his advance—razed cities, massacred and enslaved populations, thousands buried alive, pyramids of human skulls with open eyesockets "looking" to the outside. The Syrian cities of Hama and Homs capitulated at his approach. Timur happened to be in a hurry to get to Damascus at the time, and an army was coming up from Egypt, so he could not afford the delay of a siege. Their good fortune in escaping pillage and destruction was quite accidental. It did Damascus no good to surrender. From the beginning of his campaign Timur had marked that city for destruction. His first concern was that of keeping his warriors happy, and nothing made them happier than the days of pillaging, looting, and raping which Timur invariably granted them following the capture of a city.

This history of pillage and slaughter suggests an explanation for Timur's constant campaigning. Only by keeping his men on the move and providing them cities to capture and loot could he keep them satisfied. No sooner had one campaign come to an end with victory, rapine, and slaughter than another shortly got under way. When one considers the fact that although a cripple and nearing seventy Timur set out for China, one must almost conclude that he had become a prisoner either of his own driving ambition to rule the world or of his army's demand for plunder. Had he brought his campaigning to an end, he might have lost control of his army.

For a man as cruel and unprincipled as Timur, his ostensible devotion to the Muslim religion comes as a surprise. Before each battle he would prostrate himself in true Muslim fashion and offer supplication to Allah for victory. On his marches he visited any shrine he came near, and he always justified his campaigns on the grounds that the enemy were infidels, or Christians, or heretical Muslims. Yet all this was sham. He must have hoped that his prayers to Allah would inspire to greater effort those of his warriors who professed the faith he only pretended to. Subsequent scholars have left unaltered the judgment that the late eighteenth-century Edward Gibbon made regarding the genuineness of Timur's faith, that his "superstitious reverence for omens and prophecies, for saints and astrologers, was only affected as an instrument of policy."[8]

In addition to terror and religion, Timur used the more conventional weapon of spying on the enemy as a means for winning his battles. The spy system which he maintained was staffed with men who could speak the languages of the different peoples they might encounter. When it was necessary, for example, they could pass themselves off as Jews and quote the Talmud. Months before Timur met the foe on the battlefield he had sent his spies to bring him all the information he felt he should have. According to Arabshah, these men "brought to him events and news from the furthest borders, described to him what things excelled there and were remarkable, made known to him the weights received there and the prices of things, marked their posts and cities, mapped their roads, rough and smooth, showed their houses and settlements, set forth distances, long and short, and the defiles and wide spaces and borders and bounds to east and west and the names of cities and villages and titles of caravanserais and clans and the people of every place and their leaders, amirs, magnates, excellent men, nobles, rich and poor, and the name, surname, title, and family of everyone and the craft which they practised and tools which they used. And in this way he marked those things with his attention and by his prudence had all the kingdoms in his power."[9] In possession of such information, Timur not only could move his army at an unusually fast pace, but would already have determined before he laid siege to a city what wealth he could expect to find there and which artisans he would be taking back with him to Samarkand.

Timur's army remained in character and organization essentially that of his predecessor, Genghis-khan. It was nomadic in the main, its strength centered in its horse-archers, who were inured to the physical demands of riding long distances in the shortest possible time and under the most adverse conditions. From childhood these men practiced the two skills they would later excel at as warriors, that is, riding horses and shooting arrows. It is said that the only sport these nomads enjoyed was hunting, for they could ride horses and use their bows. Because of their mobility and their endurance—they often rode by moonlight or with the aid of great torches—Timur's warriors frequently came upon an enemy's army and cities long before they had been expected. And even though the Mongol horse was as tough as its rider, one could track the route Timur's army had taken by the corpses of the horses that had been ridden to death.

In the management of his army Timur retained the decimal organization which Genghis-khan had employed. He divided his men into companies of ten, one hundred, one thousand, and ten thousand, with each unit under its individual commander. Every man had his assigned place, which he was not to leave under any circumstances. The horse-archer carried a single-edged sword with a sharp, curved point, a bow and quiver, and a shield. He wore a pointed helmet and a coat of mail and had his hair in a pigtail. His mount carried some protective material about its chest and shoulders. Each two men were required to take a spare mount to serve the one who would first need it. Timur made use of foot soldiers, something Genghis-khan had not done, although they normally performed tasks other than that of fighting. They might serve as sappers and miners, to man the siege machines, to operate the flamethrowers, or to help with the transport of ladders, scaffolding, and tools. Since Timur never appeared to be lacking in siege equipment when he reached an enemy city, the number of men assigned such subsidiary roles may have equaled that of the warriors themselves. Timur used gunpowder, but for blowing up walls, not for firearms.

Of Timur's principal enemies, Turkey and Egypt, Egypt was the first of the two Timur decided to humble. This ancient country had passed through eras of greatness and decline and was enjoying one of its more prosperous moments under the rule of its Mameluke sultan. The first Mamelukes to come to Egypt had been slaves, chiefly Turks and Circassians, who were brought from Russia, the Caucasus, and central Asia to shore up the Egyptian army and to serve as bodyguards for the sultan. In 1250 the Mamelukes replaced the decadent Ayyubid dynasty with a sultan of their own. Shortly after they crushed a Mongol army some thirty miles north of Jerusalem (1260), then suppressed the last of the surviving Crusader principalities in Syria. While the Mameluke regime had lost much of its earlier vigor, in Barquq it had found a sultan who dared defy Timur and threatened him with the same treatment his predecessors had given the Mongol invaders a century and a half before.

It was Timur's good fortune in the summer of 1400, as he started west on a campaign which was to take him to Syria, that Barquq was no longer around. He had died the year previous and left an uneasy throne to his young son, Faraj. Because of dissension at home over his succession, Faraj would be lucky to hold on to his crown, let alone defeat the formidable Timur. In any event, Timur had not been waiting for Barquq's death before forcing the issue with an enemy he had been planning to conquer. He had a case against Barquq for having executed his envoy. If he was concerned about having some excuse for attacking Egypt, he could have found it in the young sultan's refusal to recognize his suzerainty and to return fugitives who had fled to his court.

As it happened, it was Turkey and not Egypt that first suffered Timur's attack in the summer of 1400. Bayazid, the Turkish sultan, had overrun principalities in eastern Anatolia which had once been under Timur's control, including the city of Sivas on the Halys River. Timur must have deemed it dangerous to move south into Syria without first capturing Sivas and cutting off that Turkish salient which might otherwise have threatened his rear should Bayazid decide to undertake an offensive of his own.

Early August found Timur and his army before the walls of Sivas. The city's fortifications were strong enough to hold for almost a month. They managed to withstand the constant assaults Timur's men made and the damage done by the flame- and stone-throwing machines. What proved fatal in the end was the slow but deadly work done by thousands of sappers, most of them slaves, who undermined the walls. When the city finally fell, the children were herded together and trampled under the hooves of the Mongol horsemen. The Armenian defenders were buried alive, thousands of young women were carried off to grace Mongol harems, and all the remaining men and women, except for Muslims who could ransom themselves, were massacred.

At the appearance of Timur, the sultan of Baghdad went to Bayazid for refuge, but Timur passed by the Ottoman empire. He would deal with its sultan later, after he had disposed of Egypt to the south. His first objective was Aleppo, among the cities of Syria second only to Damascus in size and prosperity. The ever-cautious Timur slowed his march as he approached the city when he learned that a large army had been gathering to meet him, with recruits coming from as far south as Jerusalem. The defenders of Aleppo may have construed Timur's slow advance as weakness. They decided to meet him outside the city, which only expedited their destruction. For three days Timur let his men pillage the city after which he had the population massacred and the city razed.

The terrible fate of Aleppo led Hama to submit forthwith, then Homs and Baalbeck, by which time, early 1401, Timur was nearing Damascus. Timur had planned to destroy this metropolis since its enormous size and wealth would provide the sultan of Egypt an excellent base from which to conduct campaigns to the north against his own empire. But Timur would take his time, since confusion and dissension among the city's authorities—the Syrians and the Egyptians—promised to make his task easier. Faraq had come from Egypt with an army, but he had done so with considerable misgivings since he feared a defeat at the hands of Timur would cost him his shaky throne. Scarcely had he reached Damascus and skirmished with Timur's army than he hurried back to Cairo upon learning that several of his emirs had already turned back without his permission.

Damascus closed its gates and prepared for Timur's assault, while continuing negotiations with the Mongol leader, who had his camp just outside the walls. Ibn

Khaldun, the noted Arab historian, who had come from Egypt with Faraj and who had remained in the city, is our best source for what happened. It appears Timur expressed a desire to see the scholar, so Ibn Khaldun was let down over the walls by means of a rope, since the group which opposed discussing terms with Timur was in possession of the city's gates. For a period of thirty-five days, according to Khaldun's testimony, he visited with Timur and engaged in learned conversations with him on a variety of subjects. Timur asked Khaldun to prepare a detailed geographical study of Maghrib, roughly the region of north Africa west of Egypt, which would give mountains, rivers, and cities "in such a manner that I might seem actually to see it."[10] Was this a mark of Timur's natural curiosity or did he wish to have such information against the day he might wish to take his horse-archers into that distant land?

The first ransom Timur agreed to accept for the price of the city's freedom was one million dinars. When the city leaders delivered this amount, he raised his demand to ten million dinars, then insisted that the wealth of all the merchants and all the wealthy men who had fled the city be turned over to him, together with all the beasts of burden and all weapons. After he had thus assured the city's complete inability to defend itself, he charged the inhabitants with being schismatic Muslims and gave his warriors permission to begin their looting and pillaging. Whether by intent or accident, the city caught fire and was shortly a smoking ruin. Among the famous structures destroyed was the great mosque where thousands had taken refuge. They were killed when the leaden roof fell in. Except for artisans and craftsmen, men who possessed some skill Timur felt Samarkand could use, all the others were slain or enslaved.

Following the fall of Damascus, Timur sent a force to take Antioch, while he led the bulk of his army back to Sivas. He may have intended to strike directly at Bayazid, but since the army he had sent to retake Baghdad had failed in its mission, he marched there himself. It required a siege of six weeks before the Mongols captured the city. Almost a century and a half had passed since Hulagu, Genghis-khan's grandson, had captured and ravaged that city (1258). Now it suffered an even more thorough pillaging. Except for a few ruined monuments, all that remained when Timur and his Mongols rode away were one hundred twenty towers that they had erected from the heads of 90,000 inhabitants they had slaughtered. Timur was now finally ready to bring to bay the last and probably the most dangerous of his enemies, the Ottoman Turkish sultan, Bayazid.

The Ottoman Turks had a long acquaintance with the Mongols; in fact, they had been forced westward out of Turkestan because of pressure from the Mongols. Early in the fourteenth century they had made their way across Asia Minor and under their leader Osman (Othman), who gave his name to the tribe, had established a principality of their own in the northwestern part of the peninsula (Bithynia). Osman's son Orkhan extended Ottoman rule over the greater part of Asia Minor by absorbing what remained there of the dominions of the Seljuk Turks. These Seljuk Turks had moved into that area three hundred years earlier, in the eleventh century, and had erected a powerful empire of their own, which at its height included Syria, Asia Minor, Persia, and Mesopotamia. Traditions of both the Seljuk and Ottoman Turks found their origins in the same Ghuzz tribe.

In 1345 Orkhan took the critical step which was to lead to the extension of the Ottoman empire to Europe when he married the daughter of John V Cantacuzenus, a claimant to the Byzantine throne in Constantinople. The troops he brought to Europe to aid his father-in-law were shortly bolstered with others that in 1354 seized the Gallipoli isthmus. In 1361 he captured Adrianople, the capital of Thrace, after which it served as the capital of European Turkey until 1453 when the Turks gained possession of Constantinople. In 1387 the Turks occupied the great seaport city of Salonika. They were in Europe to stay.

What facilitated these early Turkish successes and others to come was the political fragmentation of the Balkans. Several factors had produced and were aggravating this fragmentation. One factor was what might be called the national aspirations of several of the region's peoples to stake out little empires of their own. Bulgars, Bosnians, Serbs, Hungarians, and Wallachians all had ambitions of ruling themselves, usually within frontiers contested by their neighbors. The peoples of the area were also divided in their religious loyalties, many of them Latin Christians, more of them Greek Orthodox. Neither group wasted any love on the other.

The Byzantine empire, which at one time had exercised effective authority over the greater part of the region, was now the weakest of the group. It had never recovered the vitality it had enjoyed before 1204 when the Crusaders (Fourth Crusade) stormed the city and snuffed out its existence. In 1261 it had revived, but with little more than the city of Constantinople to remind the world of its former greatness. Dynastic controversies kept it in a weakened condition, while Serbia to the west and the Ottoman Turks to the east menaced its existence. Venetians and Genoese meantime siphoned off much of the city's commercial business for themselves.

It was Murad I (1362–89) who placed the Ottoman state on a solid base from which it went on to establish its hegemony over the Balkans and Asia Minor. In 1387, with the help of men supplied him by the vassal Christian states of the Balkans, Murad reduced Karaman, which was the most powerful of the principalities of Asia Minor still not under his rule. With its submission, all of Asia Minor had accepted his authority save distant Sivas whose ruler could count on

Mongol help to maintain his independence. Murad spent the year 1388 reestablishing Turkish authority in Bulgaria and Bosnia. In June 1389, at Kossovo, he confirmed his rule over the entire area when he overwhelmed an allied army of Bulgarians, Wallachians, Bosnians, and Serbs.

The hard-fought victory that the Turks gained at Kossovo inaugurated a period of Turkish domination that was to endure for four centuries. Just before the battle a Serbian patriot assassinated Murad, so Kossovo also marked the accession of his brother Bayazid, known in history as the "Thunderbolt" for the speed and power with which he struck his enemies. In 1390 Bayazid added the sister of the despot of Serbia to his harem. This may have been the most important step he took, since it brought him the help of the heavy-armed Serbian horsemen. It required several more years to force the emirs of Asia Minor, who had revolted upon news of Murad's death, back under Turkish rule. By 1393 when Bayazid had accomplished this, he had also chastened the rebellious Bulgarians and deprived them of their autonomy. He even obliged the Byzantine emperor to demolish the new fortifications he had thrown up about Constantinople.

The rise of Turkish power and its advance toward the Danube had meantime aroused universal concern in western Europe. Most immediately disturbed was Sigismund, the king of Hungary, whose realm lay in the path of Turkish expansion. While Sigismund had gained some minor successes in the course of fighting the Turks, he appreciated the dangerous threat they posed for him and his country. Also deeply concerned was Manuel II (1391–1425), the Byzantine emperor, whose very capital was being hemmed in by the Infidel, and also Pope Boniface IX, who each year saw more Christian lands being engulfed by the Muslim tide. In response to the appeals of Boniface, Manuel, and Sigismund, one of the largest Crusader armies ever assembled gathered from many of the countries of western Europe. Knights from England, France, Italy, Poland, Bohemia, and Germany came to join the Hungarians, who under Sigismund were awaiting them at Buda. Most noticeable for their absence were the Christian warriors from the Balkan states. Those who would be fighting in the coming battle at Nicopolis would do so under the Turkish standards of Bayazid.

The question of how many Crusaders converged on Buda poses the usual problem when medieval sources are studied. How unreliable these can be is suggested by the statement of one chronicler who says the Christian army numbered 100,000 men, of whom 200,000 were lost! But several modern writers do place the size of the Crusader army at 100,000. They accept the figures given by contemporary writers, and why not? Nicopolis proved a battle of immense importance. Delbrück is stingiest of all. He reduces the entire Crusader army to something between 9,000 and 10,000 men, with scarcely more than 7,500 of these taking part in the battle. All were mailed horsemen, however; there is no mention of foot soldiers. Finally, there were Venetian and Genoese boats on hand that had come up the Danube from the Black Sea to lend their assistance.

When Bayazid learned of the Crusader army at Buda, he suspended his siege of Constantinople and began preparations to meet the Christian host. For the moment he was in no hurry. He wished to give the Crusaders time to move deeper into his country. After two weeks when he did set his army on the march, he moved with such speed that he outran the scouts that the Crusaders had sent to bring them information. As a result he surprised the Crusader army, which he found laying siege to Nicopolis.

Nicopolis was the principal Turkish fortress on the Danube. Since the Crusaders lacked siege machines, they had settled themselves around the town in the hope of starving it into submission. Before the Christians realized what had happened Bayazid had taken a strong defensive position about five miles to the south of Nicopolis on a plateau a half-mile wide and protected on both sides by ravines. The Crusaders would have to attack him from the valley below.

This unlucky development did not disturb many of the Crusaders, howver, least of all the French. They were supremely confident of annihilating the unorganized rabble they expected to encounter. They had come, in the words of Froissart, "to conquer the whole of Turkey and to march into the empire of Persia."[11] Rather than have second thoughts about the foe who had outgeneraled them by seizing a strong defensive position, they quarreled among themselves as to who should have the honor of first attacking the Infidel and routing him.

Such confidence was not shared by Sigismund; indeed, the overconfidence of his allies occasioned him and his Hungarians deep anguish. They had learned from experience how fierce the Turkish warriors were, and they knew that these Turks had extended their control over the Balkans not by luck and against weak resistance, but by hard, persistent campaigning against soldiers who were among the toughest in the world. Sigismund argued long that he and his Hungarians should be first to meet the enemy. Not only had they fought him before, but the Hungarian army included horse-archers, not unlike those they would be meeting in the Turkish army. But the French insisted that they should be first to strike a blow, and to their regret, they had their way.

Several parallels have been drawn between the battle fought here at Nicopolis between the Crusaders and the Turks and that fought at Crecy between the English and the French. Most significant is the fact that the victors in both battles occupied strong defensive positions that the enemy approached from lower ground. At Crecy, furthermore, the French had not attacked in an organized mass, but in sallies and waves, and so did the Crusaders at Nicopolis. Another circumstance that may establish a third parallel between Nicopolis and Crecy is the probability that the victors in both cases enjoyed a slight superiority in numbers.

The scholar encounters the same problem in stating the size of the Turkish army at Nicopolis as he did in the case of the Christian army. Christian sources of the period confront the reader with hopelessly exaggerated figures, no doubt in the hope of accounting in the most charitable way for the overwhelming defeat that the Crusader army suffered. In view of the strategy which the Crusaders employed, or rather the lack thereof, there remains no necessity of crediting the Turks with numerical superiority to explain their victory. The 400,000 men in the Turkish army suggested by one medieval writer is palpably absurd, and also unrealistic is the 100,000 which several modern scholars propose. Delbrück, who tends to be a conservative judge in his use of the statistics furnished by medieval chroniclers, scales down their figures to a Turkish army of some 11,000 to 12,000 men. This would leave Bayazid a distinct advantage in manpower and one which the defensive position he held would tend to magnify.

The different kinds of warriors that Bayazid had under his command may also have represented something of an advantage. The men supplied by the sultan's Christian subject states included both horsemen and foot soldiers. In terms of equipment and armaments the heavy-armed horsemen resembled the knights in the Crusader army, although their number was smaller. The majority of Bayazid's Christian allies came from Serbia, where the prince was a brother-in-law of the sultan. These Serbs are said to have fought valiantly both at Nicopolis and later at Angora.

The Turkish warriors in Bayazid's army included highly disciplined soldiers together with others having less professional training. Among the latter would be counted light-armed horsemen, a kind of irregular cavalry that might ride ahead of the main army in order to disrupt the enemy's formation or harass him about his flanks. On occasion such light-armed horsemen served as decoys and simulated flight after the first encounter. The unsuspecting enemy would dash forward in expectation of an easy victory, only to be caught in a trap.

The real strength of the Turkish army in the late fourteenth century lay in the Sipahis and Janissaries. The Sipahis were mailed horsemen, and Orkhan is credited with having introduced them. They served initially as an imperial bodyguard. As their number grew, they came to constitute the core of the army. Their principal weapon was the bow and arrow, or at least this was the weapon they employed against the enemy when they charged on their speedy horses. Once they had expended their arrows and had come to close quarters they used lances, scimitars, and daggers. Man to man they were no match for the more heavily armed western European knight, but the combination of speed and arrows often sufficed to bring them a victory before they had actually closed with the enemy.

The most uniquely Turkish branch of Bayazid's army was the Janissaries, or "new troops." The majority of these warriors had been taken from their homes when still boys as a kind of tribute which the sultan exacted from the peoples, mostly Christian, whom he subjugated. They were reared in their own special quarters, given highly specialized training as archers, and indoctrinated by dervishes into the religion of Islam. They did not marry or have families, and they knew no home other than their barracks and no masters but their commanders and the sultan. That they gained renown for their skill as warriors and also for their unquestioned loyalty to the sultan is understandable. They served as foot-archers. When an able commander could synchronize their attack with that of the Sipahis, they made the Turkish army one of the best, if not the best, of the period. While the most glorious pages in the history of the Janissaries lay in the future, they already numbered some 5,000 here at the close of the fourteenth century. They appear to have distinguished themselves in winning the victory for the sultan at Nicopolis.

Even before the Christians and Turkish hosts joined battle at Nicopolis, the principal weakness of the Crusader army had come to view. This was the absence of a unified command. Sigismund, king of Hungary, was only officially in charge. Had he not consented to permit the French to advance first against the enemy, for example, they would have done so on their own. Sigismund could never even be certain that the Wallachians and Transylvanians who were his subjects would respect his orders. His army, in short, possessed the chief weakness of the traditional feudal army.

Sigismund, in a last desperate effort to persuade the French to permit him and his Hungarians to be first to advance against the Turks, sent his marshal and then came to implore them in person. But the French insisted on having their glory. In traditional knightly fashion they charged up the hill against the Turkish vanguard composed of irregular cavalry and foot-archers, the latter probably Janissaries. In vain did Sigismund urge them to slow their advance and wait for the main army to catch up. They refused and, as expected, had no difficulty scattering the Turkish horsemen they met. It was a different story with the Janissaries. Not only did the movement of the French grind to a halt, but in the midst of a bitter struggle with the Janissaries they suddenly found themselves attacked on their flanks and rear by the Sipahis who had remained hidden behind a hill. Within a short time they were encircled and annihilated.

By the time Sigismund had come up with his army and his German and Polish allies it was too late. The Wallachians and Transylvanians did not even wait to fight. When they saw the horses that the French knights had ridden up the hill gallop back riderless, they simply left the field. Sigismund was among the few to escape. He was persuaded to leave the field and flee by boat down the Danube. Although the battle ended with the destruction of the Crusader army, the fighting must have been furious. It is said that Bayazid was so incensed over the large number of casualties he had suffered that he ordered all prisoners over twenty slaughtered and those younger enslaved, except for the few for whom a ransom could be expected.

The destruction of the Crusader army at Nicopolis cleared the decks for the decisive clash between Bayazid and Timur. Given the character of the two men, a battle to the death that would leave one the unquestioned victor was inevitable. Timur could not rest until all rulers along the ever-lengthening borders of his empire had accepted his suzerainty. Bayazid would be content with nothing short of ruling a powerful empire that would stretch from the Danube to the Euphrates and perhaps even to the Nile.

It was Timur who forced the issue. Shortly after Bayazid returned to his siege of Constantinople, Timur demanded the surrender of Ahmed Jalayir, the sultan of Baghdad. A defiant Bayazid promptly cut off the beard of Timur's envoy, then sent back an insulting reply. His missive as reported by Arabshah read: "I know that this speech will rouse you to invade our countries: but if you should not come, may your wives be condemned to triple divorce." To which Timur is said to have exclaimed: "The son of Othman is mad, for he was prolix and sealed the purpose of his letter with the mention of women." For according to Arabshah, among the Mongols "the mention of women is a crime and grave offence, so much so that they do not even pronounce the word woman and studiously avoid it, saying, if a daughter is born to one of them: 'One who hides behind the veil has been born,' or 'a mistress of the bed,' or 'a veiled one,' or something of that sort."[12]

As the fatal moment approached when Bayazid and Timur would clash, the Christian world took heart. What popes and Christian Europe had long hoped to see, a war between Muslims and Mongols, appeared finally about to come to pass. Particularly grateful for the approaching contest was Constantinople, whose walls were again being invested. John, the regent of Constantinople, opened negotiations with Timur, as did Charles VI of France. Even the tiny state of Trebizond sent him tribute and offered him the use of its port. The Genoese who controlled Pera, the part of Constantinople above the Golden Horn, promised to send ships and to block any Turkish reinforcements which might wish to cross from Europe to Asia Minor should Bayazid do battle there.

Timur no doubt took these pledges for little worth. He knew all Christian states would like nothing better than Bayazid and himself to destroy each other. None of these states would bestir itself, in any event, until it had become reasonably clear which side would triumph.

In the late spring of 1402 Timur held a grand review of his forces at Sivas where he had ordered them to gather for final preparations for the campaign against Bayazid. Detachments arrived from all parts of his empire. Most of the warriors were horse-archers, some wearing coats of mail, others armor plate. Those from Samarkand were especially colorful in their brilliant outfits, furnishing therewith convincing evidence of the enormous amount of loot which Timur had accumulated in his capital and of the workmanship of the artisans he had brought there. Each company had its colored banners—crimson, yellow, white, purple, and others—with matching saddles, clothes, shields, quivers, belts, and bucklers.

Bayazid, for his part, gathered his army at Brusa, capital of Turkish Asia Minor. There had come his own Turkish troops, the Janissaries and Sipahis, together with the heavy-armed horsemen from Serbia and other horsemen and infantry supplied him by his Christian vassals in the Balkans. Warriors, possibly equal in number to these "European" forces, arrived from the various principalities of Asia Minor, some of which had once been subject to Mongol lords who had fled to Timur when the Turks had overrun them. There were no troops from Egypt. Faraj had ignored Bayazid's appeal for assistance.

From Brusa, Bayazid led his army toward the east. He followed a road that took him through the defiles and valleys about Tuqat, roughly paralleling the course of the Halys River some seventy-five miles to the south. The road that he used was the shortest to the eastern provinces of Asia Minor, and Bayazid's information had it that Timur would be approaching via that route. He should have waited for Timur in his well-watered camp in Angora, and modern writers fault him for not doing so. But Bayazid had supreme confidence in the ability of his army to defeat Timur, a confidence strengthened by what had recently happened at Nicopolis. He did not relish the thought of Timur's moving into his domain and pillaging its towns and villages. Bayazid might also have feared Timur would take his time in giving battle, something he himself could ill afford to do. The longer the interval after Nicopolis during which Timur would be tying down his forces in Asia Minor, the greater the opportunity for the Christian nations to recruit a new Crusader army.

Timur could tarry. For him there was no danger of revolt brewing in his rear, so let Bayazid make the first move. He knew Bayazid could not wait and might even do something foolish in his anxiety to hurry the matter to a head. Instead of leading his army westward along the shortest route, which would have had him meeting Bayazid head-on, Timur decided to take the longer route, an easier one, along the Halys River. On the way through this river valley his men would find plenty of plunder for themselves and ample pasture for their horses. This somewhat indirect route would also bring him to the rear of Bayazid's army, which would close the door to any retreat on the part of the Turks should Timur gain the victory.

Six days of marching from Sivas brought Timur and his army half the distance to Angora, that is, to Qaysariyah, where his men rested for another four days. Four more days of riding carried them to Qir Shahr, then another three days to Angora, during which Timur hurried his men along by forced marches in the hope of surprising the Turks. Once there he occupied the camp Bayazid had left less than two weeks before, circled it with ditches and palisades, cut off the water supply to the city, and invested it. He was about to make a final assault on the city's walls when he learned that Bayazid had turned his army about and was approaching from the east.

For Bayazid and his army, the march back to Angora had become a nightmare. The men were already tired when word reached Bayazid that Timur had bypassed him, and the sultan had no choice but order his men to turn about and return to Angora. His fear that Timur might have taken over his camp proved well founded as did his fear that Timur would have destroyed all possible sources of water. For the Turkish army the situation was truly desperate. Bayazid's men were worn out and thirsty, and there was no hope of finding water. "For them the day was lost before it had begun."[13]

The two armies met on Friday, July 28, 1402, to the north-east of Angora, in the plain of Chibukabad, the probable site of a great victory that the Roman Pompey gained over Mithradates in 65 B.C. Bayazid dared not wait to rest his men since their thirst was intolerable. He needed to fight to get to water. He placed his right wing under command of Lazarovic of Serbia, his brother-in-law, and gave him some Turkish horsemen to support his heavy-armed cavalry. His left wing he assigned to his son, Sulayman; it was composed of troops from Macedonia and from Asia Minor. Many of the latter were from principalities once under Timur's suzerainty. The center, made up of Janissaries and Sipahis, he kept for himself. Other horsemen he held in reserve.

The army with which Timur opposed Bayazid had thirty elephants from India in the front line. Both armies came equipped with Greek fire, but neither the fire nor the elephants played a significant role. It was to be a contest between armies of horsemen. "Probably no greater cavalry battle has ever been recorded in history."[14]

Because this battle between the two most powerful men in the world was to have major consequences, both contemporary and modern writers tend to grow lyrical in assessing the number of men in the respective armies. The modern scholar Grousset declares almost a million men were engaged. The Bavarian Schiltberger—he had survived the Christian defeat at Nicopolis and was taken into the Turkish service—says Bayazid had 1.4 million men under his command and Timur 200,000 more. The most conservative figure gives approximately 20,000 to each side. The case against much larger armies rests on the argument that larger forces could not have marched through Anatolia in the manner of Timur's and Bayazid's armies; neither could a Mongol army much larger than 20,000 have found space for itself within the fortified camp at Angora.

Still, it was not size or courage that decided the battle, or possibly even the thirst and weariness of Bayazid's men. Timur outgeneraled his opponent as Bayazid had outgeneraled the Crusaders at Nicopolis. He positioned his army to the west of Bayazid where he could cut off his retreat, and he had his army well rested and eager to fight. Above all, during the months preceding he had his agents moving among the Bayazid's Mongol troops, and the agents had succeeded in corrupting them. These warriors had promised to desert Bayazid once the battle was joined. They may have been unwilling allies of Bayazid in the first place, and they knew their former lords were with Timur. They must, furthermore, have felt confident Timur would win, and they knew how handsomely the Mongol general rewarded his troops. It is also likely they did not relish the thought of battling their fellow Mongols.

About ten in the morning to the sound of trumpets and drums the battle was joined. That the battle raged until nightfall comes as a surprise since what apparently decided the issue was the desertion of the Mongol warriors in the Turkish army. This must have happened early in the battle. First those from Sarukhan, Aydin, Mentesha, and Kermiyan left their position, then those from the other eastern principalities. Had these deserters left the field, their action might not have proved fatal, but they remained to fight and struck Sulayman's left wing from the rear while it was being pounded by Timur's main force from the front. Lazarovic and his Serbian heavy-armed horsemen had meantime pushed forward so far against their opposition that Bayazid sent warning to pull back lest they find themselves surrounded. Then when Lazarovic learned of Sulayman's plight, he led his horsemen to the rescue and covered the retreat of the sultan's son. The last Turkish group to continue the fight was the center, where Bayazid had his Janissaries and Sipahis fighting furiously until the end. Just before dark Bayazid decided to flee, but his horse was killed under him, and he was taken captive.

Timur sent a force to pursue Sulayman, who had escaped to Brusa with a large part of his father's treasure. By the time Timur's men reached Brusa, Sulayman had gone, so the Mongols contented themselves with pillaging and firing this important trade center. Without any great opposition, Mongol forces then spread over Asia Minor to the Hellespont and the Aegean, plundering as they went, with Timur following after in more leisurely fashion. By December he had reached Smyrna, the property of the Knights of St. John and the last Christian stronghold in Asia Minor. The Turks had failed in several attempts to capture the city, but Timur wasted scarcely two weeks before its walls. As usual it was his sappers who expedited matters by undermining the fortifications. When these collapsed, both garrison and population were put to the sword.

Timur now returned to Samarkand. He had accomplished what he had planned to do. Constantinople and Pera agreed to pay tribute, as did Sulayman, Bayazid's son and heir, and Faraj, the sultan of Egypt. Timur treated Bayazid with courtesy, it is said, although he kept him in chains at night and during the day had him travel in a litter carried on two horses and surrounded by a grille. This grille must have suggested the early story that he was confined to an iron cage and that he died from mistreatment, a story which Gibbon has dismissed as fiction. None the less, Bayazid's health seems to have deteriorated immediately, and he died early in March (1403). As fortune would have it, not much more time was allotted Timur. Once back in Samarkand he promptly began preparations for a campaign into China. He left the city in late December 1404, but grew ill shortly after and died on January 19. He was buried in Samarkand in a coffin of ebony.

The principal consequence of the great battle fought at Angora was the fifty-year respite Timur's victory gained for the city of Constantinople. That metropolis might otherwise have fallen to the Turks in 1402 instead of 1453. While its eventual fall was probably inevitable, those fifty years enabled western Europe to recover itself following the catastrophe at Nicopolis. Had the Turks on their road to conquest not been halted at Angora, they might shortly have captured not only Constantinople but Budapest and Vienna as well. It is also significant that following Angora the Turks moved their Asiatic capital from Brusa to Adrianople, a step that may have encouraged them to concentrate their efforts on expansion in Europe rather than in the Near East.

NOTES

PREFACE

1. Fletcher Pratt, *The Battles That Changed History* (New York: Hanover House, 1956), p. 12.
2. Helen Waddell, *The Desert Fathers* (Ann Arbor: University of Michigan Press, 1957), p. 35.
3. J. Otto Maenchen-Helfen, *The World of the Huns* (Berkeley: University of California Press, 1973), p. xxvi.

CHAPTER 1: MEDIEVAL WARFARE

1. See H. Mattingly, trans., *Tacitus on Britain and Germany* (Harmondsworth: Penguin Books Ltd., 1951), p. 112.

CHAPTER 2: THE BATTLE OF CHALONS

1. Dante, who refers to Attila as a "scourge on earth," has him plunged in a river of boiling blood. *Inferno*, XII, 135.
2. Jordanes, *The Origins and Deeds of the Goths*, trans. by Charles Mierow (Princeton: Princeton University Press, 1908), pp. 39-40.
3. *Ammianus Marcellinus*, trans. by John Rolfe, *The Loeb Classical Library* (Cambridge: Harvard University Press, 1939), III, pp. 381-87.
4. J. Otto Maenchen-Helfen, *The World of the Huns* (Berkeley: University of California Press, 1973), p. 204.

5. They may be more precisely classified as Indo-Iranian nomads. They were the only non-Germanic people of the migration period to make important settlements in western Europe.

6. The exact "legal" relationship of the Vandals with the empire remains a point of dispute. They may have enjoyed the status of *foederati*. See Frank M. Clover, "Flavius Merobaudes, A Translation and Historical Commentary," *Transactions of the American Philosophical Society*, 61 (1971), pp. 52-54.

7. From a fragment (*Fragmenta Historicorum Graecorum*) cited by Maenchen-Helfen, *The World of the Huns*, p. 38.

8. Jordanes, *The Goths*, p. 57.

9. C.D. Gordon, *The Age of Attila* (Ann Arbor: University of Michigan Press, 1960), p. 95.

10. Ibid., p. 96.

11. This was a title held by the leading generals in the eastern Roman Empire. In the western empire it became the rule in the fifth century, for only one man to have that title. He was, therefore, the commander in chief.

12. "I disregard the often told melodramatic story of the vicious Princess Honoria, her clandestine engagement to Attila, and what follows from it. It has all the earmarks of Byzantine court gossip." Maenchen-Helfen, *World of the Huns*, p. 20.

13. Jordanes, *The Goths*, pp. 57-58.

14. The *laeti* were Germans who had been settled on lands within the empire. In return for these lands they were to do military service. *Foederati* were troops supplied by allied peoples along the frontier who were pledged to defend that frontier.

15. Of four Frankish units listed in the *Notitia Dignitatum* in c. 425, all were cavalry regiments. See Bernard S. Bachrach, *Merovingian Military Organization* (Minneapolis: University of Minnesota Press, 1972), p. 14.

16. "I refrain from trying to reconstruct the tactics of the battle; any such attempt only leads to arbitrary suppositions. The confused and contradictory information of Jordanes reveals that he himself had no understanding of how the battle took

its course." Ulf Täckholm, "Aetius and the Battle on the Catalaunian Fields," *Opuscula Romana*, 7 (1969), p. 267.
17. Bernard S. Bachrach, *A History of the Alans in the West* (Minneapolis: University of Minnesota Press, 1973), p. 66.
18. This is how Jordanes describes the situation: "The battlefield was a plain rising by a sharp slope to a ridge, which both armies sought to gain; for advantage of position is a great help. The Huns with their forces seized the right side, the Romans, the Visigoths and their allies the left, and then began a struggle for the yet untaken crest." Jordanes, *The Goths*, p. 61.
19. Charles Oman in his *History of the Art of War* (London: Methuen, 1898), p. 21, credits the defeat of Attila to the Visigothic cavalry, which rode down the more lightly armed Hunnic horsemen.
20. *Cambridge Medieval History* (Cambridge: University Press, 1936), I, p. 398.

CHAPTER 3: THE BATTLE OF THE YARMUK

1. J.J. Saunders, *A History of Medieval Islam* (New York: Barnes & Noble, 1965), p. 14.
2. Philip K. Hitti, *History of the Arabs* (London: Macmillan, 1970), p. 25.
3. Ibid., p. 19.
4. Andreas N. Stratos, *Byzantium in the Seventh Century* (Amsterdam: Adolf M. Hakkert, 1972), p. 43. Also see Hitti, *Arabs*, p. 26.
5. Hitti, *Arabs*, p. 145.
6. See the description of Khalid's maneuver, p. 72.
7. Philip K. Hitti, *The Origins of the Islamic State*, a translation of the *Kitab Futuh Al-Buldar* (Beirut: Khayats, 1966), p. 211.
8. Stratos, *Byzantium*, p. 49, n. 162.
9. Stratos, *Byzantium*, p. 47, n. 50.
10. Hitti, *Arabs*, p. 150.
11. Omar, in Mecca, must have been confident his Arabs would destroy the Byzantine army, since here at this critical stage

in the campaign he demoted Khalid, his ablest general, and gave the command of the Arab forces to another. See note 13.

12. Of such Arab allies, Edward Gibbon observed: "Their service in the field was speedy and vigorous; but their friendship was venal, their faith inconstant, their enmity capricious." *The Decline and Fall of the Roman Empire* (New York: Random House, 1932), III, p. 64.

13. Khalid had actually been relieved of his command by Omar just before the battle, but Abu Ubayda, the man who replaced him, kept this information a secret until victory had been won, lest the transfer of authority arouse dissension among the Arab chieftains. Omar did not doubt Khalid's generalship, rather his lack of administrative ability, which the conquered area would most need in the years to come.

CHAPTER 4: THE BATTLE OF HASTINGS

1. Frank Stenton, *Anglo-Saxon England* (Oxford: Clarendon Press, 1943), p. 588.

2. Frank Stenton, *The Bayeux Tapestry* (New York: Phaidon Press, 1957), p. 16.

3. A castle of the simple *motte* and *bailey* type is shown in the Bayeux Tapestry. The *motte* was a mound of earth surmounted by a palisade and a wooden keep and girdled by a ditch. Around this was a courtyard, called a *bailey*, which was in turn protected by a ditch and a palisade. Here the garrison had its quarters and supplies. Under heavy attack the men would move inside the *motte* area.

4. The chronicler says Harold "was pierced in the eye," although this is doubted.

5. See G.N. Garmonsway, trans., *The Anglo-Saxon Chronicle* (London: J.M. Dent and Sons Ltd., 1953), p. 199.

CHAPTER 5: THE BATTLE OF HATTIN

1. As quoted in T.S.R. Boase, *Kingdoms and Strongholds of the Crusaders* (London: Thames and Hudson, 1971), p. 126.

2. See Charles Oman, *A History of the Art of War* (London: Methuen, 1898), pp. 306-14, for this quotation and those immediately following.
3. Oman, *Art of War*, p. 67.

CHAPTER 6: THE BATTLE OF BOUVINES

1. William, Eleanor's first son by Henry, died in infancy. Four sons reached maturity: Geoffrey, Henry, Richard, and John.
2. The wound was caused by a bolt shot from a crossbow.
3. See also J.F. Verbruggen, *The Art of Warfare in Western Europe during the Middle Ages* (New York: American Elsevier, 1976), pp. 223-28, who suggests 5,000 or 6,000 foot soldiers for Philip's army, 7,500 for Otto's.
4. Ibid., p. 228
5. Ibid., p. 236. Verbruggen believes 169 imperial knights were slain.

CHAPTER 7: THE BATTLE OF CRECY

1. The staple was essentially the principal market or trading center.
2. A son, born posthumously, died five days after birth.
3. One chronicler says the rain reduced the tensile qualities of the crossbow cords. See Charles Oman, *A History of the Art of War* (London: Methuen, 1898), p. 610, note 1.
4. Edouard Perroy, *The Hundred Years War* (London: Capricorn Books, 1951), p. 119.

CHAPTER 8: THE BATTLE OF ANGORA

1. See J.H. Sanders, trans., *Tamerlane, or Timur the Great Amir*, from *The Arabic Life by Ahmed Ibn Arabshah* (London: Luzac and Co., 1936), pp. 1-2.
2. See Walter J. Fischel, *Ibn Khaldun and Tamerlane* (Berkeley: University of California Press, 1952), p. 47.
3. The terms *Mongol*, *Tatar*, and *Tartar* are used indiscriminately, although Mongols and Tatars were originally

distinct tribes in Mongolia. *Tartar* is a corruption of *Tatar*. The term was applied to Mongols by medieval Christians possibly because they looked upon these Mongols as demons from the underworld (*tartarus*).

4. Arnold Toynbee, *A Study of History* (abridgement of volumes 1-7) (New York: Oxford University Press, 1946), vol. 1, 345.

5. Thomas Ollive Mabbott, ed., *Collected Works of Edgar Allen Poe* (Cambridge: Harvard University Press, 1969), vol. 1, p. 33.

6. Hilda Hookham, *Tamburlaine the Conqueror* (London: Hodder and Stoughton, 1962), p. 198.

7. See H. Mattingly, trans., *Tacitus on Britain and Germany* (Harmondsworth: Penguin Books Ltd., 1951), p. 80.

8. Edward Gibbon, *The Decline and Fall of the Roman Empire* (New York: Random House, 1932), vol. 2, p. 1253.

9. See Sanders, *Tamerlane*, pp. 300-301.

10. See Fischel, *Ibn Khaldun and Tamerlane*, p. 35.

11. John Bourchier, trans., *The Chronicle of Froissart* (London: David Nutt, 1903), vol. 6, p. 193 (modernized).

12. See Sanders, *Tamerlane*, p. 173.

13. Michael Prawdin, *The Mongol Empire: Its Rise and Legacy*, 2d ed. (London: G. Allen and Unwin, 1967), p. 495.

14. Lynn Montross, *War Through the Ages*, rev. 3d. ed. (New York: Harper, 1960), p. 219.

BIBLIOGRAPHY

CHAPTER 1: MEDIEVAL WARFARE

Bachrach, Bernard S. *Merovingian Military Organization, 481-751*. Minneapolis: University of Minnesota Press, 1972.

Beeler, John. *Warfare in Feudal Europe, 730-1200*. Ithaca: Cornell University Press, 1971.

Blair, Claude. *European Armour circa 1066 to circa 1700*. London: Batsford, 1958.

Cleator, P.E. *Weapons of War*. New York: Crowell, 1968.

Creasy, Edward. *The Fifteen Decisive Battles of the World*. London: H. Milford, 1915.

Delbrück, Hans. *Geschichte Der Kriegskunst*. Dritter Teil. Das Mittelalter. Berlin: W. de Gruyter, 1964.

Dupuy, R. Ernest, and Dupuy, Trevor N. *The Encyclopedia of Military History from 3500 B.C. to the Present*. New York: Harper and Row, 1970.

Fuller, J.F.C. *The Decisive Battles of the Western World*, vol. 1. London: Byre and Spottiswoode, 1954.

Fuller, J.F.C. *A Military History of the Western World*. New York: Funk and Wagnalls, 1954.

Hewitt, John. *Ancient Armour and Weapons in Europe*. Graz: Akademische Druck u. Verlagsanstalt, 1967.

Lot, Ferdinand. *L'Art Militaire et les Armees au Moyen Age en Europe et dans le Proche Orient*, vol. 2. Paris: Payot, 1946.

Mitchell, Joseph B., and Creasy, Edward S. *Twenty Decisive Battles of the World*. New York: Macmillan, 1964.

Montross, Lynn. *War Through the Ages*, rev. ed. New York: Harper, 1960.

Oman, Charles. *A History of the Art of War: The Middle Ages from the Fourth to the Fourteenth Century*, vols. 1 and 2. London: Methuen, 1924.

Pratt, Fletcher. *The Battles That Changed History*. New York: Hanover House, 1956.

Verbruggen, J.F. *The Art of Warfare in Western Europe During the Middle Ages*. New York: American Elsevier, 1977.

Wise, Terence. *Medieval Warfare*. New York: Hastings House, 1976.

Zook, David, and Higham, Robin. *A Short History of Warfare*. New York: Twayne, 1966.

CHAPTER 2: THE BATTLE OF CHALONS

Bachrach, Bernard S. *A History of the Alans in the West*. Minneapolis: University of Minnesota Press, 1973.

Bury, J.B. *History of the Later Roman Empire*, vols. 1 and 2. New York: Macmillan, 1958.

Cambridge Medieval History, vol. 1, The Christian Roman Empire and the Foundation of the Teutonic Kingdoms. Cambridge: Cambridge University Press, 1936.

Gibbon, Edward. *The History of the Decline and Fall of the Roman Empire*.

Gordon, C.D. *The Age of Attila*. Ann Arbor: University of Michigan Press, 1960.

Hodgkin, Thomas. *Italy and Her Invaders*, vol. 2. Oxford: Clarendon Press, 1892.

Hutton, Edward. *Attila and the Huns*. London: Constable, 1915.

Jones, A.H.M. *The Later Roman Empire, 284-602*. Oxford: B. Blackwell, 1964.

Jordanes, *The Origins and Deeds of the Goths*, translated by Charles Mierow. Princeton: Princeton University Press, 1908.

Maenchen-Helfen, J. Otto. *The World of the Huns*. Berkeley: University of California Press, 1973.

Thompson, E.A. *A History of Attila and the Huns.* Oxford: Clarendon Press, 1948.

CHAPTER 3: THE BATTLE OF THE YARMUK

Brockelmann, Carl. *History of the Islamic Peoples.* London: Capricorn Books, 1949.

Cambridge Medieval History, vol. 4, The Eastern Roman Empire. Cambridge: Cambridge University Press, 1923.

Gibbon, Edward. *The History of the Decline and Fall of the Roman Empire.*

Glubb, John Bagot. *The Great Arab Conquests.* London: Hodder and Stoughton, 1963.

Hitti, Philip K. *History of the Arabs.* London: Macmillan, 1970.

Jenkins, Romilly. *Byzantium: The Imperial Centuries A.D. 610-1070.* New York: Random House, 1966.

Saunders, J.J. *A History of Medieval Islam.* New York: Barnes & Noble, 1965.

Shaban, M.A. *Islamic History A.D. 600-750.* Cambridge: Cambridge University Press, 1971.

Stratos, Andreas N. *Byzantium in the Seventh Century.* Amsterdam: Adolf M. Hakkert, 1972.

Vryonis, Speros. *Byzantium: Its Internal History and Relations with the Muslim World.* London: Variorum Reprints, 1971.

CHAPTER 4: THE BATTLE OF HASTINGS

Barlow, Frank. *William I and the Norman Conquest.* New York: Collier, 1965.

Brooke, Christopher. *Europe in the Central Middle Ages, 962-1154.* New York: Rinehart and Winston, 1964.

Brooke, Christopher. *From Alfred To Henry III, 871-1272.* Edinburgh: T. Nelson, 1961.

Douglas, David C. *William the Conqueror.* Berkeley: University of California Press, 1964.

Hollister, C. Warren. *Anglo-Saxon Military Institutions.* Oxford: Clarendon Press, 1962.

Hollister, C. Warren. *The Impact of the Norman Conquest.* New York: Wiley, 1969.

Körner, Sten. *The Battle of Hastings, England, and Europe, 1035-1066.* Lund: C.W.K. Gleerup, 1964.

Loyn, H.R. *The Norman Conquest.* London: Hutchinson, 1965.

Poole, Austin Lane. *Medieval England.* Oxford: Clarendon Press, 1958.

Sayles, G.O. *The Medieval Foundations of England.* London: Methuen, 1948.

Stenton, Frank. *Anglo-Saxon England.* Oxford: Clarendon Press, 1943.

Stenton, Frank. *The Bayeux Tapestry.* London: Phaidon Press, 1965.

CHAPTER 5: THE BATTLE OF HATTIN

Baldwin, M.W. *Raymond III of Tripolis and the Fall of Jerusalem, 1140-1187.* Amsterdam: Adolf M. Hakkert, 1969.

Boase, T.S.R. *Kingdoms and Strongholds of the Crusaders.* London: Thames and Hudson, 1971.

Brundage, James A. *The Crusades: A Documentary Survey.* Milwaukee: Marquette University Press, 1962.

Gabrieli, Francesco, trans. *Arab Historians of the Crusades.* London: Routledge and Kegan, Paul, 1969.

Hindley, Geoffrey. *Saladin.* London: Constable, 1976.

Hitti, Philip K. *History of the Arabs.* London: Macmillan, 1970.

La Monte, John L. *Feudal Monarchy in the Latin Kingdom of Jerusalem, 1100 to 1291.* Cambridge: Medieval Academy of America, 1932.

Lane-Poole, Stanley. *Saladin and the Fall of the Kingdom of Jerusalem.* Beirut: Khayats, 1964.

Mayer, Hans Eberhard. *The Crusades,* translated by John Gillingham. Oxford: Oxford University Press, 1972.

Munro, Dana C. *The Kingdom of the Crusaders.* New York: Appleton-Century, 1935.

Setton, Kenneth M., ed. *A History of the Crusades,* vol. 1, The First Hundred Years, edited by M.W. Baldwin. Philadelphia: University of Pennsylvania Press, 1955.

Smail, R.C. *Crusading Warfare, 1097-1193.* Cambridge: Cambridge University Press, 1956.

CHAPTER 6: THE BATTLE OF BOUVINES

Appleby, John T. *John, King of England.* New York: Knopf, 1959.

Barraclough, Geoffrey. *The Origins of Modern Germany.* Oxford: B. Blackwell, 1947.

Cambridge Medieval History, VI, Victory of the Papacy. Cambridge: Cambridge University Press, 1929.

Fawtier, Robert. *The Capetian Kings of France*, translated by Butler and Adam. New York: St. Martin's Press, 1962.

Hampe, Karl. *Germany under the Salian and Hohenstaufen Emperors*, translated by Ralph Bennett. Oxford: B. Blackwell, 1973.

Kantorowicz, Ernest. *Frederick II*, translated by E. Lorimer. London: Constable, 1931.

Packard, Sidney R. *Europe and the Church under Innocent III.* New York: Holt, 1927.

Painter, Sidney. *The Reign of King John.* Baltimore: Johns Hopkins Press, 1949.

Petit-Dutaillis, Charles. *The Feudal Monarchy in France and England.* London: K. Paul, Trench, Trubner, 1936.

Poole, A.L. *From Domesday Book to Magna Carta, 1087-1216.* Oxford: Clarendon Press, 1951.

Smith, Charles E. *Innocent III: Church Defender.* Baton Rouge: Louisiana State University Press, 1951.

CHAPTER 7: THE BATTLE OF CRECY

Burne, Alfred H. *The Crecy War.* London: Eyre and Spottiswoode, 1955.

Cambridge Medieval History, VII, Decline of Empire and Papacy. Cambridge: Cambridge University Press, 1932.

Froissart. *Chronicles.*

Gibbon, Edward. *The History of the Decline and Fall of the Roman Empire.*

Hay, Denys. *Europe in the Fourteenth and Fifteenth Centuries.* New York: Rinehart and Winston, 1966.

Jenkins, Helen. *Papal Efforts for Peace under Benedict XII, 1334-42.* Philadelphia: University of Pennsylvania Press, 1933.

Lucas, H.S. *The Low Countries and the Hundred Years War.* Ann Arbor: University of Michigan Press, 1929.

McKisack, May. *The Fourteenth Century.* Oxford: Clarendon Press, 1959.

Perroy, Edouard. *The Hundred Years War.* London: Capricorn Books, 1951.

Power, Eileen. *The Wool Trade in English Medieval History.* Oxford: Oxford University Press, 1941.

Ramsay, James. *Genesis of Lancaster, 1307-99*, vol. 1. Oxford: Clarendon Press, 1913.

CHAPTER 8: THE BATTLE OF ANGORA

Atiya, Aziz Suryal. *The Crusade in the Later Middle Ages.* London: Methuen, 1938.

Cambridge Medieval History, vol. 8, The Close of the Middle Ages. Cambridge: Cambridge University Press, 1936.

Fischel, Walter J. *Ibn Khaldun and Tamerlane.* Berkeley: University of California Press, 1952.

Gibbon, Edward. *The History of the Decline and Fall of the Roman Empire.*

Grousset, René. *The Empire of the Steppes: A History of Central Asia,* translated by Naomi Walford. New Brunswick: Rutgers University Press, 1970.

Hookham, Hilda. *Tamburlaine the Conqueror.* London: Hodder and Stoughton, 1962.

Inalcik, Halil. *The Ottoman Empire,* translated by Norman Itskowitz and Colin Imber. London: Weidenfeld and Nicolson, 1973.

Lamb, Harold. *Tamerlane the Earth Shaker.* New York: R.M. McBride, 1928.

LeStrange, Guy. *Clavijo's Embassy to Tamerlane 1403-6.* London: G. Routledge and Sons, 1928.

Prawdin, Michael. *The Mongol Empire: Its Rise and Legacy.* London: G. Allen and Unwin, 1967.

Tamerlane, or Timur the Great Amir, translated by J.H. Sanders from *The Arabic Life By Ahmed Ibn Arabshah.* London: Luzac, 1936.

Vernadsky, George. *The Mongols and Russia.* New Haven: Yale University Press, 1953.

Waugh, W.T. *A History of Europe from 1378 to 1494.* New York: Methuen, 1932.

INDEX